Felix Cadet

Port-Royal Education

Felix Cadet

Port-Royal Education

ISBN/EAN: 9783337039066

Printed in Europe, USA, Canada, Australia, Japan

Cover: Foto ©ninafisch / pixelio.de

More available books at **www.hansebooks.com**

PORT-ROYAL EDUCATION

SAINT-CYRAN; ARNAULD; LANCELOT; NICOLE; DE SACI;
GUYOT; COUSTEL; FONTAINE; JACQUELINE PASCAL

EXTRACTS, WITH AN INTRODUCTION,

BY

FÉLIX CADET

INSPECTOR GENERAL OF PUBLIC INSTRUCTION

TRANSLATED, WITH AN INDEX, BY

ADNAH D. JONES

NEW YORK
CHAS. SCRIBNER'S SONS
1898

TABLE OF CONTENTS.

PAGE

INTRODUCTION.—Origin of the *Petites Écoles* of Port-Royal—Ideas of Saint-Cyran on Education—His collaborators, Lemaître, de Saci, Fontaine—The real masters: Lancelot, Nicole, Guyot, and Coustel—Analysis of their works—Wallon de Beaupuis, Arnauld 1

Of the education of girls at Port-Royal according to the constitution of the monastery and the rule of Jacqueline Pascal 46

Reasons which led to the closing of the schools and the destruction of Port-Royal—General criticism . . 58

EXTRACTS.

SAINT-CYRAN.—Origin of the *Petites Écoles* . . . 69
LANCELOT.—Charity of M. de Saint-Cyran towards children . 71
LANCELOT.—Saint-Cyran's literary theory . . . 82
DE BEAUPUIS.—Regulations for the school of Le Chesnai . . 86
DE SACI.—Letter on Education 92
FONTAINE.—Conversation between Pascal and M. de Saci on Epictetus and Montaigne 95
LANCELOT.—A new method of learning to read . . . 110
Of the Verb 111
ARNAULD.—Questions of grammar 117
ARNAULD.—Regulation of studies 123
NICOLE.—Design of the New Logic 128
Reply to the principal objections . . . 132
Of bad reasoning in civil life 139
Rules of the method in the sciences . . . 152

	PAGE
GUYOT.—On teaching reading and writing. Exercises in translation, elocution, and composition	154
NICOLE.—General views on the education of a Prince	167
Special advice concerning studies	171
Of the means of preserving peace with men	181
ARNAULD.—Eulogy on Descartes' philosophy	193
COUSTEL.—Rules for education	201
Of civility and politeness in children	211
ARNAULD.—On the persecutions of Port-Royal	218
MÈRE AGNÈS.—Constitutions of the monastery of Port-Royal	221
JACQUELINE PASCAL.—Regulations for the children of Port-Royal	226
BESOGNE.—Sister Anne Eugénie, mistress of the boarders	245
NICOLE.—A recreation at Port-Royal	247
APPENDIX.—A study of the writers of Port-Royal by Father Bouhours	249
INDEX	256

PORT-ROYAL EDUCATION.

INTRODUCTION.

THE *Petites Écoles* of Port-Royal had but a short and troubled existence. Their foundation goes back to the year 1637,[1] but their real organization only dates from 1646. Several times broken up in consequence of theological disputes excited by Arnauld, or because of the war of the Fronde, they were finally closed by the king's command in March, 1661.[2]

They hold, nevertheless, an honourable place in the history of pedagogy. If they lasted but a short time they shed a brilliant light, and exercised, as much by the character and talents of the masters as by the reform in methods of teaching and the books which they produced, a considerable influence, which on certain points is still active.

The first idea of their foundation belongs to the illustrious Duvergier de Hauranne, abbé of Saint-Cyran.[3] He was so profoundly moved by the importance of the education of the young, that he did not scruple to apply to this work the saying in the

---

[1] In 1637 we see the beginning of this celebrated community of recluses, which was formed outside the monastery of Port-Royal, and which brought up in the knowledge of letters and the practice of Christian piety a few children of good birth, whose parents wished to spare them the irregularities which were too general among young men attending college. (Preface to the *Nécrologe de Port-Royal*.)

[2] The nuns were allowed to receive boarders again from 1669 to 1679. (See note to p. 47.)

[3] Born at Bayonne in 1581, he was appointed to the Abbey of Saint-Cyran, in La Brenne, "a desert country where everything was lacking," said Lancelot (*Mém. sur M. de Saint-Cyran*, t. i. p. 288), on the frontiers of Touraine, Berry, and Poitou.

gospel referring to salvation : "*But one thing is needful.*" In his eyes the well-being of families, of the State and of the Church had its source and origin in this; all irregularities had no other origin or cause than bad education. Thus he thought no expressions sufficiently strong to condemn the negligence of parents in respect to this, nor any commendations sufficiently high to praise the devotion of persons who dedicated themselves to the education of young children. "There is no occupation," he said, "more worthy of a Christian in the Church, there is no greater charity after the sacrifice of one's life. . . . The guidance of the most tender soul is a greater thing than the government of a world." He was indignant, as if it were an absurdity and a folly, at men seeking after the positions of seneschal and master of the stables, and looking upon the education of reasonable creatures as the lowest employment.[1]

"I confess," he said to Fontaine, "that I should consider it a religious duty if I could be of use to children." "I should have been delighted to pass my whole life in it," he wrote to Lancelot. At the period when Vincent de Paul began to devote himself to the work of the Foundling Hospital, Saint-Cyran had for a moment "the desire of sending far and wide to collect young orphans in order to rear them in his abbey." In fine, when his ideas were more settled, his scheme was simpler, and it would require all the decision of Father Rapin to arouse in him the least ambition of taking the education of the young out of the hands of the Jesuits. The letter that he wrote from the prison of Vincennes speaks of a sort of "nursery for the Church," in which he would have brought up "six children chosen throughout the

---

[1] It has required much time to change men's ideas on this point. Two hundred years after Saint-Cyran, Channing notes with pleasure the progress made: "Men are beginning to understand the dignity of the schoolmaster. The idea is dawning on us that no employment is comparable to that of the education of the young in importance and value. That the talent of training the young in energy, truth, and virtue is the first of all the arts and sciences, and that consequently the encouragement of good masters is the most sacred duty that society has to fulfil towards itself." (*Œuvres Sociales*, trans. Laboulaye, p. 177.) Our schoolmasters have no longer to strive against the indifference and contempt of society; they have to guard themselves against the feeling of pride that their new position in public opinion might cause in them. It is only in this way that they will preserve the sympathy of everyone.

Introduction. 3

city of Paris." In a conversation, related by Lancelot, referring to another school which he was to entrust to M. Singlin, Saint-Cyran said "that he was far from making grand plans, that he did not wish to do anything brilliant, and that he should be contented to bring up there a dozen children at most in Christian virtue." (Lancelot, *Mémoires*, t. i. p. 291.)

His arrest and detention at Vincennes from 1638 to the death of Richelieu, whom he survived but a few months, did not permit him to carry out this modest plan. He had to restrict himself to personal efforts on several occasions,[1] but especially to excite, by his example and exhortations, devotion as disinterested as his own, but better guided, and therefore more efficacious. He sometimes said that he would have gone to the world's end to find a competent master. (Lancelot, t. i. p. 129.)

Saint-Cyran, then, was really the inspirer and mover of the pedagogic work of Port-Royal,[2] and there is a real interest in carefully seeking out his principal ideas on education.

I purposely set aside all his theological principles on the original fall of man, on the natural corruption of human nature, on the eternal damnation of infants dying unbaptized, and all the consequences which he logically deduces from them as to the end of education, and the direction to be given to it. Modern pedagogy is a secular science which must not wear the garb of any religious system. It cannot accept discussion on this ground, which has only a purely historical interest. Its starting-point is different, as is also its end. The child is,

---

[1] We see him in prison educating the young child of a poor widow. Lancelot (t. i. p. 133) shows him to us engaged in educating the two sons of the lieutenant of whom he had much to complain on account of his ill-treatment.

[2] We read, nevertheless, in the supplement to the *Nécrologe de Port-Royal*, p. 398 : "The establishment of the *Petites Écoles de Port-Royal* was due to the solicitation of this illustrious magistrate (Jérôme Bignon). M. de Saint-Cyran had often conversed with him about his views on the Christian education of children, and M. Bignon, after having long pressed him to put them in execution, demanded, as a tribute due to their mutual friendship, that the pious abbé should undertake to bring up his sons, Jérôme and Thierri Bignon, in a Christian manner. It was on their behalf that the *Petites Écoles* were started outside Port-Royal de Paris by MM. Lancelot and De Saci, while their sister, Marie Bignon, was educated within the convent."

in its view, a personality necessarily imperfect, in which good and evil are mingled, and not a *child of perdition*, as Guyot said, who must be snatched from the devil. It takes seriously, but not tragically, this severe and delicate work of education that Saint-Cyran calls "a tempest of the mind." (Letter to M. de Rebours.) It does not consider that the chief object of education is to preserve baptismal innocence in children by withdrawing them from the world and even from their families, to work solely for their salvation, and, by preference, within the walls of a cloister. It proposes to develop in them the knowledge of truth and the practice of virtue, to prepare them to fulfil the various duties that await them in life, profoundly convinced that the surest way of fulfilling our destiny, whatever it may be, is first to act our part as men.

Saint-Cyran demands in the first place that the family should completely cede its rights to him. If he undertakes the charge of a child, he wishes "to be entirely its master"; whether it be the son of the Duchesse de Guise, or the child of a poor cabinetmaker, this condition is a *sine quâ non*.[1]

Then he attaches a very great importance to the choice of his scholars, to discerning whether they are apt for study, or fit only for manual labour. "It is very remarkable," observes Lancelot with some reason (t. ii. p. 194), "that he is in nowise guided by their natural abilities in making this distinction, but by the seeds of virtue which he sees that God has sown in their hearts." A young child, eight or nine years old, who appeared a prodigy of intellect, had been put into Lancelot's hands. Saint-Cyran in prison wished to see him, and on the statement of his master that nothing had been observed in him that proceeded from corruption, but only a strange eagerness for knowledge, joined to great inquisitiveness and an ardent

---

[1] Mme. de Maintenon dreads the influence of the family no less. She writes to Mme. de la Mairie, March 5th, 1714: "The first impressions given to children in most houses are almost always vicious; we see them come to us untruthful, thieves, and deceitful . . . They must be shown that we know very well that they have seen these things done in their families, but that they must not do them any more." The girls of Saint-Cyran could only see their relations *once every three months for half an hour at most*.

Introduction. 5

desire to obtain advantages, "he decided off-hand that it was not at all necessary to put him to study, and this was absolutely carried out." He added that "sometimes out of a hundred children not one ought to be put to study." His fear was lest he should burden the Church with a number of people whom she had not called, and the State with a multitude of idle persons who thought that they were above everybody because they knew a little Latin, and who considered themselves dishonoured by following the profession in which their birth would have placed them. Those only in whom great docility and submission, with some mark of piety and an assured virtue, had been perceived ought to receive intellectual culture.[1]

We shall not be surprised that he paid little attention to physical education. Christian spirituality has been too much in fault in regarding the body as the origin of the passions, and of irregularities of conduct, and as an enemy to be fought and mastered; it was the Renaissance, that is to say, the return to classical antiquity, which enlarged the domain of pedagogy and restored their due share to hygiene, games, and physical exercises. Rabelais and Montaigne in the sixteenth century, Locke in the seventeenth, Rousseau in the eighteenth, Hufeland in the nineteenth, brought about the success of this salutary reaction, and convinced educators that it was necessary to attend to the child's health before thinking of his intellectual and moral culture. These pre-occupations of modern pedagogy seem scarcely to have attracted the attention of Saint-Cyran, who was too much engrossed by his religious ideas. Only one passage, and that of small importance, has a bearing on the method of feeding.[2]

But he seems to me to have very well understood the necessity

---

[1] Our ideas are broader and more generous, and we open the book of knowledge to all. There is nothing better or more necessary for the proper working of our political institutions; but it would be wise also not to cast all minds in the same mould, and, in order to make enlightened citizens, not to inspire them with a distaste for manual labour. Our curricula, well filled, too uniform, and not sufficiently adapted to the needs of the various localities, are, perhaps, not irreproachable in this respect.

[2] He recommends, in a conversation with Lemaître, the watching over the inclinations of children which tend towards "idleness, untruthfulness, and eating, *on account of their constitution which demands it*," and the accustoming them "to eat all kinds of vegetables, cod-fish, and herrings."

of not overpressing the child by too early intellectual labour. "I should think I had done a great deal," he says very sensibly, "although I had not advanced them much in Latin up to the age of twelve years, by causing them to spend their early years in the close of a house or monastery in the country, and by giving them all the pastimes suitable to their age." The monastery excepted, this reminds us of the negative education extolled by Rousseau.

Saint-Cyran sacrificed intellectual to moral education too much. "He remarked," said Lancelot (t. ii. p. 195), "that, generally speaking, knowledge did more harm than good to the young. And once he made me attentively consider this saying of St. Gregory Nazianzen, who said that the sciences had entered the Church, like the flies in Egypt, to cause a plague." His sombre and exclusive theory ill qualified him to appreciate literary beauties. Is it not strange to hear him say seriously during a visit to Port-Royal to the children who were studying Virgil, "You see that author? He has procured his own damnation, yes, he has procured his own damnation, in making these beautiful verses, because he made them through vanity and for glory; but you must sanctify yourselves in learning them, because you must learn them to please God, and render yourselves fit to serve the Church." What a strange idea! To study like "a college scapegrace," Rousseau would say, the fourth book of the Æneid, even the Eclogues of Alexis and Gallus (Saci and Guyot translated these works for their pupils), with the aim of pleasing God and serving the Church. What a narrow and strained conception of the utility of poetry. Is it not sufficient to justify such a study that it purifies the taste, ennobles the feelings, and excites admiration by the contemplation of the beautiful? What fanaticism to condemn with so much assurance those who have rendered us this eminent service by their masterpieces.

Let us first recommend to our masters for the teaching of morality the precept that the Mother Agnès recalls to the memory of a sister on the subject of religious instruction, "There are some truths that should rather be felt than learnt." (*Lettres*, t. ii. p. 444.) What practical results can we expect to obtain if we teach duty like a theorem in geometry? It is not a question of setting out learned abstractions, logical deductions, or methodical classifications. The heart and conscience must be educated, moral feeling must be awakened and strengthened, the love of what is good must be inculcated, good habits must be formed. Saint-Cyran will be of use to us, especially in what concerns moral education.

A real knowledge and a sincere love of children inspired these pedagogic directions which I sum up from Lancelot: Before all things, to gain their confidence by a calculated gentleness, by a really paternal love, and a seemly familiarity; to bear their faults and weaknesses patiently; to show still more charity and compassion towards those who are seen to be more unformed and backward; not to dishearten them by a too severe look and a too imperious manner; to know how to condescend discreetly to their humour for a time, in order to strengthen these young plants, sometimes even to ask instead of commanding; to descend to their level in order to raise them to our own; to watch continually in order to preserve these tender souls from evil, sometimes to punish ourselves for their faults, for which we should always fear we may be partly responsible, either through hastiness or negligence; to pray to God before correcting them, in order not to give way to a movement of ill-temper; to warn them at first only by signs, then by words, reprimands, and threats; to deprive them of some pleasures, and to resort to corporal punishment only in the last extremity; *plus prier que crier*, to ask rather than scold, he said, by a happy play of words; or, to sum up all in the formula that 'pleased him, to speak little, bear with much, and pray more. But for him the principal points in the good education of children were the good example to be set them, together with perfect order in the school.

Lemaître, the great orator, the first of the solitaries of Port-Royal, was also one of the earliest to second Saint-Cyran in the execution of his projects. The young Andilly and Saint-Ange were entrusted to his care. A touching passage in the *Memoirs* of Dufossé shows him at work:—

"I remember that, scholar though I was, he often made me go to his room, where he gave me very solid instruction in studies as well as in piety. He read to me, and made me read various passages from the poets and orators, and pointed out all their beauties, both their strong sense and their diction. He taught me also to read verse and prose as they should be read, which he did admirably himself, having a pleasing voice, and all the other qualities of a great orator. He also gave me several rules for good translation, in order to enable me to advance in it."[1] It is well known that he took charge of the education of Racine.

His younger brother, M. de Saci, who, after Saint-Cyran and M. Singlin, was the director of Port-Royal, took part incidentally in the teaching. With Lancelot, Saint-Cyran had especially entrusted him with the education of the two sons of M. Bignon. His letter, which we publish under the title of *Patience and Silence*, is an admirable page of pedagogy. His influence on classical studies was more considerable; to him we owe a translation of the *Fables* of Phædrus,[2] and of three comedies of Terence.[3] It is to be noticed with what "ingenious charity" the man of letters, enamoured with noble antiquity, endeavours to conciliate the cultivation of good taste with respect for morality, and the quite new importance that he attaches to the study of the French language. ". . . Many persons of quality complain nowadays with great reason," says he in the preface, "that when their children are taught Latin it seems that they unlearn French, and that in aspiring to make them citizens of ancient Rome they are made strangers in their own country . . . After having learnt Latin and Greek for ten or twelve years we are often obliged to learn French at thirty."

His intellect, full of fire and light, with a certain charm and sprightliness, and his especial talent for poetry, were celebrated at Port-Royal. Fontaine has preserved his first piece. It is a letter of thanks, half prose, half verse, to his mother for a

---

[1] *Mémoires pour servir à l'hist. de Port-Royal*, 1739, p. 156.
[2] The *Fables* of Phædrus, the freedman of Augustus, translated into French with the Latin opposite, to serve for a good understanding of the Latin tongue, and for translating well into French. (1647.)
[3] The Comedies of Terence (Andria, Adelphi, Phormio), translated into French and rendered with propriety, by changing very little, to serve for a good understanding of the Latin tongue, and for translating well into French, by the Sr. de Saint-Aubin. (Paris, 1647.)

present of four purses that she made to him and his three brothers. Forced wit and an affected style give themselves free scope. "We see in it," he says, "in a small space, the most illustrious prisoner in the world (gold); and our hands have enchained him who disposes of the liberty of all men :—

"That superb metal, to which so many mortals
Dedicate so many vows, raise so many altars ;
Son of the Sun of the Heavens and Sun of the earth," etc.

The four purses, of different colours, are compared at first to a beautiful flower-bed, then to the whiteness which when the sun is hidden adorns

"That great blue veil that covers all the sky";

then to the lily and the rose, which

"Both redouble their natural beauties";

then to the sun's rays on the "soft ivory" of the snow; at last "to the thousand deep red roses" of the dawn.

"I shall always admire these purses as marvels, and I shall love them as my little sisters, since they are in some sort your daughters, and I am truly your very humble and very obedient son, De Saci."

This poetical talent, such as it was, was utilized in 1654 to reply to the facetious jests of the Jesuits in their almanack entitled, *The Rout and Confusion of the Jansenists*. De Saci, with the applause of Arnauld [1] (Saint-Cyran would have energetically condemned such a freak), composed, in trifling verses of eight feet, the *Enluminures de l'almanach des Jesuites*. I will only quote one specimen, which has at least the historical value of verifying how superior the Jansenists were to the Jesuits pen in hand :—

"There are none, even your booksellers,
Who do not value your adversaries,
Whose fine books have always,
Notwithstanding your noise, so great a vogue.
But yours, so magnificent,
Are the seniors in the shops,
And always stay at home
As if they were in prison.

---

[1] Arnauld undertook, at a great expense of erudition and logic, to justify this pamphlet, in his *Application des règles des Pères à l'almanach*.

> Every other book is asked for,
> Seen, prized, and bargained for ;
> But they are recluses,
> Whom no man has ever seen.
> All the leaves collected
> Are ream on ream piled up
> And, the attics being full of them,
> They are the guardians of the shops.
>   There the mice run over the pages
> Of your admirable works,
> And the troop of noble rats
> Make them their food and their good dishes."
>
> (6th illustration, p. 24.)

Naturally, Lancelot applied to de Saci to versify the *Garden of Greek Roots* (1657). The prologue well preserves the imprint of its author :—

> "Thou, who cherishest the learned Greece,
> Where of old wisdom flourished ;
> Whence theological authors
> Have borrowed their sacred terms
> To be of our great mysteries
> The august depositaries,
> Enter this GARDEN, not of flowers
> Which have only useless colours,
> But of nourishing ROOTS
> Which make learned minds."

In truth, de Saci, wholly given up to piety, looked with some contempt on all secular studies, and thought that reading the classical authors was dangerous for those who could not "pick up some pearls from the dunghill, whence arose even a black smoke which might obscure the wavering faith." Religion is his sole thought: "The chief end of education ought to be to save the children and ourselves with them." We see him in his admirable conversation with Pascal, firm and intrenched in his faith, despise the fine-drawn reasoning of Epictetus and Montaigne, and enthusiasm for science, "those dangerous viands served up on handsome dishes" to people "who are sleeping, and who think they eat while sleeping."

Fontaine describes him admirably in this passage : "No one ever saw M. de Saci take an interest in those inquisitive sciences (the system of the world by Descartes, animal-machines).

Smiling good-naturedly when anyone spoke to him of these things, he showed more pity for those who paid attention to them than desire to attend to them himself. He said to me one day, speaking to me privately on the subject, that he wondered at the action of God with regard to these new opinions; that M. Descartes was with respect to Aristotle like a robber who came to kill another robber and carry off his booty; that Aristotle, little by little, had at last become the master of the ministers of the Church. 'I saw at the Sorbonne,' he said to me, 'and I could not see it without a shudder, a doctor who quoted a passage from the Scriptures, and another who boldly refuted him by a passage from Aristotle. . . . Aristotle having usurped such authority in the Church, was it not just that he should be dispossessed and overthrown by another tyrant, to whom, perhaps, the same thing would happen one day?" (*Mémoires*, t. iii. p. 75.)

What a narrow-minded opinion, and what a prejudice! Sainte-Beuve answers him roundly: "Jansenius made a disturbance in the bosom of the Church; Descartes made a revolution everywhere." (t. iii. p. 120.)

We recall his smart paradox on the inutility of travelling: "Travelling was seeing the devil dressed in every fashion— German, Italian, Spanish, and English."

De Saci's chief work was his translation of the Bible, of which the publication, begun in 1672, was not finished till 1707, twenty-three years after his death. Reading and meditating on the sacred books, and making their reading and meditation easier for the faithful, was the chief business of his life. "With my Bible," said he, "I could go to the end of the world." It is curious and interesting to mark the hesitation and the scruples of the translator. He had translated at first in a style that his friends thought too elevated, and then too bald. He set to work a third time, trying to keep a middle course. Sainte-Beuve amends the cutting sentence of Joubert, "De Saci has shaved, powdered, and curled the Bible, but at least he has not rouged it," by this sprightly remark, "It would suffice to say that he has *combed* it." (t. ii. p. 362.) The celebrated translator passed judgment on himself a few months before his death:—

"I have endeavoured to remove from the Holy Scripture

obscurity and inelegance; and God has willed until now that His Word should be enveloped in obscurities. Have I not, then, reason to fear that giving, as I have tried to do, a clear version, and one perhaps sufficiently correct with regard to purity of language, is *resisting the designs of the Holy Spirit?* I know very well that I have not aimed at the graces and niceties that are admired in society, and that might be sought at the French Academy. God is my witness how much horror I have always had of these ornaments. . . . But I cannot hide from myself that I have endeavoured to render the language of Scripture clear, pure, and conformable to the rules of grammar. . . . Shall I not, then, have reason to tremble if the Holy Ghost, having until now set aside the rules of grammar, and having visibly despised them, I now take the liberty of reducing it to these rules . . . ?" (Fontaine, *Mémoires*, t. iv. p. 322.)

Evidently de Saci had not such soundness of taste as he had tenderness of conscience and ardour in devotion; but with these few reservations, how much admiration this pure and regular life, so enamoured of perfection, so full of self-sacrifice and charity, deserves! One touching trait will suffice to depict this noble soul. When he came out of prison in 1668 what will it be thought that he demanded of the friendship of Le Tellier, who was afterwards chancellor? "He begged him to use his influence with the king to obtain permission from his majesty that from time to time persons of whose fidelity there could be no doubt should go to the Bastille to see what was going on there, in order that poor prisoners who spend years there without anyone even remembering why they have been imprisoned, should not be left in perpetual oblivion." (Leclerc. *Vies intéressantes*, t. iv. p. 56.)

But the real masters of Port-Royal were those who were entrusted with the teaching at the time of the organization of the *Petites Écoles* in 1646. Lancelot and Nicole, Guyot and Coustel, under the management of M. Wallon de Beaupuis, but in reality under the powerful influence of Arnauld, the heir to the authority of Saint-Cyran and the author or inspirer of most of the classical books of Port-Royal.

The most distinguished master was Claude Lancelot. Of all the recluses of Port-Royal he devoted himself the most entirely to education, and composed the greatest number of classical works. He was born at Paris about 1615. Having early resolved to devote himself to God's service, he entered in 1627 the community of Saint Nicolas du Chardonnet, where he remained ten years studying the fathers of the Church, and regretting that he did not find men like St. Chrysostom, St. Ambrose, and St. Augustine. "If there were only one," said he, "I would start at once and go and seek him, even to the world's end, to throw myself at his feet and receive from him so pure and beneficial a guidance." (*Mémoires*, t. i. p. 5.)

It was then that he heard the abbé of Saint-Cyran spoken of as a man of the early centuries, and he put himself under his spiritual direction with unbounded submission and admiration. "I confess," he said, "that it was one of my devotions to pause sometimes and contemplate M. de Saint-Cyran as one of the most living images of Christ that I had ever seen. (*Mém.* t. ii. p. 204.)

He entered Port-Royal January 20, 1638, a few months before the arrest of Saint-Cyran, to share the life of penitence of the early solitaries, then not very numerous. They were soon obliged to disperse, but in order not to abandon the task that had been entrusted to him, Lancelot was sent to La Ferté-Milon with M. Vitard, then twelve or thirteen years old, in order to take charge of his education. On his return to Paris in October, 1639, he started for the abbey of Saint-Cyran, whence he returned in October, 1640, to take charge of the two children of M. Bignon, the Advocate-General, and afterwards of a little boy whom Saint-Cyran sent to him, the care of whom he shared with de Saci because he was occupied in the mornings in the sacristy of Port-Royal.

He published in 1644 the *New Method of Learning the Latin Tongue with Ease*. The preface and the address to the reader state precisely the reform introduced into the teaching. The rules are given in French. The "minutiæ of grammar" are rejected. "I have been careful to avoid some observations that seemed to me not very useful, remembering the excellent saying of Quintilian, that it is part of the science of a really skilful grammarian to know that there are some things that are not worth knowing. But I hope," he adds, "that the substantial and judicious remarks of these authors,[1] in order to thoroughly understand the ground of the Latin language, . . . will show with how much reason the same Quintilian said that those are very much deceived who laugh at grammar as a low and despicable art, since, being to eloquence what the foundation is to the edifice, if it is not firmly established in the mind all that is added to it afterwards will fall to the ground." He praises this maxim of Ramus: "Few rules and much practice," an excellent recommendation that Fénelon supports with his authority.[2]

Thus Lancelot claims to do in six months what Despautère would take three years to do. In a letter to Bussy, Corbinelli advises him to teach his daughter Latin by the method of Port-Royal: "There is only enough for a fortnight." (30 July, 1677.) Nothing shows that this was a joke on the pretension to improvise knowledge. It is only a rather strong illusion of an admirer. Lancelot had charge of the teaching of Greek and mathematics at the school in the Rue Saint-Dominique de l'Enfer in 1646. He gave, in 1655, the *New Method of Learning the Greek Language with Ease*. M. Egger, a very competent judge, notes the marked advance of this work on the books of Clénard, Vergara, and Vossius: "The barbarous quatrains that Lancelot mixes with the rules in prose in his methods have quite gone out of fashion now. But, then, it was something to employ the French language instead of Latin; it was something to have set out the declensions and conjugations at greater length; to have facilitated the effort of memory necessary for pupils in learning the vocabulary of a dead language by the choice of the most useful words." (*De l'hellénisme en France*, vol. ii. p. 60.) It was not the fault of Port-Royal that the study of Greek was not again held in honour

---

[1] He says that he had read the works of Sanctius, a celebrated professor of Salamanca, of Scioppius and Vossius, learned Dutchmen (1577–1649); he does not appeal at all to the authority of the Portuguese Jesuit Alvares, whose grammar Father Rapin accuses him of copying, but without showing any proof of it. (*Mem.* Introduc., p. 125.)

[2] "The great point is to bring a person as soon as possible to the practical application of the rules by frequent use; then he will take pleasure in noticing the details of the rules that he followed at first without remarking them." (*Lettre à l'Académie Française*, § 2.)

among us. We know with what success Lancelot imparted the knowledge of this language and the taste for its literature to Racine.

In 1657 appeared the *Jardin des racines grecques*. It would not be very useful to pause on this work, which would not interest our readers. The learned Dübner, otherwise a great partisan of the pedagogic reforms of Port-Royal, does not hesitate to call it "Ostrogothic." M. Egger declares that this book, by its errors and want of criticism, "has been one of the greatest obstacles to progress in grammatical methods among us." (*De l'hellénisme en France*, vol. i. p. 112.) After being long used in class, it was suppressed by a ministerial decree of December 4, 1863. Two passages in the preface deserve to be noticed. One relates to Comenius and his method, *Janua linguarum reserata* (the gate of languages opened), 1631. "A work estimable in itself," said Lancelot, "but not sufficiently proportioned to the title it bears, and the intention of its author." After having tried it, he thinks it long and difficult, without interest for the children, and, in fine, of very little use, because of its want of method. There is a good page of pedagogy to be gathered here.

"Besides requiring an extraordinary memory to learn it, and that few children are capable of it, I can assert, after several experiments that I have made, that scarcely any are able to retain it, because it is long and difficult and, the words being never repeated, they have forgotten the beginning before reaching the end. Thus they feel a constant dislike for it, because they always find themselves, as it were, in a new country, where they recognize nothing: the book is filled with all sorts of unusual and difficult words, and the first chapters are of no assistance for those that follow; nor these for the last, because there is no word in one which is found in the others." And he adds, with his consummate experience in teaching: "What might be called the *Entrance to languages* ought to be a short and easy method to lead us as quickly as possible to the reading the best written books, in order to learn not only the words that we lack, but also what is most remarkable in the turn and most pure in the phrase, which is, without doubt, the most difficult and most important part in every language."

The other judgment is not so well founded in reason. For the etymologies, he quotes especially the *Origines françaises* of M. Ménage, "who alone is worth a multitude of authors, because, besides drawing from the ancients, he has carefully collected what the most able men of our own times have that is curious upon this matter." If there is a book that deserves the discredit and oblivion into which it has fallen, it is assuredly this one. The philological caprices of Ménage have passed into legends. It was easy for Father Bouhours to amuse himself at his expense, to the great delight of Mme. de Sévigné.[1]

"M. Ménage especially excels in etymologies, he says with lively raillery. His mind seems to be made expressly for this science; sometimes he even seems to be inspired, so lucky is he in discovering where words come from. For example, did he not need a sort of inspiration to discover the real origin of *jargon* and *baragouin?* Jargon, according to him, comes from barbaricus. Here is its genealogy in direct line : barbarus, barbaricus, baricus, varicus, uaricus, guaricus, guargus, gargo, gargonis, JARGON. Baragouin is a near relation of jargon : barbarus, barbaracus, barbaracuinus, baracuinus, baraguinus, BARAGOUIN. Nothing is clearer nor more precise. And I have no doubt that M. Ménage is very pleased with himself at this new discovery; for formerly he did not think that jargon and baragouin were of the same country, nor came from the same stem. He insists, in his *Origines de la langue française*, that jargon is Spanish and baragouin Bas-breton, . . . so true is it that words like men come from where one wills. However this may be, we are indebted to M. Ménage for a great deal of similar knowledge; it is he who, with that faculty of divination that M. de Balzac attributes to him, has discovered that *laquais* came from verna, vernula, vernulacus, vernulacaius, lacaius, laquay, LAQUAIS; that *boire à tire-larigot* came from fistula : fistula, fistularis, fistularius, fistularicus, laricus, laricotus, LARIGOT. . . All that is very fine and curious."

---

[1] "I read the angry books of Father Bouhours, the jesuit, and of Ménage, who tear each other's eyes out and amuse us. They say what they think of each other, and often insult one another. There are, besides, some very good remarks on the French language. You cannot think how amusing this quarrel is." (16 September, 1676.)

In 1660 Lancelot, under the supervision of Arnauld,[1] edited one of the most important works of Port-Royal, the *Grammaire générale et raisonnée*, containing the grounds of the art of speaking, explained in a clear and natural manner, the reason for what is common to all languages, and the principal differences that are met with in them, with several new remarks on the French language.

This compendious but incomplete work was a bold conception for the time, the influence of Descartes and his unflinching confidence in the power of the reason are felt in it. It incited the researches of the philosophical grammarians of the eighteenth century, du Marsais, Duclos, Condillac, and de Tracy. This was the best that could be done until the discovery of Sanscrit, with a wider knowledge of languages and their filiation and history permitted Grimm, Humboldt, Bopp, Burnouf, Diez, Michel Bréal, and Littré to substitute the sure method of history, phonetics, and comparison for the brilliant but barren speculations of philosophical abstraction.

If we no longer share the enthusiastic admiration of the worthy Rollin for this work, and no longer see the *sublime genius of the great man*, we still remain struck with this vigorous spirit of analysis and this luminous method.

At the same date the indefatigable master, under the name of M. de Trigny, completed his grammatical teaching by giving the *Nouvelle Méthode pour apprendre facilement et en peu de temps la langue italienne*, and the *Nouvelle Méthode pour apprendre facilement et en peu de temps la langue espagnole*. He had recourse to the learning of Chapelain for these two works. The second was dedicated to the Most Serene Infanta of Spain, Donna Maria Teresa, "whom all France already looks upon as her queen." A passage in the Preface to the *Italian Method* should be pointed

---

[1] "The General Grammar is the result of conversations that M. Lancelot, who was entrusted with the teaching of languages in the schools of Port-Royal, had with this great man, in the moments that the doctor was able to give up to the desire that he had to learn with him. M. Lancelot wrote out the answers that M. Arnauld gave to his questions; and thus was composed the first work that went deeply into the art of speaking, and developed the first foundations of the Logic." (*Vie de messire Ant. Arnauld*, Paris et Lausanne, 1783, t. i. p. 218.)

out to those engaged in teaching, for the proper management of the grammatical studies both of teachers as well as of students: "Whosoever wishes to learn a language with facility should as soon as possible join use and practice with precept." For the Italian, for instance, the declension of the article, and the auxiliary and regular verbs—some three or four pages—are all that it is necessary to know in order to begin construing an author. "After that the rules for the irregular verbs may be learnt, or at least read attentively; the rest of the grammar may almost be left to the teacher to be applied in practice."

With respect to the grammar of the French language, which is obviously lacking in the collection, and which was demanded abroad,[1] particularly by Daniel Elzevier, the famous bookseller of Amsterdam, Lancelot replied to Dr. Saint-Amour, who had to make the proposal, "that he had several times resolved upon undertaking this work, but that he had always found so many difficulties, and so little likelihood of being able to surmount them, that he had been obliged to give it up." Saint-Amour returned to the charge two or three times, but always without success, Lancelot never ceasing to object how much "he had been repelled every time he had wished to undertake it."

After all, the Port-Royalists rendered a greater service to the French language than drawing up its grammar: they gave it an important place in classical studies by their methods drawn up in French, and no longer in Latin; and by their translations they invigorated it from the sources of antiquity, and cleared it of pedantry and scholasticism. They won theology for it as Descartes did philosophy and Corneille the high style of poetry. The grave and learned works that issued from Port-Royal, more attentive to matter than form, to truth and virtue than to beauties of style, drew admiration even from its enemies. Father

---

[1] Among ancient works that the study of our language produced we may cite:
PALSGRAVE, l' *Esclaircissement de la langue françoyse* (1530); LOUIS MÉGRET, le *Tretté de la grammere françoeze* (1550); RAMUS, *Gramere fransoeze* (1562).

VAUGELAS in 1647 published only detached remarks on the French language, and not a methodical treatise. In 1714 FÉNELON expressed a wish that the French Academy would add a grammar to its dictionary.

Annat had not more brilliantly combated Pascal than the learned Father Pétau had attacked Arnauld, and Father Rapin does not stint his praises of the book on Frequent Communion (1643), "Nothing had been seen better written in our language." (*Mémoires*, t. i. p. 22.) He does not do less justice to Pascal. "Men had," he says, "so little experience of a manner of writing resembling that of the *Letters to a Provincial*, that they could form no conjectures sufficiently clear to point to anybody with certainty, because they had never seen anything of this character in our language." (*Mémoires*, t. ii. p. 380.)[1] Mme. de Maintenon, whose profound antipathy for "those gentlemen of Port-Royal" is well known, asserts that the works "contain a venom so much the more dangerous as their style is more pleasing to the natural taste, and elevates the mind. For myself, I have never liked any of their books, although they are very fine." (*Instruction à la classe bleue*, 1705.)

The influence of these models for the perfecting of the language was deep and lasting. "By employing themselves for twenty years after the *Provincials* in dexterously finding fault with the style of Pascal the jesuits learnt to write well. By ironically pointing out the rather uniform gravity,[2] the long periods, and at times unusual expressions of the other writers of Port-Royal, they tried their hand at a style which was more easy and flowing without being less correct.[3] (Villemain, *Préface du Dictionnaire de l'Académie*.)

This service was more valuable than the composition of a French Grammar.

To return to Lancelot. When in 1661 the *Petites Écoles* were

---

[1] There is no one, even to the venomous Father Brisacier, who does not admit the literary merit of the *Heures de Port-Royal;* he calls them "a sink of errors, a grenade of impiety, a common sewer of all the works of Calvin collected in *good French* under the specious title of *Office de la Vierge*." Quoted by ARNAULD, *la Morale pratique des jésuites*, t. viii. p. 162.

[2] A curious note of Bossuet on his reading, dated 1669, contains this information: "Some books of MM. de Port-Royal, good to read because *gravity* and *grandeur* are found in them, their prefaces by choice; but their style has *little variety*. Without variety there is no pleasure." (FLOQUET, *Études sur la vie de Bossuet*, t. i. p. 378.)

[3] Father Bouhours, the author of the *Entretiens d'Ariste et d'Eugène* (1671), must especially be named. The second dialogue is entirely devoted to a serious study of the language of Port-Royal.

finally closed by the king's command, he had been for some time in charge of the education of the Duc de Chevreuse, as we see by the address of a letter of Chapelain: "*A M. Lancelot, précepteur du Marquis de Luynes, à Port-Royal.*"
In 1663 he published four treatises on poetry—Latin, French, Italian, and Spanish. He was probably working on that *Recueil de poésies chrétiennes et diverses*, dedicated to Mgr. le prince de Conti, which appeared in 1671 in three volumes under the name of . . . (the reader may guess a hundred times), under the name of La Fontaine; his friendship for Racine and Boileau brought him into contact for a short time with Port-Royal. In offering this collection to the prince, he acknowledges that he has done little more than lend his name.

> "Those who by their labour have brought it to this state
> Might offer it to thee in more brilliant terms;
> But, fearing to emerge from that profound peace
> Which they enjoy in secret, far from noise and the world,
> They engage me to bring it to the light for them."

Lancelot had for two years been entrusted with the education of the princes de Conti. Fontaine has preserved the interesting report that he sent to M. de Saci on the employment of the day by his pupils, and the distribution of their studies. He preferred to resign his position in 1672, rather than consent to take his pupils to the theatre. His inflexible strictness cannot escape the reproach of inconsistency justly thrown on him by Sainte-Beuve : "Of what use is it, O Lancelot, to teach children so well—Greek, Spanish, Italian, and the niceties of Latin— and to forbid them afterwards to go to the theatre and hear Chimène, to permit neither the *Jerusalem*, the *Aminta*, *Théagène*, the Anthology, nor all Catullus? This prohibition and interdiction extended, in fact, beyond childhood, and in part existed for grown-up men. Was it possible? Was it reasonable? Of what use was it to teach so much and so well, if it were not to put men in a position to use this knowledge later? Why should I not enjoy the honey and the flowers of this Greek whose Roots I have devoured? The child who will write *Bérénice* said this to himself one day, and he leaped over the obstacle. He flew over the hedge like the bee." (*Port-Royal*, t. iii. p. 531.)

This was the end of the pedagogic career of Lancelot, who henceforth devoted himself to the religious life in the abbey of Saint-Cyran under the direction of M. de Barcos. On the death of this abbé, in 1678, great troubles arose in the abbey, and Lancelot was exiled, on the pretext of jansenism, to Quimperlé in the remotest part of Britanny,[1] where he died on April 15, 1695, leaving behind him a venerated memory. The history of French pedagogy cannot leave in oblivion the name of this educator who devoted himself unreservedly to children, and who so well understood that pedagogy should be in the heart still more than in the head, and that the master should feel "the love of a father" for his pupils. "A preceptor who was not in that frame of mind would never do anything . . . . If, on the contrary, he were so, this love would make him find more ways of being useful to his scholars than all the advice that might be given him." (Letter to M. de Saci on the education of the princes de Conti.)

Nicole shed more lustre than Lancelot by his talents as a writer and moralist, so much praised by Mme. de Sévigné and Voltaire. In reality he was much less the man of Port-Royal. He scarcely knew Saint-Cyran, and did not altogether admire him when he compared him to a field, "capable of producing much, but prolific in briars and thorns," and he even went so far as to speak of his gibberish. He acknowledges that he kept himself a little aloof. "I was for five or six years in a place where they usually opposed to de Saci, M. Singlin, M. N. and M. N. on one side and myself on the other." (*Essais*, t. vii. p. 180). On the death of de Saci he did not approve of the marks of veneration and tenderness lavished by the nuns on their beloved confessor; and he wrote to Mlle. Aubry, begging her not to mention it, that for thirty

---

[1] Nothing more is heard of him except one curious circumstance related by Arnauld to M. du Vaucel and Mme. de Fontpertuis, March 16 and 17, 1689. James II., King of England, who had been dethroned, arrived at Kimperlay (*sic*). "A great supper was awaiting him in the abbey where brother Claude Lancelot is . . . . M. d'Avaux seated him at table by his side . . . Who would have thought that a monk exiled to Britanny would have had the honour of supping with a king ?"

years he had suffered from this unreasonable assiduity of the devotees.

M. de Beaubrun, in the interesting portrait that he has drawn of Nicole, goes so far as to say : " He was a jansenist, perhaps, only through fear of displeasing M. Arnauld, since after 1689 he wrote to Father Quesnel that for more than thirty years he had had the thoughts that he had expressed in his treatise on *la Grâce générale*, that is to say that he was writing in favour of jansenism, while he had in his mind a system diametrically opposed to it." (*Vie manuscrite*, a passage quoted by Sainte-Beuve, t. iv. p. 516.)

Nicole, besides, was less exclusively attached to the *Petites Écoles*. He divided his time between the care of his pupils, his theological studies, and his preparation for the licentiate's degree, which he did not renounce until 1649. A manuscript biographical notice from Holland thus describes the more restricted part that he took : " M. Nicole only directed the studies of the young people at Port-Royal. The young gentlemen were themselves much inclined to study; they only needed to have the best passages of the Greek or Latin authors pointed out to them. M. Nicole was there to inspire them with the taste for them. M. Nicole was to them rather an adviser than a master, as this name is understood now." (Quoted by Sainte-Beuve, t. iv. p. 599.)

His talent as a teacher was very remarkable. Father Rapin (*Mém.* t. ii. p. 254) relates that Singlin heard him discourse on an eclipse of the sun, got him to talk on various subjects, and brought him under the notice of Arnauld, who hastened to associate him with himself, and being unable to do without him, soon carried him off to the schools. He was well qualified for teaching *belles-lettres* and philosophy.

"M. Nicole," says Besogne (t. v. p. 225), "studied under his father all the authors of profane antiquity, both Greek and Latin.[1] At the age of fourteen he had finished the usual course of the humanities, he had so much aptitude and penetration of mind joined to a most excellent memory. It was sufficient for

---

[1] Nicole, *Essais de morale*, t. viii. p. 193, admits that he had not read Demosthenes.

him to read a book once in order to retain its substance, and at an advanced age he told his friends that he had forgotten nothing that he had read in his youth. He knew his Virgil and Horace perfectly. A short time before his death he gravely recited a number of verses of the Æneid. The author who pleased him most, and whom he willingly re-read for his good latinity, was Terence. He was accustomed to say that the best passages of these authors were like fine models that it was necessary to have in the mind in order to write fine works; that a man who was not provided with these fine models, and who undertook to compose, might indeed write fine things, but it was as if he printed in Gothic characters; while he who had made these fine passages his own was in a position to print in fine Roman characters, which it was a pleasure to read."

This extensive and varied knowledge, this wide and curious reading, which give a peculiar character to Nicole among the solitaries of Port-Royal, lacks, however, the keen feeling for beauty. A passage in one of his letters is truly singular for a professor of the humanities; he does not conceal his contempt for the impassioned admirers of the ancients: "For myself," he adds, "*I take pleasure in discovering the falsehoods and great delusions in these same books.* I find a quantity of them." This is a very unfortunate turn of mind, and would be calculated to vitiate and sterilize all literary teaching. "The pleasure of criticism," says La Bruyère, "takes from us the faculty of being deeply touched by very fine things."

Nicole has an unfortunate kind of prejudice against the whole of ancient literature.

Recalling to mind that Saint-Cyran never read the books of heretics "without having performed the exorcisms of the church, because he said that they were written by the spirit of the devil, and that there was in these books an impression of error," he adds, "But do not all the books of the pagans come from the same source?" (t. xii. p. 176.)[1] Happily he corrected this

---

[1] It is unpleasant to see Port-Royal, which stigmatized the ineptitude of Father Garasse, in agreement with him on this point, in better terms, however: "It is true that the greatest captains in the world, who in old times filled the earth with the signs of their triumphs, are now like hodmen

sally himself, and felt the moral value of ancient literature. (See p. 180.)

What shall we say of several of his criticisms on French literature? Did he not arouse the anger and ingratitude of Racine by calling the dramatic poets public poisoners? The great Corneille, whose theatre breathes in the highest degree heroism and the sentiment of duty, finds no favour in his prejudiced eyes, and he pronounces, even in the case of the *Cid* and *Horace*, the words corruption, barbarism, criminal aims.

"One cannot better prove the danger there is in all comedies than by showing that those even of this author are contrary to the spirit of the Gospel, and that they corrupt the mind and heart by the pagan and profane sentiments that they inspire." (*Les Visionnaires*, Avertissement, p. 22.) Bossuet, unfortunately, has not been more just towards Corneille.

The genius of Pascal also has partly escaped Nicole. He proclaims him, indeed, "one of the great minds of this age" (*Essais*, t. iii. p. 3); he quotes the *Pensées* as one of the most useful works to put into the hands of princes (see p. 179); but he goes so far as to call him "a gatherer of shells," and nearly made the abbé de Saint-Pierre, to whom he said this enormity, doubt the discernment of the moralist. (*Ouvrages de morale et de politique*, t. xii. p. 86.)

With what strange freedom, in a letter to the Marquis de Sévigné, he reproaches Mme. de la Fayette with wishing to impose admiration of these *Pensées* without "telling us more particularly what we ought to admire in them," and to reduce us "to pretend to think admirable what we do not understand!"

We cannot but praise the wisdom and prudence of the editors, while regretting it, that in publishing the *Pensées* they thought of excising some passages in which the royal majesty was treated with small respect, some assertions which furnished matter for new discussions, and some attacks on the "worthy Fathers."

---

and stable-boys in hell; it is true that the devil has taken the greatest philosophers of Greece, the wisest councillors of the Areopagus, the most famous orators of Rome, the haughtiest princes of heathendom, the most learned physicians of the universe; it is true that they are all in the pay of Lucifer." (P. GARASSE, *Doctrine curieuse*, p. 867.)

Introduction.

We can understand, strictly, that Arnauld should write to M. Perrier, who defended the work of Pascal: "A man cannot be too precise when he has to do with such ill-natured enemies as yours. It is much more to the point to avoid carping criticisms by some slight change, which only softens an expression, than to be reduced to the necessity of making apologies. . . ." (20 Nov., 1660.)

But that anyone should have the idea of correcting Pascal's style, of remodelling his phrases, of changing such and such a familiar and original expression, such and such a lively and dramatic turn, shows an aberration of mind, an absence of criticism, and a want of taste that we cannot describe; and we have some trouble to understand that this was, in great part, the work of him whom Bayle calls the finest pen of Port-Royal, and whom the papal nuncio named the golden pen.[1]

This imperfection of his literary sense, taste, and imagination is equally betrayed in the only book relating to the teaching of *belles-lettres* on which Nicole worked, *Epigrammatum delectus* (A Selection of Epigrams, 1659). A preface and a dissertation, both in Latin, indicate the aim and plan of the work—to cultivate the mind, and to protect the morals. The worthy Nicole "shuddered with horror at the sight of the obscenities of Martial and Catullus, whose works eternal oblivion or the flames ought to have destroyed." But as "remedies are drawn from the viper and flowers are found among poisons," he sets to work to make a selection of the most elegant pieces. He would perhaps have acted as wisely in not including the construing of these authors in a programme of classical studies. This kind of work is of a very limited and secondary character.

The dissertation on true and false beauty, on the nature and the different kinds of epigrams, notwithstanding the praises of Chapelain[2], ill-satisfies the reader. Father Vavasseur, "the best humanist of his time," in the opinion of the abbé d'Olivet, the

---

[1] See in Havet's edition, especially pp. 13 and 267, two specimens of this literary profanation.
[2] 9 September, 1659, letter to d'Andilly: "I have seen nothing better written in the didactic style, nothing more judicious, more chaste, more clearly set forth in the nature of the epigram, in fine, more instructive."

historian of the French Academy, has roughly handled him, and not without reason. Was it not sufficient for the theory of this kind of poetry which only admits of a few verses to demand naturalness and simplicity, a witty and pointed turn, grace and delicacy? Instead of that, Nicole discourses gravely on the nature and source of the beautiful; he lays down this principle, sufficiently vague, however, that it is especially in conformity with the nature of things and with our nature; he reduces its conditions to three—the agreeableness of the tone, the propriety of the words, and the truth and naturalness of the thoughts; he thinks that he has thoroughly examined his subject, although he admits himself that all this has little to do with the epigram, in proclaiming the weakness of human nature as the reason of metaphors. It is this that appears so chaste to Chapelain. Nicole then explains how, in consequence of these premisses, he has been obliged to reject from his collection false, mythological, equivocal, hyperbolical, doubtful, vulgar, spiteful, verbose, or common epigrams. After which, but a little late, he takes in hand the definition and form of the epigram, and admits two kinds—the sublime, grand, and magnificent kind, and another a little lower in style but more useful in application.

The best thing in this ill-balanced dissertation is the ideas rather carelessly thrown out at the end, where Nicole, without circumlocution, praises, especially in the epigram, the ingenious point that penetrates the mind deeply, or its simplicity and playfulness, and the art of treating the subject without excess or defect, without obscurity or complication, by cleverly leading up to the effect; and he quotes Martial, who is a master of this art. Martial and Port-Royal! Does not the approximation of these two names excite the most legitimate astonishment? All Nicole's dissertation, however, falls to pieces at this simple remark of Voltaire: "The epigram should not be placed in a higher rank than the song ... I should advise no one to apply himself to a style that may bring much disappointment and little glory." (*Œuvres*, t. xxxix. p. 212.)

Nicole took a large share in the composition of the *Logic, or the Art of Thinking*, but the firmer hand and more liberal mind of Arnauld are perceived in this work. Arnauld, alone at Port-Royal, is sincerely Cartesian; he declared himself a partisan of the new philosophy on the appearance of the *Discours de la Méthode* in 1637. In his lectures at the college of Le Mans[1] he dictated the new principles to his pupils. When he sent to Father Mersenne his objections to the *Meditations* of Descartes, which appeared in 1641, he wrote these explicit words: "You have known for a long time in what esteem I hold the person of M. Descartes and the value I set upon his mind and teaching."

In June, 1648, he writes to Descartes himself that he has "read with admiration and approved almost entirely of all that he has written touching the first philosophy" (*i.e.* Metaphysics). He held these opinions all his life.

It was in vain that Leibnitz, in that interesting correspondence from 1686 to 1690, which has been published in our time, showed him how much was lacking in the philosophy of Descartes, that he was not satisfied with the definition of the body by extension nor with that of the soul by thinking, nor[2] of the conditions of the perfection of God and of the immortality of the soul, nor of the automatism of animals. Arnauld remains convinced of the soundness of the doctrine of Descartes, and does not cease taking up its defence. In 1692 he repels the attacks of Huet, Bishop of Avranches, as in 1680 he had done those of Lemoine, Dean of the Chapter at Vitré. He appeals to the principles of Descartes against the Calvinists in the *Perpétuité de la foi*, so far as to make Jurieu say that the theologians of Port-Royal were more attached to Cartesianism than to Christianity. (*Politique du clergé de France*, p. 107.)

Elsewhere he sadly wonders that the Inquisition has not put the works of Gassendi, who had employed his whole mind to ruin spiritual philosophy in favour of the doctrines of Epicurus, in the Index, and that it had, in fact, placed the *Meditations* of Descartes in it.

---

[1] At Paris, in the rue de Reims, then in 1682 rue d'Enfer; in 1761 it was united with the Collège Louis le Grand.

[2] Bossuet supports him: "Every time that M. de Leibnitz," he replies to him, "undertakes to prove that the essence of the body is not in its actual extent any more than that of the soul in actual thought, I declare myself on his side. (*Œuvres*, t. x. p. 97.)

Nicole is much less firm in his attachment to Cartesianism. With his turn of mind, readily sceptical in everything that does not relate to faith, he takes pleasure in disparaging philosophy. "If I had to live over again I think that I would so act as not to be put in the number of the Cartesians any more than in that of others. . . . In truth, the Cartesians are worth little more than the rest, and are often prouder and more self-sufficient; and Descartes himself was not a man who might be called a pious person." (t. viii. p. 153–156.)

We shall be less astonished at seeing a professor of philosophy treat with so little respect him whom history calls the father of modern philosophy when we read the judgment that he pronounced on the real founder of ancient philosophy.

"Socrates . . . . is a man full of small ideas and petty reasoning, who looks only on the present life, a man who finds pleasure in discoursing on truths for the most part useless, and which only tend to enlighten the mind with respect to a few human objects." (t. xi. p. 119.)

It would be difficult to have a more narrow and unjust prejudice and to decry thus gratuitously one of the most real glories of humanity; the immortal thinker who recalled men to the study of themselves, who preached to them temperance and justice and the dignity of labour, who courageously opposed the sophists, the ethics of pleasure and passion, the politics of force, and who crowned this disinterested and useful life by a heroic death.

Although, then, Nicole passes for the author of the two discourses prefixed to the *Logic*,[1] the merit of the firm and courageous attitude of the authors towards Aristotle and scholasticism must especially be attributed to the influence of Arnauld.

---

[1] Arnauld only speaks of the first of these discourses in this note to Mme. de Sablé: "All that I can do to reconcile myself with you is to send you something that will amuse you for half an hour, and in which I think you will see expressed a part of your ideas respecting the folly of mankind. It is a discourse that we have been thinking of prefixing to our *Logic*. You will oblige us by sending us your opinion of it when you have seen it, for it is only persons like yourself that we would have for judges of it." (19 April, 1660.) It is in the second, which answers the objections, that the hand of Arnauld is visible.

Introduction. 29

In the struggle of the Cartesian philosophy to free modern thought from the heavy yoke of Aristotle and scholasticism, we know with what prudence[1] Descartes had in 1637 undertaken the destruction of the ancient philosophy by proclaiming the right of free examination, provisional doubt, and the criterion of evidence.

"My intention is not to teach here the method that each man must follow to properly guide his reason, but only to show how I have tried to guide my own." (*Discours de la Méthode*, i.)

".... Setting forth this writing only as a history, or, if you like it better, as a fable. ... My design has never extended further than trying to form anew my own proper thoughts, and to build on a foundation which is entirely my own." (ii.)

He writes to Father Mersenne in 1641: "I will tell you, between ourselves, that these six meditations contain all the foundations of my physics; but do not say so, if you please, for those who favour Aristotle will perhaps make more difficulty in approving of them; and I hope that those who read them will insensibly get accustomed to my principles, and will recognize their truth before perceiving that they destroy Aristotle's."

We shall understand this prudence if we remember that Giordano Bruno, who, among other misdeeds, had opposed the philosophy of Aristotle at Paris, was burnt at Rome in 1600; that Vanini, in 1619, at Toulouse was condemned for his philosophical opinions to have his tongue cut out and afterwards to be hanged and burnt; that Galileo, who had been severely admonished in 1616 by the congregation of the Index, had to go to Rome in 1633 to solemnly abjure his theory of the movement of the earth.

The *Logic* of Port-Royal, published in 1662, lays down clearly and boldly the right of human reason before the jurisdiction of authority: " It is a very great restraint for a man to think himself obliged to approve of Aristotle in everything, and to take him as the guide to the truth of philosophical opinions. ... The

---

[1] Bossuet thinks it excessive: "M. Descartes has always feared to be remarked by the Church, and we see him take precautions against that, some of which run to excess." (Lettre à M. Postel, docteur de Sorbonne, 24 mai, 1701.)

world cannot remain long under this constraint, and insensibly regains possession of natural and reasonable liberty, which consists in approving what it judges to be true and rejecting what it judges to be false."

To appreciate at its real worth the boldness of these resolute declarations, we must remember that in 1670, the general of the jesuits wrote to all the houses of the society to oppose Descartes' philosophy, and that shortly afterwards the University presented a petition to the Parliament to forbid its teaching. The *Arrêt Burlesque*, composed by Boileau in 1675, did ample justice to it.

"The Court having examined the petition .... setting forth that for several years an unknown person, named Reason, had attempted to enter by force the schools of the said University .... where Aristotle had always been recognized as judge, without appeal, and not accountable for his opinions ...; having examined the treatises, entitled *Physics of Rohault, Logic of Port-Royal* ...

"The Court .... has maintained and kept, maintains and keeps, the said Aristotle in full and peaceable possession of the said schools. ... And, in order that in the future he be not molested, has banished in perpetuity Reason from the schools of the said University; forbids him to enter them and disturb or molest the said Aristotle in the possession and use of the same, on pain of being declared a jansenist and friend of innovations. ..."

The greatest merit of the *Port-Royal Logic* is to have introduced Cartesiansm into teaching. It proclaims aloud that it has borrowed some reflections "from the books of a celebrated philosopher of this age, who has as much clearness of mind as there is confusion in the others." It sets forth, like Descartes, in the name of the famous axiom, "I think, therefore I exist," the evidence of conscience as the criterion of truth, and the four rules of his *Method* as the best guarantee against error, and for discovering the truth in human sciences.

It was indeed the spirit of Descartes that suggested to the authors their small confidence in the rules of logic, and the infallibility of the syllogism, their title of "Art of thinking" instead of "Art of reasoning," their carefulness in forming the judgment by replacing the abstract and conventional examples by instructive examples taken from the different branches of knowledge, to give to logic at once more interest and especially more practical utility, and to bring it out of the school and make it useful for the study of the sciences as well as for the conduct of life.

These solid merits have made this work a classic. Excepting certain defects of plan and proportion, easily explicable by the haste in which the work was composed, by the collaboration of two authors, and by the successive additions that they made to it, there is really but one fault, but it is a grave one, to be found with the *Logic*, namely, that it is so full of the spirit of Descartes that it escapes the influence, not yet very marked it is true, of Bacon.[1] A theologian and geometrician, Arnauld has explained the method of deduction, and completely neglected the method of induction, observation, and experiment which are suitable to the physical and natural sciences. It was in vain that the illustrious Chancellor of England, in the *Novum Organum*, in 1620, with the enthusiasm of an apostle, had invited men to lay aside the sterile dogmatism and the compilations of pretended scholars, and to interpret the great book of nature by a patient observation of facts;[2] "not to cling, so to say, to empty abstractions and pursue unrealities like the common logic, but to anatomize nature, to discover the real properties of bodies, and their well-determined actions and laws in matter" (*Nov. Org.* ii. § 52.); to give up the syllogism as "an instrument too weak and coarse to penetrate into the depths of nature." (*Nov. Org.* i. § 13.)

A very remarkable chapter, in which we recognize the delicate hand of Nicole, his talent for analysis and his gentle raillery, namely, that on *fallacies in life*, permits us to study the moralist under his true aspect.

We know what an impassioned cult Mme. de Sévigné did not cease to profess for the moral philosophy of Nicole, notwithstanding

---

[1] Nevertheless we find the Advocate-General Bignon, one of the great friends of Port-Royal, speaking at length of Bacon to a traveller who came from England. (*Vie* par l'abbé Pérau, vol. ii. p. 92.) Descartes, in his *Letters* (t. ii. pp. 324, 330, 494), approves of Bacon's method, and thinks it proper for those who wish to work at the advancement of the sciences. He always calls him Verulamius, from the barony of Verulam that he possessed.

[2] "What it is necessary, so to say, to attach to the understanding is not wings, but on the contrary lead, a weight which may restrain its flight," he says in his figurative language. (*Nov. Org.* i. § 104.)

the bitter criticisms of her son,[1] who openly declared the *Traité de la connaissance de soi même* "distilled, sophisticated gibberish in several passages, and, above all, wearisome almost from one end to the other." She proclaimed it "admirable, delightful"; she is "charmed" with it; it is a pleasure which "carries her away." She felt a lively pleasure in seeing "the human heart so well anatomized, and its depths searched with a lantern." "It is a treasure to have such a good mirror of the weaknesses of our heart." (vol. i. 71.) This patient, ingenious, sometimes playful and gently satirical analysis of weaknesses, eccentricities, prejudices, and illusions gave satisfaction to her fine and delicate mind, as the purity and severity of the morality did to the nobility of her sentiments and the respectability of her life.

The *Essais de morale* comprise six volumes, to which may be added two other volumes of Letters, which are not the least interesting part of the works of Nicole. No comprehensive plan binds these various *Essais* together, because they were composed from day to day as opportunity offered. The first are well developed and very methodical treatises, in which the author feels himself at his best, because he finds something "to prove and to settle." Then they are only very short articles, and at last simple detached thoughts.

Nicole rarely raises his voice to the pitch of the keen eloquence of Pascal; he lacks authority and real passion in order to move us profoundly; he leaves us cold, and makes us smile rather than tremble when, for instance, he represents the whole world under the power of the demon, as "a place of execution . . . full of all instruments of men's cruelty, and filled on the one side with executioners, and on the other with an infinite number of criminals abandoned to their rage. . . . We pass our days in the midst of this spiritual carnage, and we may say that we swim in the blood of

---

[1] Ch. de Sévigné thus terminates a letter to his mother: "And I tell you that the first volume of the *Essais de morale* would appear to you just as it does to me, if La Marans and the abbé Têtu had not accustomed you to fine and elaborate things. This is not the first time that gibberish appears to you clear and easy; of all that has been said of man and the heart of man, I have seen nothing less agreeable; those portraits in which everyone recognizes himself are not there. Pascal, the *Port-Royal Logic*, Plutarch and Montaigne speak very differently; this man speaks because he wishes to speak, and often he has not much to say." (2 February, 1676.)

sinners, that we are all covered with it, and that this world which bears us is a river of blood." (*De la crainte de Dieu.*) He does not succeed better in his picture of the conscience of the sinner at the moment that he appears before his judge; he compares it to "a vast but dark chamber, that a man works all his life to fill with adders and serpents. . . . When he is thinking least of it, the windows of this chamber opening all of a sudden and letting in the broad daylight, all the serpents awake suddenly, and springing upon the wretch, they tear him to pieces with their bites," &c. (*Du jugement.*) To represent the primitive corruption of man, "let us imagine," says he, "a universal plague, or, rather, an accumulation of plagues, pests, and malignant carbuncles with which the body of a man may be covered, &c.; this is an image of the state in which we are born." (*De la connaissance de soi-même.*) There is always the same weakness and impotence with the same exaggeration.

Sometimes Nicole gives a smart and clever touch, that sets off the expression and renders the truth pleasing. Here are two passages of a letter which deserve to be extracted:—

"The young children of our villages have a very amusing custom when they go in procession after Easter. He who carries the bell separates himself with a few companions a quarter of a league from the main body of the procession, and if he meet another bell they come to action; they knock their bells against each other, and do not finish the contest until one of the bells is broken. After which there is nothing more to be said, for no one can doubt on which side victory is. It is much to be wished that it were the same in the conflict of caprices, and that the one that is broken should be so plainly and incontestably broken that there could be no doubt about it," &c. (*Essais*, t. vii. p. 31.)

And a few pages further on: "I should even dare to tell you (*provided that* you do not take my comparison too literally, and *that* you do not take it into your head to conclude *that* I accuse you of drunkenness) *that* I should wish *that* one should do with regard to imputations *that which* they say *that* the Breton girls do with regard to the fault *which* prevails in that country, *which* is that of getting intoxicated; for, as they suppose *that* there is no man *who* is exempt from it, they will not marry one, it is said, without having seen him drunk, in order to know by that whethe he is merry or quarrelsome in his cups." (*Essais*, t. vii. p. 35.)

We have said that the jansenists use long and cumbrou sentences. This quotation is a sufficiently demonstrative proof o it. The matter is here spoilt, as if designedly, by the form. Bu at Port-Royal it was thought derogatory to Christian humility t pay attention to style, and Nicole declares to Mme. de la Fayett that he does not think it a great evil to be a bad author. (t. viii p. 261.)

The neglect that he suffered because he would not take up th quarrels of Port-Royal to the end inspired this gentle and witt raillery:—

"It is the same with friends as with clothes. Some are onl good for summer, others for winter, others for spring and autumn But as we only put off our summer clothes after the season i past, and keep them for another year, it is necessary in the sam way to keep our friends, although they may not be good at al times, and to reserve them for those when they may be useful Some are only good for the month of July, that is to say, whei there is no cold to fear, and their number is sufficiently great. (*Essais*, t. vii. p. 167.)

But most often Nicole, without bestowing much care on th form (he declares that he is incapable of a double attention) follows his thought, and conducts his fine and delicate analysi at a uniform and rather monotonous pace. He has been unde no illusion with regard to this, and his declaration is mos explicit: "As there are painters who, having little imagination give all their characters the same features, there are also peopl who always write in the same manner, and whose style is alway recognizable. No one ever had this defect more than I." Nicole wa not the man to make Bossuet change his opinion on the judgmen already delivered by him in 1669: "The style of MM. de Port Royal has little variety; without variety there is no pleasure. We know the passionate outburst of J. le Maistre: "Nicole, th coldest, the greyest, the most *leaden*, the most insupportable o the bores of that great and tedious house."

We are here a long way from the enthusiasm of Mme. d Sévigné: "What language! what skill in the arrangement o the words! One thinks one has only read French in this book." (12 January, 1676.)

It is precisely in the arrangement of the words and the turn of the phrase that Nicole seems to us absolutely wanting in skill. The expression is well chosen, exact, sometimes profound, often fine and delicate. But it most often loses a portion of its good qualities and charms, because it disappears as if drowned in a drawling and cumbrous sentence, overloaded with incidental or subordinate propositions, which the habitual employment of the present participle makes still heavier. Here is a sufficiently striking example. Nicole has been moved by the gloomy theories of La Rochefoucauld, and he writes: "So many secret affectations glide into friendships, that I scarcely dare to say that I love anyone, for fear that all I feel for him may not be reduced to loving myself, there being nothing more usual than only to love in others the favourable sentiments that they have for us, when we imagine we love what God has put in them." (t. vii. p. 40.) On reading such phrases, and they abound in Nicole, we might say, "What a creditable scruple! What tact in putting us on our guard without discouraging us by a bitter and trenchant condemnation of friendship!" But we should never say, "What skill in the arrangement of the words! What a writer!" La Rochefoucauld draws this praise from us at the very time that we repudiate these distressing calumnies against the human heart.

Notwithstanding her admiration, Mme. de Sévigné had too much good sense and soundness of judgment not to take exception several times to the essence of the ideas, and not to point out contradictions in them. Even in that famous *Traité de l'art de vivre en paix avec les hommes*, of which she said she would like "to make broth and swallow it," she agrees with her daughter that if peace and union with our neighbour are so precious, and require so many sacrifices, "there is no way after that of being indifferent to what he thinks of us," and that she is "less capable than anyone of understanding this perfection which is a little above human nature." Her judgment is more severe on the *Traité de la soumission à la volonté de Dieu:* "See how he represents it to us as sovereign, doing all, disposing of all, regulating all. I agree to it, that is what I believe; and if, on turning over the leaf, they mean the reverse, to keep on good terms with both sides, they will have on that, with respect to me, the fate of those political opportunists, and will not make me change." (25 May, 1680.)

Would anyone believe that she is speaking of her beloved Nicole in that curious letter of July 16, 1677? "There is the prettiest gibberish that I have ever seen in the twenty-sixth article of the last volume of the *Essais de morale*, in the treatise *de tenter Dieu*. That is very amusing; and when, besides, we are submissive, that morality is not unsettled by it, and that it is only to confute false reasoning, there is no great harm; for if they would keep silence, we would say nothing; but to wish to establish their maxims by every means, to translate St. Augustine for us, lest we should ignore him, to publish all that is most severe in him, and then to sum up, like Father Bauny, for fear of losing the right of scolding; that is provoking, it is true. . . . May I die if I do not like the jesuits a thousand times better; they are at least consistent, uniform in doctrine and morals. Our brethren speak well and conclude ill; they are not sincere; here I am in Escobar. You see very well, my daughter, that I am playing and amusing myself."

On looking closely into the *Essais* of Nicole it would not be difficult to point out many exaggerations and inexact ideas, false wit, "refinements of spirituality," a certain want of vigour and authority, of impulse and enthusiasm for what is good.[1]

Is it well to preach such enervating doctrines to prepare us to cultivate our faculties in order that we may better fulfil our destiny and courageously perform the duties of life? "Man's real science is to understand the nothingness of the world, and his true happiness to despise it." (t. vii. p. 3.) "The world is but a great hospital full of patients." (t. vii. p. 209.) "The conversation of the world is almost constantly the school of the devil." (t. x. p. 198.) "The devil is the greatest author and the

---

[1] Joubert, who calls Nicole "a Pascal without style," and praises, not the form, but "the matter, which is exquisite," admits, however, that in his *Essais* "the morality of the gospel is perhaps a little too much refined by subtle reasoning." (Vol. ii. p. 165.) Thus Nicole undertook to show an officer "a hundred deadly sins of which he had never heard, and which he did not know at all." (*Essais*, t. vii. p. 151.)

greatest writer in the world, as well as the greatest speaker, since he has a share in most of the writings and speeches of men." (t. xii. p. 176.) "If Christ brought any science into the world it was that of despising all the sciences which are the subject and foundation of the vanity and curiosity of men."[1] (t. xi. p. 89.)

What shall we say of the reflections suggested to him by his asthma? "The world values only the talents of action, and to be good for nothing is to be a subject for its abhorrence. This, however, is a very false judgment, which has its source only in the vanity natural to man, and if we were well rid of it we should find more happiness in the deprivation of the talents that I call the talents of impotence than in all the great qualities." (t. vii. p. 162.)

There can be nothing better than for the moralist to put us on our guard against the dangers of ambition. But is it not forcing the note and missing the aim to lay down this principle: "No person is permitted to endeavour to raise and better either himself or his family"? (t. xi. p. 321.) What father of a family, seeking very legitimately to prepare a better position for his children, would take seriously the reasons appealed to by Nicole, that it is rendering our salvation more difficult, and forsaking the example of Christ, whose whole life was only a continual abasement and humiliation?

Mme. de Sévigné thinks that description of society very amusing in which, thanks to cupidity, very obliging people build and furnish our houses, weave our stuffs, carry our letters, run to the world's end to fetch provisions and materials, or cheerfully render us the lowest and most laborious services. The idea is neither correct nor sound. It has a paradoxical turn, which

---

[1] How much better Bossuet keeps within bounds and reconciles everything: "I am not one of those who make much of human knowledge, yet, nevertheless, I confess that I cannot contemplate without admiration the wonderful discoveries that science has made in order to investigate nature, nor the many fine inventions that art has found to adapt it to our use. Man has almost changed the face of the world. . . . He has mounted to the skies; to walk more safely, he has taught the stars to guide him in his travels; to measure out his life more evenly, he has forced the sun to render an account, so to say, of all his steps." (*Sermons*, 4ᵉ semaine de carême.) Such language honoured the pulpit; Nicole only made a canting discourse.

would make it accepted with more propriety in a humorous writer. In a serious moral lesson it is needful to adopt another tone, and to speak in better terms of that admirable harmony of economical interests that Bastiat has so eloquently described, and which so happily inspired the fine sonnet of M. Sully-Prudhomme. The poet, awaking from a dream, in which he believes himself for an instant abandoned by the labourer, the weaver, and the mason, and seeing with pleasure everybody at work, far from stigmatizing them with the name of grasping, finds only a cry of thankfulness in his heart:—

" And since that day I have loved them all ! "

Is not that grave discussion of seventeen pages on this strange question, *May a person entirely devoted to God have his portrait taken for his friends and neighbours* mere sentimentalism? Christ did, it is true, send to Abgarus, King of Edessa, the impression of His countenance on a cloth, but that was to induce him to be converted. "It would be criminal in us to wish to be considered and loved as the Son of God wished to be considered and loved." (t. viii. p. 196.) And the scene of the staircase? A female devotee was showing Nicole out . . . to honour the steps of Jesus Christ! Notwithstanding his edification at the reply, he endeavoured, but in vain, to show her that useless steps could no more honour those of Christ than words without deeds and without necessity could honour His words, "She did not well understand my reply, and continued to honour Jesus Christ by showing me out." (t. vii. p. 185.)

Even in serious matters Nicole, by his turn of mind, gives a euphuistic character to the moral lesson, and thus impairs its gravity.

Ancient philosophy and Christianity have both recommended as one of the most useful exercises the examination of the conscience, the regulation of the employment of time, incessant watchfulness over our bad propensities, in order to remedy the evil at once. Let us listen to Nicole: "To facilitate this practice, let her imagine that a person who resembles her, that is, who has the same maladies as she has, asks her advice, and that she prescribes all that comes into her mind; let her write down her thoughts on this subject, and let her play the directress with respect to this person, who will not be different from herself. There is nothing but what is reasonable in that, for we are, in fact, double. It is a *sort of game* that I propose, but which will not fail to relieve the mind." (t. vii. p. 47.)

After having written much to dissuade from marriage, does he not ruin his whole argument by this subtle distinction, that he has spoken "as a mere advocate" and not "as a judge," or by this comparison with a person who, being questioned about two roads, contents himself with showing the one he knows best?

As he pleases himself immoderately in his letter to Mlle. Aubry, the directress of the school that he founded at Troyes in 1678, in developing that affected allegory of the pustules (envy, jealousy, malignity), and as he is proud of his analysis, how the Hôtel of Rambouillet would have applauded! "You did not yet know that one of your duties was to cleverly pierce these pustules of the soul; I tell you so now." (t. viii. p. 58.)

To resume, it would be difficult to conclude, with Mme. de Sévigné, that all that "is of the same stuff as Pascal." And if we cede this point, it would be on condition of immediately adding this witty *repartie* of M. V. Fournel: "Yes, but the tailor is different."

His contemporaries boast of his "golden pen." Nicole lacks many things for posterity to ratify this eulogy. Like all the writers of Port-Royal, by an exaggerated scruple of piety, he treats the question of style too disdainfully as a vanity. He is little concerned about negligence of style, the matter alone deserves his attention. Truth appears to him worthy of respect, however she may be clothed. The only question is to know if we are not wanting in respect and compromising her influence by refusing her the garb that is most becoming to present herself to the world and to succeed. Nicole says elsewhere to Mme. de La Fayette that he does not write for the public, but only to employ himself and occupy his mind;[1] that his writings were not made

---

[1] Nicole even says, humorously enough, of an apology that he had composed, that his only aim was "to procure sleep . . . It seems to me that it is a very legitimate purpose to wish to sleep." When his system of *General*

to be printed. When the opportunity made him hastily take up the design of publishing them, "being very much occupied with other things, I satisfied myself by reading them over quickly, paying special attention to the matter. So that not being capable of a divided attention, I am astonished how many inexact expressions have escaped me.[1] All that I can do, then, is to beg intelligent persons to say nothing about them, and to let this edition be exhausted under favour of the indulgence of the public. I shall be more exact another time if I have leisure; and if not I shall put up with the reputation of writing badly, which is not a great evil." But, then, why print? Posterity only collects and preserves well-finished works. Voltaire is a little premature in this prophecy: "The *Essais de morale*, which are useful to mankind, will not perish." (*Siècle de Louis XIV.*, Ecrivains.) D'Aguesseau, like Rollin, had already recommended to his son only "the first four volumes of the *Essais de morale*, which are more carefully finished than the rest, and in which it is easier to perceive a plan and regular order." (4th Instruction.) In our time M. Silvestre de Saci has reduced to one volume his *Choix de petits traités de morale* (1857, 16mo), and doubtless the few readers of an author formerly so much appreciated might easily be counted. He suffers the natural law of retaliation. He has not thought sufficiently of us, and we forget him. What a disillusion would not Mme. de Sévigné suffer on vainly seeking the name of her favourite author in the fine study of M. Prévost-Paradol on *les Moralistes français*. The eminent critic has not given him the most humble place between Montaigne, La Boétie, Pascal, La Rochefoucauld, La Bruyère, and Vauvenargues.

There is among the *Essais de morale* a tract which more especially interests us, *De l'éducation d'un prince*. It does honour to the educators of Port-Royal. We extract a few thoughtful pages, in which the reader will find useful subjects for meditation. What a fine and broad definition! "The aim

---

Grace was attacked, he answered the objections by repeating his saying: "It is a sort of narcotic that I have always used." (Quoted by Sainte-Beuve, t. iv. p. 492.)

[1] We read in the same letter: "I should not dare to say to what the corrections that I might make, if I had leisure, would amount, there are so many things to observe when negligence of style is to be avoided."

of instruction is to carry the mind to the point that it is capable of attaining." This is a manly sentence that redeems many discouraging phrases on the vanity of curiosity and on the contempt for the sciences. Nicole is not less happy, both in thought and expression, when he points out to the masters that their part is "to expose to the inward light of the mind" the object of their lessons, and that without this light "instruction is as useless as wishing to show pictures during the night. The mind of children is almost entirely full of darkness, and only catches glimpses of small rays of light. Thus everything consists in husbanding these rays, in augmenting them, and in exposing to them what one wishes them to understand. . . . We must look where there is light, and present to it what we wish to make them understand." A perusal of this little tract cannot be too much recommended. A great deal of practical advice on the different branches of teaching will be found in it. It is one of the most authoritative and suggestive books of Nicole.

After Lancelot and Nicole, the most eminent name is that of Coutel, or Coustel (1621-1704). Lemaître, in a memoir inserted in the *Supplément au Nécrologe*, enters in May, 1650, the arrival at Port-Royal des Champs of "M. Coutel, Picard, sçavant en grec et en latin." Since the establishment of the *Petites Écoles* in the rue Saint-Dominique-d'Enfer (1646) he had been placed in charge of a division of six pupils. It was only in 1687 that he drew up the *Rules for the Education of Children*, a work dedicated to Cardinal Furstemberg, whose nephews he had educated. It is the most complete and methodical work of Port-Royal on pedagogy that remains to us. The matter is worth much more than the form. Coustel was far from being a good writer, but he was an earnest and devoted teacher, modest and sensible, who knew children well and loved them. The prolixity, negligence, and commonplace of his style condemned him to a prompt oblivion.

As to Guyot, it is strange that the historians of Port-Royal have not given him a short notice. Besogne declares that "nothing is known of him." Guyot was, however, one of the masters on the first foundation, and is the author of numerous publications. We owe him A New Translation of the Captives of Plautus, 1666; Moral and Political Letters of Cicero to his friend Atticus, 1666 ; A New Translation of a New Collection of the Best Letters of Cicero to his Friends, 1666 ; Letters of Cicero to his Common Friends, and to Atticus, his Particular Friend, 1668 ;[1] A Political Letter of Cicero to his Brother Quintus, and Scipio's Dream, 1670 ; A New Translation of the Bucolics of Virgil, 1678 ; Moral and Epigrammatic Flowers from Ancient and Modern Writers, 1669. And at the beginning of several of these works he has developed, in very extended and important prefaces, several of the pedagogic reforms in the realization of which he had collaborated in the *Petites Écoles*.

The reason of the silence of Port-Royal on this master, who played such an active part, has been given by Barbier, in a notice on Th. Guyot (*Magasin encyclopédique*, August, 1813) ; he did not remain faithful to Port-Royal. One of his works, published in 1666, is dedicated to Messeigneurs de Montbaron, students with the R.R. P.P. Jésuites at the College of Clermont, "that celebrated school," says he, "that piety has dedicated to science and virtue." He disowned his old friends in their misfortune, and paid court to their relentless persecutors. Nevertheless, some extracts from one of his prefaces, on teaching reading, on the study of the French language, and on the advantages of oral instruction, will be read with interest.

It is proper to devote a few lines at least to the austere and venerable Wallon de Beaupuis, director of the *Petites Écoles de Port-Royal*. Born at Beauvais in 1621, he commenced his studies in the college of that town, partly under the celebrated Godefroi Hermant ; then, after a fourth year of rhetoric with the jesuits at

---

[1] The translator causes a smile when, under pretence of politeness, he introduces into the letters of Cicero and his friends our French forms : "*Monsieur votre frère, madame votre mère, mademoiselle votre fille, madame votre femme,*" transforms Balbus into M. Lebègue, and Pomponius into M. de Pomponne ! But what is more serious is that in an excellent preface, which sums up all education in "precision of mind and rectitude of will," he several times compares the child to a bird in a cage ! "By restraining and confining him within the limits of a strict discipline, *as in a cage*, to teach him to be wise and virtuous . . ." (p. 114). "As far as possible, all the openings of the cage, which give to this spirit the greatest desire to go out, must be closed. Some open *bars* . . . . to live and be in health ; this is what we do with *nightingales* to make them sing, and to *parrots* to teach them to talk" (p. 127). "More than one *cage* is necessary for him to live and to render him capable of instruction " (p. 137).

Paris, he studied philosophy with Arnauld at the College of Le Mans, and then theology at the College of Clugny. The book on *Fréquente Communion* won him over to Port-Royal, where he was admitted in 1644. He was entrusted with the charge of the school in the rue Saint-Dominique; then, in 1653, with that of Le Chesnai, of which he has left us the regulations. He was engaged, besides, in collecting extracts from the Fathers to aid Arnauld and Nicole in the composition of their works. After the breaking-up of the *Petites Écoles* he was ordained priest, notwithstanding his resistance, and was for some time preceptor to the two young Periers, Pascal's nephews; then, in 1676, he had the direction of the seminary at Beauvais. Disgraced at the end of three years, and deprived of all employment, he passed the remainder of his life in the most austere retreat, without any other recreation than an annual journey to Port-Royal. He died in February, 1709, at the age of 87, bearing witness to himself that "by the grace of God he had sought always and above everything the supreme good." His work at Port-Royal was more religious than pedagogic.

Dr. Antoine Arnauld [1] deserves a place of honour among the pedagogues of Port-Royal, although the great business of his life had been to fulfil the last vow of his dying mother, that of Saint-

---

[1] Antoine Arnauld was born at Paris, February 6, 1612. He was the twentieth child of the celebrated advocate Arnauld, who, in 1594, had defended the University against the jesuits with so much vehemence. This was the most illustrious conquest of Saint-Cyran during his imprisonment. Entirely devoted to Port-Royal, to which he made a donation of his property, priest and doctor in 1641, he devoted his life to the defence of religion and morality. His very numerous works, almost exclusively polemical, form no less than forty-two folio volumes. The greater number have suffered the fate reserved for this kind of books. "The fire and division becoming extinct," says La Bruyère, "they are like last year's almanacks." His treatise, *De la fréquente Communion* (1643), deserves special mention. "This book caused something like a revolution in the manner of understanding and practising piety, and also in the manner of writing theology. . . . It was, to say truth, the first manifestation of that Port-Royal of Saint-Cyran, which until then had remained rather in the shade, in a sort of mystery conformable to the character of the great director." (SAINTE-BEUVE, t. ii. p. 166.) Almost always compelled to hide and to fly, he died in exile at Brussels, 8 August, 1694. His burial place was kept secret, lest the jesuits should have him disinterred, as they did Jansenius.

Cyran, and his own oath as doctor, namely, the defence of the truth. It was in the midst of his constantly-recurring struggles against the jesuits Sirmond, Pétau, Nouet, Brisacier, Annat, and Maimbourg, against the faculty of theology, against the assembly of the clergy, against the archbishops of Paris, Péréfixe, and Harlai, against the archbishop of Embrun, against the doctors Morel and Lemoine, against Richard Simon, against Jurieu, against the bishops of Lavaur and Vabres, against Malebranche, against the calvinists, and against Nicole himself, that the indefatigable athlete, as if in play and to fill up his scanty moments of leisure, composed his most justly estimated works. The *Grammaire générale et raisonnée* is, to tell the truth, all his own. His letter to some members of the Academy on the difficulties of French syntax bears witness to the power and acuteness of his criticism, and would alone suffice to justify the estimate of Bossuet —a sound and powerful arguer.

We know the occasion on which he composed the *Logic*, or the *Art of Thinking*. "One day," says Besogne, "when M. Arnauld was conversing with several persons, among whom was the young duc de Chevreuse, the son of the duc de Luines, he told this young nobleman that if he would give himself the trouble he would engage to teach him in four or five days all that was worth knowing in *Logic*. The proposition surprised the company a little. They conversed about it for some time. At last M. Arnauld, who had made the offer, resolved to make the trial. He set to work to compose a short abridgment of *Logic*, which he hoped to finish the same day. But, while reflecting, so many new thoughts occurred to his mind that he employed four or five days, during which he formed the body of the work. The paper was put into the hands of the young duke, who reduced it to four tables, and by learning one each day he knew the whole at the end of four days, so that the prediction of four or five days came true to the letter." (t. v. p. 524.)

He composed his *Elements of geometry* in the same way, at a moment's notice, so to say, during a slight illness, in a few days of liberty in a country house at Le Chesnai, "without any book." And if we may believe a note of the editor, Pascal had judged this work so favourably that he had burnt an essay on this science when he saw the manner in which Arnauld had remedied the confusion imputed to Euclid.

Is it not very touching to see him engrossed with a question of pure pedagogy in the midst of the worry of persecution, and at a time when he was obliged to hide? "You will laugh," he writes, January 31, 1656, to the Mother Angélique, "at what gives me occasion to write to you. There is a little boy about twelve years old who does not know how to read. I wish to try if he can learn by M. Pascal's method. I therefore beg you to finish what you have begun to set down in writing." (t. i. p. 101.) It is not impossible that the Mother Angélique laughed when she received this letter;[1] we, however, are not tempted to do so; we admire the good heart that reveals itself with such amiable simplicity.

M. Sainte-Beuve has devoted the last chapter of his third volume to the most eminent students of Port-Royal (Jérôme and Thierry Bignon, Racine, Le Nain de Tillemont, &c.). I am happy to fill up a grave lacuna by adding the name of Boisguilbert to his list.

In the Advertisement to the reader, in one of his translations, the precursor of the economists, whom history has finally avenged of the scorn of Voltaire, thus expresses himself: "Although it seems that in our days all the sciences have been carried to the highest point that they can ever attain, we may say that that of making Greek and Latin writers speak our language has gone further, nothing being able to be added to the works of those gentlemen of the Academy, of Monsieur d'Andilly, who seems to have surpassed himself in his Josephus, and of *those famous anonymous writers so celebrated throughout France;* so I shall candidly confess that if I am sufficiently happy that this small work is not found very imperfect, I owe it *to some education that*

---

[1] I judge so by this detail that the abbé Racine relates: Some of the sisters asked the Mother Angélique whether their novices and boarders would not be restored to them. "My daughters," she replied, "do not trouble yourselves about that. I am not anxious about whether your novices and boarders will be restored to you, but I am that the spirit of retirement, simplicity, and poverty shall be preserved among us. Provided that these things continue, *laugh at all the rest.*" (*Abrégé de l'histoire ecclesiastique,* t. x. p. 541.)

I received among them in my youth."[1] (*Roman History*, by Herodian, 1675.)

The thinker and patriot, whose enthusiastic eulogy [2] Michelet so justly made, is not one of the least glories with which Port-Royal may adorn herself.

OF THE EDUCATION OF GIRLS AT PORT-ROYAL.

"At Port-Royal," writes M. Cousin, "the women are, perhaps, more extraordinary, and assuredly quite as great as the men. Is not the Mother Angélique the equal of Arnauld by her intrepidity of soul and elevation of thought?[3] Is Nicole much above the Mother Agnès? She has more energy with as much gentleness. And did not their niece, the Mother Angélique de Saint-Jean, use, in the government of Port-Royal, a prudence, ability, and courage that her brother, the minister, might[4] have envied her? Who among the men has dared and struggled more, and has suffered more, and more patiently than all these women? They also have known and braved persecution, calumny, exile, and prison. . . ." (*Jacqueline Pascal*, p. 491.)

But if these persons are morally equal, is it the same with their pedagogic work? We have not, so to say, any information about the education of the girls at Port-Royal.[5] We know, in

---

[1] The names of Boisguilbert and his brother are, in fact, mentioned in the *Vies intéressantes et édifiantes*, p. 86.

[2] "May we see on the bridge of Rouen, opposite Corneille, the statue of a great citizen who, a hundred years before 1789, sent out from Rouen the first sound of the Revolution with as much vigour and more gravity than Mirabeau did later!"

[3] "M. d'Andilly said to me, 'Count all my brothers, my children, and myself as fools in comparison with Angélique.' Nothing that has come out of those parts has ever been good which has not been amended and approved by her; she is steeped in all the languages and sciences; in fine, she is a prodigy." (*Lettre de Mme. de Sévigné*, 29 Nov., 1679.) Sainte-Beuve equally pays homage to this great mind: "No character in our subject appears to us more truly great and *royal* than she—she and Saint-Cyran." (t. iv. p. 160.)

[4] M. de Pomponne, secretary of state, chargé d'affaires étrangères from 1671 to 1679.

[5] Here are a few dates of the establishment of the schools, and a few figures for the number of pupils. In 1609, the date of the reformation of the monastery by the Mother Angélique, the Sister Louise Sainte-Praxède de Lamoignon was appointed mistress of the boarders, as being the most

a general manner, that it was much praised and sought after. Testimony in its favour is not wanting. "A great number of girls brought up in this monastery," says Racine, "might be cited who have since edified the world by their wisdom and virtue. We know with what feelings of admiration and thankfulness they (women of quality) have always spoken of the education that they had received there." The abbé Fromageau, who was sent by the archbishop of Paris, May 9, 1679, to make an inquiry by the king's order, dwelt at length, Besogne relates (t. ii. p. 507), "on the excellent education that was given to the children of whom he mentioned, as an example, the young demoiselle Bignon." A few days after, the archbishop "exhausted himself in eulogies of the virtue of the nuns, and of the excellent education they gave to the children.[1] And when the president de Guedreville, whose daughter was a boarder at Port-Royal, came to inquire what grave reason caused the dismissal of the boarders, the prelate assured him of the irreproachable management of the house, and of the excellence of the education that was received there."[2]

But there is an absolute want of proofs. Where are the programmes of studies? What methods did the mistresses employ? What books did they put into the hands of their pupils? What traces have they left of their teaching and of

---

capable of any of the twelve professed nuns of Port-Royal. The monastery was transferred in 1626 to the faubourg Saint-Jacques (now the *Maternité*). The house of Port-Royal des Champs was re-opened in 1648. In 1661, at the time of the closing of the schools, there were 21 boarders in Paris, and 20 at the Champs. Besogne gives the list of them. (t. i. p. 412.) At the "peace of the church" in 1669, the boarders were again admitted into the two houses, henceforth completely separated. But on the death of the duchesse de Longueville (1679), the king ordered them to be definitely sent back to their parents. Besogne counts then 42 pupils. Nicole had founded a girls' school at Troyes in the preceding year. The teaching sisters, or black sisters, who were in charge of it were ordered not to teach any more in 1742, and in 1749 were dispersed. This last information is furnished us by M. Th. Boutiot. (*Histoire de l'instruction publique et populaire à Troyes pendant les quatre derniers siècles*, 1864.)

[1] "There was nothing to find fault with in the education that she gave to the children, he told the abbess; on the contrary, nowhere was it so good." (*Hist. gen. de P.-R.*, t. vii. p. 318.)

[2] Clémencet makes him say: "They train the boarders perfectly well, not only in piety and morals, but also by forming their minds; there is no place where they would be better for all things than there.

their system of education? Racine indeed tells us: "They were not satisfied with training them up in piety; they also took great pains to form their minds and reason, and laboured to render them equally capable of becoming some day either perfect nuns or excellent mothers." (*Abrégé de l'histoire de Port-Royal.*) The programme certainly is excellent; it is very unfortunate that the proofs in support of it are absolutely wanting.

The respectable du Fossé (*Mémoires pour servir à l'histoire de Port-Royal*, p. 378) extols the merits of Mother Angélique Arnauld, who for twenty-seven years was at the head of the community. He praises her ability "in making shrines, like the most clever architects, or wax figures better finished than those that are seen at Benoit's; in writing letters that touch the heart and elevate the mind"; he praises her sound piety, her profound humility, her ardour for penance, and her contempt of the world. But there is not a word relating to education. And, in fact, the Mother Angélique in her *Entretiens et Conférences* has never treated a question having a bearing on education. Once only a sister consulted her about the absence of mind that children caused her. The answer was so short that the poor sister did not understand it, and dared not press the matter.

On the other hand, there are many passages not very encouraging as to the intellectual development of the pupils.

Page 377: "The demon delivered a discourse on philosophy which lasted two hours, the most lofty and elegant that this philosopher had ever heard. He was quite delighted with it; but the moment it was finished he forgot it so entirely that he could not even remember a single word . . .; this discourse, which appeared so admirable and was so useless, shows that all human sciences are but vanity, and that they are often more hurtful than useful, because they puff up the mind."

Page 399: "Rejoice, ye poor and unlearned, without books, without reading or elevated conversation, in preparing your vegetables, in boiling your pot, if you are satisfied with your condition, if you are contented to be the least in the house of God, if you have no desire for another condition; the Son of God came for you. Have no care, He Himself will convert your heart: fear not the lack of instruction."

Judging from the writings of the Mother Agnès, teaching appears to be an unpleasant task imposed on the sisters :[1] "You must not, if you please," we read in a letter of March 18, 1655, to the sister Marie-Dorothée Perdreau, "desire to be exempt from the service of the children, although it may be unpleasant to you; for, since we receive them in this house, the lot may fall upon you as well as another." The Constitutions force them, nevertheless, on this course, while recommending them to apply themselves to their task with "great disinterestedness, dreading this task on account of the many opportunities there are for making mistakes, for diverting oneself too much, and losing the spirit of meditation, which it is not easy to preserve in such a great employment." Want of professional qualification, far from being taken into consideration in the interest of the children, is precisely a motive for the superiors for choosing the nuns who, for the work of their salvation, need to be humbled and to suffer. "Do not put forward as an excuse," the Mother Agnès writes again, "that you do not discharge this duty well, and that you make many mistakes, for it is for that very reason that perhaps it will be found fitting to leave you there still, that you may better understand your incapacity . . . God permits the children not to behave to you as they ought that these insubordinate pupils may make you suffer and humble yourself." (Faugère, t. ii. p. 465 and 461.)

This is doubtless very edifying but not very pedagogic, and the children appear to be sacrificed too much to the moral advancement of their mistresses. We cannot, however, but pay tribute to their devotedness and self-abnegation. They are also, as far as it is possible to judge by the very rare passages that refer to them in the voluminous writings of Port-Royal, imbued with an admirable sense of their responsibility. "She was so humble," says the *Nécrologe* of D. Rivet, speaking of the sister Marie de Sainte-

---

[1] Dufossé admits it implicitly : "Although the order which obliged the nuns of Port-Royal to dismiss their boarders (1669) caused them much distress on account of the young girls who were so unjustly deprived of a pious education, it was, nevertheless, easy to console themselves on their own account because of the relief that they received from it, and the incomparably greater peace that this release procured for them." (*Mém. pou servir à l'histoire de P.-R.* p. 177.)

Aldegonde des Pommares, deputy mistress, "that she took upon herself almost all the faults that the children committed, always thinking that they would not have happened except for her want of discretion or through having spoken to them roughly." (Page 5.) Similar testimony is borne to the sister Anne-Eugénie by Besogne in an interesting page that we have extracted.

The Constitutions of the monastery of Port-Royal and the Regulations for the children, by Jacqueline Pascal, the only documents that we possess, bring before us a very monastic education.

First, the parents must renounce their authority over their children and "offer them to God, unconcerned whether they are to be nuns or in society, according as it shall please God to ordain." Vocations will not be forced, but, as Jacqueline Pascal recommends, "one may make use of the opportunity to say something about the happiness of a good nun . . . . to show that the religious life is not a burden, but one of the best gifts of God." Thus the greater number of the young women renounce the worldly life. Everything contributes to this. Although the Constitutions contain this article: "The girls may be kept until the age of sixteen years although they do not wish to be nuns," the Mother Angélique gave notice to Mme. de Chazé that her daughter, who was about fifteen, "did not wish to be a nun, and that it was necessary to remove her." (Leclerc, *Vies intéressantes et édifiantes des religieuses de Port-Royal*, t. iii. p. 28.)

We may conjecture how marriage was spoken of there. Saint-Cyran, in one of his *Lettres chrétiennes et spirituelles* (they figure in the list of reading books drawn up by Jacqueline Pascal), writes: "If there were 100,000 souls that I loved like yours, I should always wish, in imitation of Saint Paul, never to see them involved (in matrimony), and would do my utmost to prevent them entering it." (t. i. p. 170.) His successor, the abbé Singlin, continues this teaching. We see him at work in the *Vies intéressantes* by Leclerc. The sister Élizabeth de Sainte-Agnès de Féron entered Port-Royal at the age of seven years. When her mother thought of marrying her "Singlin strongly represented to her all that she had to fear in an engagement of this kind. She had always had a great distaste and a terrible dread of marriage." (t. ii. p. 388.) In conformity with these ideas, the Mother Agnès Arnauld wrote, in 1634, to her nephew Lemaître to dissuade him from his project of marriage: "My dear nephew, this will be the last time that I shall use this title. . . . . You will say that I blaspheme this venerable sacrament to which you are so devoted, but do not trouble yourself about my conscience, which knows how to separate the sacred from the *profane*, the precious from the *abject*."[1]

We know with what practical good sense Mme. de Maintenon counteracted this false delicacy, and exclaimed one day: "This is what brings ridicule on conventual education!"

The boarders wore the white habit and the veil of the novices. It is not given to those who at first show some dislike to it.

How was that long day filled which began at four or half-past four o'clock for the elder and at five for the younger children?

With regard to studies, we only see reading and writing mentioned, and on festivals one hour's arithmetic.

The only reading books mentioned refer to piety: The Imitation of Christ, Fr. Luis de Granada, la Philothée, St. John Climacus, The Tradition of the Church, The Letters of M. de Saint-Cyran, The Familiar Theology, The Christian Maxims, contained in the Book of Hours; The Letter of a Carthusian Father, lately translated; The Meditations of St. Theresa on the *Pater-noster*, &c. The morning reading is taken from the service for the day, or from The Life of the Saints, and is to serve for the subject of private conversation during the day. No other books are left with the children than their Hours, Familiar Theology, The

---

[1] This is the language of the *précieuse* Armande:—
"Cannot you conceive what, as soon as it is heard,
Such a word offers to the mind that is repulsive?
By what a strange image one is smitten?
To what an offensive object it leads the thought?
Do you not shudder at it? and can you, sister,
Persuade yourself to accept all the consequences of this word?"
To which the charming Henriette answers so sensibly:—
"The consequences of this word, when I consider them,
Show me a husband, children, and a home,
And I see nothing in all that, if I can reason on it,
To offend the mind or make one shudder."
(MOLIÈRE, *Les Femmes savantes*, acte i. sc. 1.)

Words of Our Lord, The Imitation of Christ, and a Latin and French Psalter.

The regulation recommends to "exercise the memory of the children very much" in order to open their mind, to occupy them and prevent them thinking evil." But further on we see that they have to learn by heart "The Familiar Theology, the Service of the Mass, The Tract on Confirmation, then all the hymns in French in the Hours, then all the Latin hymns in the breviary; and when they have come into the monastery young, there are many who learn the whole Psalter. They have not much difficulty, provided that they are exhorted and *forced a little*." We might suspect it.

As to writing, "they write their copy or they transcribe something when they are *very good* and are permitted to do so."

We are very glad to learn from an enemy that the French language was taught them formally. "There was always," says Father Rapin, "a certain spirit of politeness in these illustrious penitents, who could not belong to a party which had learnt to write and speak well to its contemporaries without feeling the effect of this spirit. . . . Everything there was polished, even the little boarders whom they took the trouble to rear in purity of language as much as in virtue, and it was in conversing with them that Doctor Arnauld found so much pleasure in noticing that great number of new expressions that he had the art to utilize in his works, and of which he made a special study." (*Mémoires*, t. ii. p. 276.)

Let us add needlework, housekeeping, singing by notes, and we shall have gathered all we are able to learn of the programme of studies. There is no trace of the teaching of history or the natural sciences.

With regard to outside news, "they receive the announcement of the taking the veil by some sisters or some note requesting their prayers for some person or some pious undertaking."

We may at least remark in this teaching, which appears to us so inadequate, some good scholastic usages. "At the end of a lesson, three or four children are set to repeat what was told them the day before. They are not questioned in turn, in order to keep them on the alert; sometimes one, sometimes another is addressed. . . .

As to the younger children, they must not be left idle, but their time must be divided, making them read for a quarter of an hour, play for another quarter, and then work for another short time. These changes amuse them, and prevent them forming the bad habit to which children are very prone, of holding their book and playing with it or with their work, sitting sideways and constantly turning their heads."

By as much as Jacqueline Pascal is distressingly laconic, when it is a question of the intellectual development of the pupils, by so much does she please herself in setting out in detail the monastic side of their education.

We are rather shocked by the system of repression to which the girls are subjected. On every page of the Regulations one word constantly reappears, cold and pitiless, namely, silence:[1] perfect silence while rising and dressing,—strict silence till the *Preciosa* of prime,—very strict silence while at work after breakfast at half-past seven,—silence during the household work,—increased silence during the writing lesson,—silence during the two hours' duration of the service and masses in the monastery, even when they do not attend it,—silence in the refectory,—complete silence during work till vespers,—silence after the evening angelus, even in summer, when they are walking in the garden,—great silence while undressing and going to bed at eight o'clock.

Will the poor little mutes at least regain a little liberty, and give themselves up to the joy of their age " in play-time, when it seems they have a right to say many thing to amuse and recreate themselves"? Not by any means, except the very young ones, who are left to play. As to the rest, the mistresses take care to speak to and converse with them, in order to help them to say reasonable things which will enlarge their minds.

---

[1] Evidently these absolute precepts must have been very much modified in practice. The wise caution that precedes the Regulations for children (see p. 226) proves this. "It would not always be easy nor even useful to put it in practice with this severity, for it may be that all children are not capable of such strict silence and so strained a life without being depressed and wearied, which must be avoided above all things." The Mother Agnès writes, about 1660, to Mme de Foix, coadjutrix, of Saintes: "Our boarders are not constrained to keep silence, but they are carefully watched, in order that they may not converse about trifles."

Besides, they are forbidden to speak of their confessions, of the singing of the sisters, of the penances of the refectory, of their dreams, and of the parlour. They are not allowed to speak in an undertone, on pain of repeating aloud what they have said.

Play-time, however, is almost always taken up with work. "Except the very little ones, who always play, all work without losing their time, and they have made it such a habit that nothing wearies them so much as the recreations on festivals."[1] What an admission!

Two extracts (see pp. 245 and 247) permit us to penetrate into Port-Royal at this period of the day. One shows us the Sister Eugénie taxing her ingenuity to amuse the children who cannot play without her. The other, more curious, sketches a lively scene in which the children, taking part in the disputes of the day, amuse themselves by bringing Escobar to trial!

Religious exercises occupy a place very disproportionate to the age of the children, if the aim were not to train them all for the religious life.[2] Prayer is not only the beginning and end of every lesson, it recurs every hour; when the bell rings for a service in the choir work is interrupted to repeat a prayer. The scholars hear mass every day "on their knees; it has been found that this posture is not so uneasy when one has become used to it early." They go to terce and vespers on Sundays and Thursdays, to the high festivals, to the feast-days of saints,

---

[1] There is a question of recreations in the examination of the Sister Jeanne de Sainte-Domitille. "The little girls, the priest tells her, laughing, have answered: 'Alas! recreation, we did not waste our time over that, we did nothing but weep for our sins.' 'This last answer,' replied the sister, smiling, 'comes as little from the children as the preceding. In the matter of recreation they passed two hours a day in it very gaily, and have always been very pleased to go into that house, which has plainly appeared by the sorrow they showed in leaving us.'" (*Histoire des persécutions des religieuses*, p. 171.)

[2] Leclerc says of Mdlle. du Fargis, a boarder from the age of seven years: "The Mother Angélique took special care in training her in virtue, and in inspiring her with contempt of the world and of herself. She soon had the consolation of seeing that her pains and instructions produced excellent results in this young pupil. In fact, when she was of an age to choose her state of life, she formed the resolution to be a nun. "Her father cast himself at her knees. The constancy of the young novice appeared even too heroic to the Mother Angélique, who said to her, 'You must humble yourself; you are too strong.'"

doctors, and others, if they ask and deserve this favour. At eleven o'clock scrutiny of conscience. The elder girls may repeat their sexts. After recreation they sing the *Veni Creator* in preparation for religious instruction; then they are allowed the favour of telling aloud one of their faults, "they are accustomed to do so readily."¹ At four o'clock the elder girls may obtain the favour of going to vespers. At last the evening recreation ends with complines, which they may recite in summer while walking in the garden.

We cannot approve of this excess of religious practices any more than of that spirit of mortification which presents work solely as a penance, which exempts from the collation at the age of fourteen, and exhorts the children " to take sufficient nourishment as not to become feeble." ² At that age the body needs to grow and be strengthened. How much more sensible and humane is Mme. de Maintenon when, in describing a reasonable person, she shows him "eating with a good appetite, not like a glutton with his head in his plate, but gracefully and cleanly, and, since it has pleased God that we should find pleasure in eating, he takes it unaffectedly, and without any scruple."

The Mother Angélique solemnly protests before God, in a fine letter written to the queen on her death-bed in 1661, that they were not at all occupied in the monastery with the theological controversies raised by Saint-Cyran and Arnauld. Father Rapin replies by a dilemma which is not wanting in force. "If these questions are essential to faith, why deprive this house of knowledge necessary to salvation? If they are not so, but are im-

---

¹ Mme de Maintenon absolutely forbids this practice to the Ladies of Saint-Cyr : " Cultivate carefully in your young ladies the sentiments of honour . . . . and do not exact from them practices that might weaken that glory and make them bold : for example, making them acknowledge publicly humiliating faults, thinking that this would be recalling the custom of public confession, which the Church has thought it right to suppress." (*Entretien*, 1703.) Mme. de Maintenon is aiming here at the Jansenists, who had begun to revive this ancient custom.

² Besogne, praising the love of the Mother Angélique for mortification, relates that the most devout of the young girls prided themselves on emulation, and that it very nearly cost three of them very dear who "took it into their heads, in order to mortify themselves in imitation of the nuns, to gather weeds in the garden, pound them up, and swallow the juice." (t. i. p. 42.)

material, why make so much clamour about them everywhere? Why resist the Pope and trouble the Church for affairs of so little importance, that they may be ignored without any bad consequences? Is it likely that the heads of this party are so zealous in teaching their maxims to the whole kingdom, and that Port-Royal alone, where they reside, is left in ignorance of the mysteries that are taught there?" (*Mémoires*, vol. iii. p. 163.)

Two anecdotes related by Mme. de Maintenon at Saint-Cyr would tend to confirm the reasoning of the jesuit father: "When the king forbade boarders to be placed at Port-Royal Mme. la comtesse de *** withdrew her daughter, who was only twelve year old; she brought her to court, where she began to disparage all that M. de Péréfixe had done in his visit to Port-Royal. She was inexhaustible, and I could not understand how a child could speak with such boldness. During this very visit of the archbishop he made a speech to try and gain them over. After a rather long speech he asked a little boarder of nine or ten years old, who had been listening attentively, if she was beginning to be convinced of the truth of what he said. She answered him with an astonishing boldness, 'I admire the depth of the judgments of God to have given us a prelate as ignorant as you are.' And all the nuns applauded this answer. This is the submission and humility that their directors inspire in them." (*Lettres historiques et édifiantes*, vol. ii. p. 227.) No doubt the testimony of an impassioned enemy, and one very much inclined to raillery, must be a little distrusted. But putting together these facts and the recreation scene where the boarders amused themselves by bringing Escobar to trial, we conclude that they were not so entirely strangers to the religious disputes of the time. The contrary would be altogether unlikely.

But what an odious imputation, justly stigmatized by Arnauld (*la Morale pratique des jésuites*, t. viii. p. 209), theological hatred has cast on these nuns, "as pure as angels," said archbishop Péréfixe, by reproaching them with being "as proud as demons!" One of the thousand pamphlets to which the quarrel between the jesuits and jansenists gave rise, *le Pays de Jansénie*, accuses them of giving their pupils lessons in immodesty, in consequence of the doctrine of Jansenius and Saint-Cyran on grace.[1] "Do not think, my daughters," he impudently makes them say, "that the grace of God is always with us. Alas, no! There are wretched times when we are indeed compelled to sin. What should we do if God withdraws Himself? That often happens, however. Are we not indeed unfortunate? Chastity is commanded to us, and sometimes we are deprived of the strength necessary to preserve it. Remember that, my daughters, your salvation is at stake if you ignore it, and you may have need of it at some time. There are husbands who would not be so cruel to their wives if they had studied theology, for they would know that grace is often denied us, and that in that case they should rather pity our weaknesses than be angry for the faults into which we fall by the absence of the succour that God refuses to us, either to punish our infidelities or to teach us by a necessary lapse that we can do nothing without Him. It is thus," continues the pamphleteer, "that they bring up the young to that patience that results in the greatest ignominy of the sex, when solicitations are warm and opportunities present. For although they do not intend to give lessons in immodesty to their young scholars, the doctrine nevertheless leads to it." You admit it, then, venomous logician, all this argument carried to excess is nothing but an insult and a calumny. Attack opinions, but do not outrage persons. Such a proceeding, always culpable, is especially so here towards pious women whose morality no one ever thought of throwing suspicion on. It is an unqualified infamy.

Setting aside the exaggerated anxiety, the suspicious watchfulness, the constant nervousness that the nuns of Port-Royal, under the inspiration of Saint-Cyran, bring to the accomplishment of their task, we must acknowledge the accuracy of their principles with respect to moral education.

To unite a strength which restrains children without repelling them to a gentleness that wins them without enervating them; vigilance and patience; no partiality for the more agreeable and pretty children; no familiarity; great evenness of temper, for

---

[1] *Relation du pays de Jansénie*, by the Capuchin Zacharie, under the name of Louis Fontaine (1658).

too much laxity soon leads to too much severity, and it is much more painful for children to suffer these variations than to be always kept to their duty; seldom to admonish for slight faults, even to pretend not to perceive them; to reprimand without bad temper or offensive terms; "they must be convinced that they are only reprimanded for their good"; to be sparing of words in reprimanding;[1] to chastise even without speaking, in order to prevent the children telling untruths or seeking excuses; to work upon their character with discretion in private conversations; to win their entire confidence, and to be on guard against their cunning; to infuse this idea into them, namely, that their progress in what is good will be measured, not by extraordinary actions, but by the accomplishment of their everyday duties, "by the fidelity they shall bring into the smallest regulations of the schoolroom, by the support they shall give their sisters, by the charity with which they shall serve them in their needs, and by the care they shall take to mortify their faults." Here, in few words, and without pretension, is an excellent line of conduct.

On the whole the girls' schools of Port-Royal affect the history of pedagogy less than the boys' schools. These mark an epoch of notable reforms and real progress. If we often disagree with their venerable masters, if we have neither the same starting-point nor the same goal, if pedagogy has cast off their theological ideas, what advantage may we not still draw from a close intercourse with them. What legitimate lessons they may continue to give us on the proper aim of studies, on the art of managing children and training their minds and hearts. Their works, one of the glories of French pedagogy, still deserve to be read and pondered. Their example especially ought to continue living. A more absolute and disinterested devotedness to the great work of education has never been seen, nor a more watchful conscience, a more sincere and active love of childhood, nor a keener desire to render study easy and attractive.

How did these humble schools raise the implacable hatred

---

[1] "Nothing weakens a reprimand more than a great many words." (Mme. de Maintenon, letter to a mistress, 1692.)

of the jesuits, a hatred that was not extinguished, even after the dispersion of the scholars and the exile or imprisonment of the masters, until the day that the very buildings were razed and destroyed and the tombs profaned?[1] What do I say? This hatred is not yet extinct, it is again revived under our eyes, and at the present time dreams of annihilating the works, and even the very names, of our pious solitaries and their friends.[2]

If the jesuits feared for a moment to see the education of youth slip out of their hands, and their colleges lose their prosperity,[3] as Racine and several writers of Port-Royal assert, they must have been promptly reassured; for the *Petites Écoles* could only be a brilliant and short-lived institution, the individual work of a few eminent masters, which was ill-adapted for imitation, and which, by its narrow limits, confined to a very small number of select pupils, could not respond to the needs of public instruction, and consequently had no future prospects.

The cause of the quarrel must evidently be sought less in the scholastic success of the masters of Port-Royal than in their growing favour with the public as spiritual directors and as writers. Father Canaye explains it candidly in that curious conversation with the Marquis d'Hocquincourt, related by Saint-Évremond who was present: "It was not their diversity of

---

[1] A letter of Feb. 2, 1712, gives frightful details; the writer had them from an eye-witness. The labourers who disinterred the bodies, and broke them when they could not lift them entire, "drank, laughed, sang, and derided those persons whom they found thus in the flesh. But the most horrible thing was that there were ten dogs in the church devouring the flesh which still remained on those limbs which were separated from the bodies, and no one thought of driving them away." (LECLERC, *Vies intéressantes*, t. iv. p. 59.)

[2] The *Catalogue mensuel de l'œuvre pontificale des vieux papiers* (the office is at Langres, Haute-Marne), in its number for April and May 1885, points out to the pious fury of devout souls 33 works to be destroyed. The names of Arnauld, Nicole, Pascal, Saci, Saint-Cyran, Duguet, &c., figure in it. A note, written in a jovial style, explains that the jansenists who did so much evil in former times snore peacefully on the shelves of libraries, and that now is a very favourable moment for laying hands on them and thrusting them all at once into the sack. Comment seems to me needless.

[3] The testimony of Bacon in favour of their talent as educators is often quoted. It is proper to set in the balance the very superior authority, in my opinion, of Leibnitz: "I am far from thinking like Bacon," he writes, "who, when it is a question of a better education, is content to refer to the schools of the jesuits." (*Œuvres*, t. vi. p. 65.)

opinions upon grace nor the five propositions which had set them at loggerheads. The ambition of governing men's consciences did it all. The jansenists found us in possession of the government, and they wished to take it from us. . . ." (*Œuvres* de Saint-Évremond, t. ii. p. 156.)

Victors along all the line, both as writers and directors of conscience, the jansenists had necessarily to succumb before the double opposition of the Church and the State.

Captivated by perfection and holiness, conceiving a very high idea of religion and morality, pushing the requirements of the Christian life, the responsibility of the priesthood, and the terrible grandeur of God to the extreme, they had bewailed the disorders of the clergy, of the Court of Rome,[1] and the monastic orders, and, like Vincent de Paul, François de Sales, de Bérulle, de Rancé, and Bourdoise, had felt deeply the need of a complete reform. With the generous but somewhat chimerical idea of restoring Christianity to its primitive purity, they expressed themselves in sharp and energetic terms on the corruption of morals and discipline in the Church. Saint-Cyran sorrowfully said that for five or six hundred years God had been destroying His Church.[2] He repeated the melancholy saying of François de Sales: "There is scarcely one competent confessor in ten thousand!" Jansenius, his companion in studies, wrote to him on April 5, 1621: "After the heretics, no people in the world

---

[1] The satirical Gui Patin is not the only person who complains of the abuse of nepotism at the Court of Rome, under the pontificate of Innocent X. (1644–1655): "The Signora Olympia, sister-in-law of the pope, who governs him body and soul, also governs the papacy. It is said that she sells everything, seizes and receives everything . . . which has drawn a joke from Pasquin, 'Olympia, olim pia, nunc harpia.'" (*Lettres*, t. i. p. 363.) The Venetian ambassador, Contarini, writes officially: "Donna Olympia sells, taxes, lets, gets presents made to her for all Government transactions, for pardons and justice; she is surrounded by a band of agents and extortioners." (Quoted by de Chantelauze, *Le cardinal de Retz et l'affaire du chapeau*, t. i. p. 296.) Pamphlets were affixed to the church doors: "Olympia primus, pontifex maximus." A medal represented her with the tiara on her head and St. Peter's keys in her hand; Innocent X. in woman's dress holding a distaff and spindle.

[2] Vincent de Paul in his deposition remembered only the second half of the phrase; but the Mother Angélique had noted down the first in writing. (See the letter of Lemaître in the *Mémoires pour servir à l'histoire de Port-Royal*, t. ii. p. 207.)

have more corrupted theology than those brawlers of the school that you know. If it had to be corrected in the ancient style, which is that of truth, the theology of this time would have no appearance of theology for the greater number of persons."

Arnauld, in his fine book, *De la fréquente communion*, in 1643, protested with unparalleled energy against the moral and religious condition of his contemporaries: "Also it is a horrible thing that never have so many confessions and communions been seen, and never more disorder and corruption ... that there was never more impurity in marriages ... more profligacy among the young ... more excess and debauchery among the common people. Who does not know that for twenty years fornication has passed among men of the world as a slight fault; adultery, one of the greatest of all crimes, for a piece of good fortune; cheating and treachery for court virtues; impiety and free-thinking for strength of mind ... fraud and lying for the knowledge of sale and trading; the rage for constant gaming as a genteel occupation for women ... the disguised simony and the profanation of church property as a legitimate accommodation which facilitates the interchange of benefices? ... I say nothing of more abominable crimes that our fathers were ignorant of, and which have broken out to such an extent in this unfortunate age, that one cannot think of them without being seized with horror." (3ᵉ partie, ch. xvi.)

And the young and ardent doctor (he was then thirty-one) did not fear to trace back to the proper person the responsibility for all these disorders: "This is what we might with truth call the greatest misfortune that could happen to the Church, if we did not add that there is a still greater, namely, that persons are found who make profession of piety, who flatter the sinners in the desires of their soul ... who seem to work for nothing else than to foster crimes by a false mildness, instead of arresting them by a just severity... They are persons who imagine that they have changed the face of a whole town, and have made it become quite Christian without any other change than that those who only communicated once a year now communicate once a month, and sometimes oftener... They admit that morals are not less corrupt than before ... yet, nevertheless, they will maintain that men are in a better condition than they were, because they tell a priest every week what they told only every month, and add every week two sacrileges to their other crimes. . ." The mild and prudent Nicole declares that he fears some extraordinary effect of God's anger "at a time when the whole Church is filled with vicious and ignorant ecclesiastics and dissolute monasteries." (*Visionnaires*, p. 179.) This was to bring on their hands many powerful enemies. It was easy to raise the hue and cry after the dangerous innovators, the new reformers, the disguised heretics, who wished, like Luther and Calvin, to ruin the Church under the pretext of reforming it.

The State, that is to say Louis XIV., maintained, besides, ineradicable prejudices against them. "The gentlemen of Port-Royal—always these gentlemen," repeated in chorus the king and Mme. de Maintenon. The sincerity of their convictions and of their apostolate is a sure guarantee to us, at least at the period with which we are occupied, that they remained strangers to political cabals, notwithstanding the accusations without proof and the perfidious insinuations of their adversaries.[1] It required, in truth, all the blindness of hatred to transform Saint-Cyran, Arnauld, Singlin, de Saci, Nicole, and Lancelot into conspirators and rioters. "Mme. de Longueville," Father Rapin relates, "said of Arnauld that he would never have been able to achieve his salvation if intrigue had been necessary to save him." (*Mémoires*, p. 240.) And this is well seen when, hidden and disguised in the duchess' house, he betrayed his incognito so artlessly.[2]

The testimony of Cardinal de Retz is very favourable to them. "They are," Besogne makes him say, "the poorest people in the world in the matter of intrigue and affairs of State; they will

---

[1] The zealous annotator of the *Mémoires* of Father Rapin is forced to admit it: "The *Mémoires* are not very explicit on the part that the jansenists took in the armaments of the Fronde, and Port-Royal wished to deny it; the pamphlets are never silent about it." (t. i. p. 252.) A high authority truly!

[2] Speaking of a new work, the doctor, who was visiting him, happened to say, "De Saci does not write so well." "What do you mean?" replied the patient, "my nephew writes better than I." In an analogous circumstance, the physician spoke of the arrest of Arnauld, "Oh! it is rather hard to believe that," replied the incorrigible doctor, "I am M. Arnauld."

not meddle with them. And far from receiving any assistance from them, they have disgusted several persons of my party and refused absolution to those who belonged to it."[1] (*Hist.* t. v. p. 546.)

But it must be acknowledged that appearances were against them. "With a facility more Christian than judicious," according to the just comment of Racine, they welcomed a number of discontented or disgraced courtiers and a number of great ladies wearied of their intrigues. Their attachment to their archbishop, the Cardinal de Retz, whose consummate perversity[2] they did not know so well as we do, and who used them to further the ends of his ambition, compromised them completely in the opinion of Louis XIV. and his ministers. Their connection with the duchesse de Longueville, the duc de Luynes, the marquis de Sévigné, Mme. de Guénégaut, the prince and princess de Conti, &c., caused the Fronde to be called the jansenists' war. Anne of Austria, indoctrinated by the marquis de Senecey, by Henri de Bourbon and the jesuits, declared "that the king would remember them when he was of age," and he did remember them, in fact. His governor, Villeroi, represented them to him as people who "wanted neither pope nor king." (*Mémoires*, du P. Rapin, t. i. p. 271.) Hence, we can understand the saying attributed to d'Harcourt, "A jansenist is very often only a man whom it is wished to ruin at court."

M. Cousin and M. Renan have said that in this struggle it was the jesuits who defended the good cause, that of human

---

[1] We see the abbé Singlin and the bishop of Alet exact from their penitents, the prince de Conti and the duchesse de Longueville, restitution of considerable sums to the poor, to repair the damages caused in the provinces by the civil wars. (BESOGNE, *Hist.* t. iii. pp. 39 and 83.)

[2] His secretary, Guy Joly, reports this cynical conversation : "My poor fellow, you lose your time in preaching to me. I know very well that I am only a knave. But, in spite of you and all the world, I wish to be so, because I find more pleasure in it. I am aware that there are three or four of you who know me and despise me in your hearts ; but I console myself with the satisfaction that I experience in imposing on all the rest by your means. People are so much deceived, and my reputation is so well established, that if you wished to undeceive them you would not be believed, which is sufficient for me to be contented and live after my own fashion." (*Mémoires.*) The admiration that Mme. de Sévigné did not cease to profess for Cardinal de Retz is well known,

liberty. Mme. de Sévigné, so attached to her friends and her brethren of Port-Royal, separates from them, in fact, on this point of doctrine. She has just been reading the Bible of Royaumont, and, after having seen the reproaches of ingratitude and the horrible punishments with which God afflicted His people, she writes: "As to myself, I go much farther than the jesuits. . . . I am persuaded that we have entire liberty. . . . The jesuits do not say enough about it, and the others give occasion for murmuring against the justice of God when they take away our liberty, or abridge it so much that it is no longer liberty." (A Mme. de Grignan, August 28, 1676.) D'Alembert twits them equally, and with spirit, on the contradiction between their inexorable dogma and their ethics: "What would be thought of a monarch who should say to one of his subjects, 'You have shackles on your feet, and you have no power to take them off; nevertheless, I warn you that if you do not immediately walk, for a long time and quite straight, along the edge of this precipice on which you are, you shall be condemned to everlasting torments'? Such is the God of the jansenists." (*Destruction des jésuites*, p. 64.)

And, in spite of all, the men of Port-Royal, vanquished, proscribed, and annihilated, make in history quite another figure than their triumphant vanquishers. By a happy inconsistency with their discouraging system of predestination, they do not the less represent, in a certain measure, liberty of conscience, the spirit of inquiry, independence of thought, and the love of justice and truth. "Their adversaries pleaded the opposite cause, namely, undisputed sway over mind and heart." (Villemain.)

By a new and still more happy inconsistency they worked with a more ardent zeal than anyone for the reform of manners. Their moral grandeur burst forth before the eyes of their most prejudiced contemporaries, and, far from diminishing with time, it shines with a purer light, in the history of French civilization, in proportion as the miserable incidents of the struggle in which they succumbed are effaced. The true reason of their success, in the opinion of their most prejudiced adversaries, was the strictness of their spiritual discipline. "The jansenists," says Father Rapin, "advanced their affairs by disguising their real

Introduction. 65

sentiments; this was by a morality that had nothing but what was beautiful and edifying." (*Hist. du jansenisme*, p. 496.) One of the least equivocal marks of heresy was purity of morals. Port-Royal[1] drew from this valuable testimony her consolation and strength in the midst of the severest trials.

I cannot speak better of the moral bearing of the work undertaken by the solitaries of Port-Royal than Henri Martin has done in that admirable and well-thought-out page of his *Histoire de France:* "Thorough sincerity in the action of man upon man, and a thorough disdain of all precautions and of all polity in things pertaining to God, characterize what may be called the method of Saint-Cyran. He desires to regenerate souls individually, not to obtain by surprise the superficial adhesion of a great number, still less to demand a verbal adhesion that the heart does not ratify. He was not the man to compel heretical populations to become Catholics in appearance. What matters appearance to him? What matter outward forms to him? It is better to gain one soul to the internal Christ than an empire to the external Church. Here Saint-Cyran touches Descartes, although turning his back on him. . . . Descartes regenerated the mind; Saint-Cyran endeavours to regenerate the heart. . . . It is for this that jansenism deserves, even at the present time, our serious study, too much inclined as we are now to place our hopes in social and collective reforms, which will remain unrealizable so long as they are not based on the reformation of the human soul. . . . We must be very self-

---

[1] The Mother Agnès writes to Mme. de Foix, April 16, 1663: "There was a jesuit who preached, this Lent, in Burgundy, that solitude, retirement, the desire for penance, love and zeal for the penitential canons, and to see the ancient penance and all the other maxims of Christian perfection re-established in the Church was the true mark of heresy. After that, must we not consider ourselves very happy, according to the Gospel?" Arnauld said, on his side, "The whole court knows that, a bishop reproving an abbé of good family because his conduct was not sufficiently regular, 'What do you wish us to do?' replied the abbé. 'If we were more regular we should be taken for jansenists, and that would mean exclusion from all dignities." (*Phantôme du jansénisme*, p. 28.) A few pages further on he quotes the words of Cardinal Bona: "What! to be poor, diligent in prayer, and to exhort the faithful to be diligent in it, to live in an exemplary manner, and to preach Christ in an apostolic manner, is that what is called jansenism? Please God we were all jansenists in this manner!" (p. 33.)

reliant in order to be as wrong as the jansenists. However far removed we may be from their doctrines, we must acknowledge that they have enhanced the moral grandeur of man; they are the Stoics of Christianity." (t. xii. pp. 84, 85.)

If they were vanquished in their generous efforts, their adversaries paid dear for their victory; they received a mortal wound from the arrow of the *Provincials*, or rather, to speak more correctly, it was the ancient faith that succumbed in this relentless conflict. Contemplating the field of battle, Boileau, who had friends in both camps, said like a satirist, "Oh! what madmen men are!" (Letter to M. Brossette.) Bayle decided in his usual manner, "It is properly a matter of Pyrrhonism." (Letter to Math. Marais.) "All that is nonsense!" exclaimed the courtiers and men of the world, according to Mme. de Choisy (letter to the comtesse de Maure, 1655); and Christians complained, with Mme. de Sévigné, of all these over-refined discussions on grace: "Thicken religion a little, it is all evaporating through being over-refined." Ridicule had invaded the sanctuary with that cloud of pamphlets that they were throwing at one another's heads, to set the laughers on its side. The titles are sufficiently significant: *A Damper for the Jansenists, The Lantern of St. Augustine, Snuffers for the Lantern, A Curry-comb for the jansenist Pegasus, Ointment for the Burn, The Country of Jansenia, Illustrations of the Jesuits' Almanack, Essay of the New Tale of Mother Goose, or Illustrations of the Game of the Constitution, The Jesuit Harlequin, The Pasquinade of St. Medard, An Apology for Cartouche, or the Villain without Reproach, by the grace of Father Quesnel, The Precept aud Pastoral Ordinance of Momus.* And what songs, quatrains, satirical prints, comedies, and public masquerades![1]

---

[1] Gerberon describes the procession organized by the jesuits of Macon: "They made all their scholars march in order, two by two, through the streets of the town, dressed in white. After them came a triumphal car, on which was a handsome young man dressed up as a girl, with everything that the vainest women use as ornaments; and in order to denote what he represented, he carried a banner, on which were read these words, in handsome characters, GRACE SUFFISANTE. Behind this car was seen another young man tied and bound, who wore a paper mitre and other pontifical ornaments to match, and who was covered from head to foot with a large black veil to denote the defeat and disgrace of Jansenius." (*Hist. gén. du jansénisme*, t. i. p. 483.)

French humour indulged in it to its heart's content, and found the subject inexhaustible. What became of religious beliefs in the midst of this universal bantering? Father Rapin has said a word which is really the best and most sensible in all his writings: "It is not by these means that the Gospel is preached and defended." (*Mém.* t. ii. p. 195.) While the pastors were fighting with their crooks, as they are shown in a print, the wolves carried off the sheep. Is this, after all, to be so much regretted? I think not; for behind incredulity and indifference walked liberty of conscience, tolerance, justice, and humanity. Maurepas, who, under Cardinal Fleury, took an active part in this trifling, was not, perhaps, wrong in saying, "We have no other means of avoiding the civil war that the jesuits wish to bring on us." (*Mém.* t. ii. p. 73.) In fact, really religious minds have no reason to complain that all this polemical theology has ceased to separate them from God; and those who are more sensitive to the love of their neighbour rejoice to see so copious a source of terrible hatred exhausted and religious persecutions for ever ended. May Port-Royal, to which we owe so many grand lessons, still secure to us, by the sight of its ruins, this glorious conquest of the modern spirit—horror of intolerance, and respect for liberty.

FÉLIX CADET.

PORT-ROYAL EDUCATION.

EXTRACTS FROM THE WRITERS OF PORT-ROYAL.

ORIGIN OF THE *PETITES ÉCOLES*.

I WISH you could read in my heart the affection that I have for children, and how there is nothing that is not modified by the reflections that the prudence of faith and grace obliges us to make. And when I formed the design of building a house which should be, as it were, a seminary for the Church, to preserve in it the innocence of the children, without which I perceive every day that it is difficult for them to become good ecclesiastics, I only intended to build it for six children, whom I would have chosen throughout the city of Paris, as it might please God that I should meet with them, and I would have given them a master especially to teach them Latin, and with him a good priest, whom I had already in view, to direct and govern their consciences. And I intended to give them for Latin (if he whom I had should happen to fail me) a man of twenty or twenty-five years of age, knowing that an older man is usually rather unfit to teach languages to children. This design having been destroyed by my imprisonment,[1] I have thought no more of it, and have given all the money that I had, except two thousand francs for this house, to the poor. It is true that finding here the son of a poor widow, who seemed to have good abilities, I have gradually taught him in my room; but a domestic disturbance[2] having driven him

---

[1] On Friday, 14 May, 1638, Saint-Cyran was taken to the Castle of Vincennes, where he remained a prisoner until the death of Richelieu.

[2] M. de Saint-Cyran, although very badly treated by the lieutenant of the governor of Vincennes, had given some attention to his two sons; and "as his zeal for the education of children was very great," says Lancelot, "he added

away, I have been obliged to continue my charity to him by sending him to Port-Royal, because otherwise he would have been ruined among the soldiers, and those who had taken him from me by their authority would have succeeded in their design of injuring him. In fact, the circumstances were such that I could not abandon him without displeasing God and violating the character that He has given me, which is a personal law, and ought rather to be obeyed than public laws.[1] But I have since willingly consented that the good work that I began with the children of M. Bignon[2] should be continued at Port-Royal, as much because it is difficult for me to interrupt what I am doing for God's service as because M. Bignon gave me two thousand francs to employ as I should think fit, and which I had determined to employ on the above-mentioned building, in order that the children might share in the charity of their father. For I am much concerned lest those who have chosen me as the instrument of some good work should not be the first to reap the benefit of it. Nevertheless, I understood this in such a manner that if the children turned out intractable and unwilling to submit to the discipline under which I wished them to live in this house, it should be in my power to dismiss them without those from whom I had received them, not even excepting M. Bignon, bearing me any ill-will for it. . . .

---

a third to them, who was the son of a poor woman, a niece of the precentor of the Sainte-Chapelle. This last soon outstripped the other two, which made the lieutenant's wife so jealous, that she forbade M. de Saint-Cyran to see any children, under the pretext that he might instil bad principles into them." (*Mém.* t. i. p. 133.)

[1] The clearness of these declarations explains the ascendancy of Saint-Cyran. He said one day to Lemaître: "You are not yet accustomed to this language, and people do not talk so in the world, but here are *six feet of ground* (*his room*) *where neither chancellor nor any one else is feared*. There is no power that can prevent us speaking the truth here as it ought to be spoken."

[2] "The establishment of the *Petites Écoles de Port-Royal* was due to the solicitations of this celebrated magistrate (Jérôme Bignon). M. de Saint-Cyran had often given him his ideas on the Christian education of children, and M. Bignon, after pressing him for a long time to put his ideas in practice, demanded as a tribute due to their mutual friendship that the pious abbé should undertake the charge of the Christian education of his sons, Jérôme and Thierri Bignon. It was on their behalf that the *Petites Écoles* were set up outside Port-Royal by MM. Lancelot and de Saci, while their sister, Marie Bignon, was educated within the monastery." (*Supplément au Nécrologe*, p. 398.)

The duty of instructing children is in itself so irksome, that I have seldom seen a wise man who has not complained and grown tired of it, however short a time he has worked at it; and the most devout men in the order of Saint-Benedict have found this penance the hardest of all. You may read an example of it in the life of St. Arsenius;[1] and for my own part I have always considered this occupation so troublesome,[2] that I have never employed any man in it to whom God had not imparted this gift;\ or if I have been deceived in my choice, I have removed him as soon as I perceived that he did not possess it. I should think I had done a great deal, although I had not advanced them much in Latin up to the age of twelve years, by causing them to pass these early years in the close of a house or monastery in the country, by giving them all the pastimes suitable to their age,[3] and showing them the example of a good life in those who were with me. . . .

Extract from a letter of M. de Saint-Cyran written from the Bois de Vincennes. (*Supplément au Nécrologe*, p. 46.)

OF THE CHARITY OF M. DE SAINT-CYRAN TOWARDS CHILDREN.

. . . He thought that the whole course of life depended on this early age, and that, provided the young were well brought up, it might be hoped that public posts would be filled with the most worthy officers and the Church with the most virtuous men, and that the Republic[4] and private families would draw from it in-

---

[1] Arsenius (350-445), governor of the children of Theodosius the Great, whose court he quitted to pass the remainder of his life in a desert of Egypt.

[2] He calls it "a tempest of the mind," on account of its religious responsibility.

[3] This wise care not to overpress the children suggested to Rousseau his theory of *negative education* up to this age of twelve years: "You are alarmed," he said, "to see the child waste his early years in doing nothing? What! Is it nothing to be happy? Is it nothing to jump, play, and run all day long? He will never be so busy in all his life." Saint-Cyran, who allows the child all the pastimes suitable to his age, is very careful to surround him with good examples.

[4] That is, the State. This sense appears very clearly from the distinction that Étienne Pasquier, in the sixteenth century, draws of "three kinds of republics: the royal, the manorial, and the popular." (*Lettres*, liv. xix. lettre 7.)

calculable advantages. So that it might be said of this good work, which is now so much neglected and abandoned, *Porro unum est necessarium*, that it is, in a sense, the *one thing needful*, since, if it were entirely successful, most other disorders would be remedied; on the other hand, if this foundation be wanting, it was a necessary consequence that the effects of it would be felt during the remainder of life.

M. de Saint-Cyran also used to say that whatever virtues parents might otherwise possess, this single point was fitted to condemn them if they did not do their duty in obtaining a good education for their children,[1] which is at the present time more rare and difficult to find than is thought. He could not sufficiently wonder at the blindness of most parents, who do not see that, even if there were no question of eternity in it, their own interest should lead them to fulfil this obligation, since it only too often happens that those whom they think they have brought into the world to be the support and honour of their family become the disgrace and ruin of it for want of a good education. He could not understand how, when it is a question of settling their children in places, in employments, and in the world, they inconvenience themselves as if they were staking everything on it, although they often only procure for them the means of ruining themselves; instead of which, when it is necessary to educate them well, for the satisfaction of their own consciences and the secure establishment of their children's well-being, they are unable to find the means for it, and complain of the smallest expense. And truly in this they show that they cannot be true Christians, since not only is acting in this way like building their house on the quicksands, but is even throwing themselves with those who compose it, and who ought to support it, into the flood which beats against it. He deplored the misfortune of our age, in which the devil had found a much easier means than did formerly that Pharaoh, king of Egypt, who was only his shadow, of ruining the children of the Church; this plague being so much the more

---

[1] Saint-Cyran, in a letter addressed to a person of quality, says: "As they hasten to baptism they should hasten to education, and all that is done for children without that brings the malediction of God on the father and mother, who are the visible guardian angels." (*Lettres chrétiennes et spirituelles de Saint-Cyran*, 1685, t. ii. p. 326.)

appalling, as he often makes use of the negligence or avarice or other passions of their parents in order to ruin them, instead of which the Israelites felt at least their ill-fortune, and did all in their power to save their children from the rage of the tyrant.

He admired the Son of God, who, in the highest functions of His ministry, would not that little children should be forbidden to approach Him; who embraced and blessed them; who has charged us so strictly not to despise or neglect them, and who has spoken of them in such favourable and astonishing terms as to astound those who offend the least of them. Thus M. de Saint-Cyran always showed a kindness for children that went even so far as a sort of respect, to honour in them the innocence of the Holy Ghost who dwells in them. He blessed them and made the sign of the cross on their foreheads, and when they were able to understand it, he always spoke some kind word, which was like the seed of some truth that he threw out in passing, and in the sight of God, that it might germinate in due season. Once when he came to see us he went into the children's class-room, and as he always had a cheerful look and a heart inclined to do good, he said, caressing them : "Well, what are you doing? for you must not lose time, and what you do not fill up the devil takes for himself. . . ." They showed him their Virgil that they were studying, and he said, "Do you see all those beautiful verses? Virgil, in making them, procured his own damnation, because he made them through vanity and for glory. But you must save yourselves in learning them, because you ought to do it for the sake of obedience and to fit yourselves for serving God."

A boy of whom he had taken charge during his imprisonment, and to whom he afterwards continued his kindness, having fallen into evil courses, gave him so much pain that he told me that all his troubles in prison were nothing compared to this affliction. After his release he wished him to visit him every day, and received him, and left whatever occupation he was engaged in, even his great work, in order to speak a kind word to him, or to try and lead him back to God. He did not succeed, however, and this would be a story[1] worth writing at length, to show how

---

[1] "For nothing," said Lancelot, who had been entrusted with the education of this boy, and shared the work with M. de Saci, "shows more

unfathomable are the judgments of God, and that the prayers of the saints do not suffice to avert the perdition of those whom God has abandoned. This boy, having begun by stealing an old skull-cap from M. Singlin,[1] and selling it for two liards in order to have something to gamble with, and afterwards taking all he could pilfer, advanced by such rapid strides towards his ruin, that he even took the silver spoons, fell into all kinds of debauchery, and became at length a thorough rogue, as his mother herself once told me. . . .

M. de Saint-Cyran thought so highly of the charity of those who employed themselves in bringing up children in a Christian manner, that he said there was no occupation more worthy of a Christian in the Church; that after the love of which it is said, *majorem haec dilectionem nemo habet*[2] (St. John xv. 13), which makes us willing to die for our friends, this was the greatest; that it was the shortest way of going back in his mind and expiating the faults of his youth; that one of the greatest consolations we could have in dying was that we had contributed to the good education of some child; and that, in fine, this employment was sufficient by itself to sanctify a soul, provided it had been carried out with charity and patience. He said that we ought to be, not only the guardian angels, but in some sort the providence of children who were committed to our charge, because our chief care should be always to attach them to what is good with gentleness and charity, as we have need that God should attach us to it and make us do it. He usually reduced what it is necessary to do with children to three things: to speak little, bear with much, and pray more.

---

plainly that a person does not do all the good he imagines in undertaking the care of a child if he does not seriously devote himself to it and take all necessary trouble. He acts then like a nurse, who should be satisfied with giving the breast to her nursling at stated hours, and should expose it the rest of the time to whatever might happen. This poor child then, not being sufficiently watched over, fell into disorderly ways." (*Mém. de Saint-Cyran*, t. i. p. 133.)

[1] Singlin, confessor of the nuns at Port-Royal for twenty-six years, then superior of the two houses *des Champs* and the *Faubourg Saint-Jacques* for eight years, died 1664.

[2] "Greater love hath no man than this, that a man lay down his life for his friends."

He desired that we should bear with their faults and weaknesses, in order to induce God to show mercy to ours, and perhaps afterwards to strengthen these young plants when they should learn what patience we have exercised towards them. He added that we should have still more charity and pity for those whom we saw to be more unformed and backward. . . . He could not bear that anyone should employ too severe looks and too imperious a manner, which had something of disdain, or was likely to intimidate them and make them pusillanimous,[1] which is expressly forbidden us by the Prince of the Apostles.

On the contrary, he wished a suitable familiarity to be used with them, which should win them by a calculated gentleness and a truly paternal love, and which should lead us to be very condescending to them, since if they had no confidence in us, and did not perceive that we felt kindly towards them, it would be impossible to do anything.[2] And this explains why he often condescended in prison to play at ball on a table with children of seven or eight years old.

He did not wish the teachers to have recourse hastily to the use of the birch, unless for very serious faults, and then only after having employed all other means of punishment. For he desired them to bear with their faults in order to put themselves to the test before God, and to do nothing rashly, and also to pray for them before punishing them; then he wished them to be warned by signs only, then by words, and after several reprimands to employ threats, that they should be deprived for a time of

---

[1] The recommendation is excellent, but how is it to be reconciled with the precept to annihilate our own will? The Mother Agnès wrote, 30 April, 1652, to Mdlle. Perdreau: "Read, in *L'Amour de Dieu* of the saintly bishop of Geneva, what he says on the *death* of the will."

[2] "Leading them with watchfulness and gentleness," said Saint-Cyran, in a letter to a person of quality, "and sometimes requesting instead of commanding them, and complying a little with their humour for a time in order to lead them to act without such compliance in the future. . . . Only care must be taken to use this compliance with much circumspection and impartiality, always bearing in mind that we must not stop there, and that, if we are obliged to condescend to them, it is only in order to raise them to our own level and to withdraw them little by little from their inferior position, and not to satisfy our own inclinations by following theirs, and to indulge ourselves with them in an indolent compliance so easy to our nature." (*Lettres chrétiennes et spirituelles*, 1685, t. ii. p. 326.)

something they liked, or of play, even of their luncheon or part of their breakfast, and that the birch should be used only in the last extremity and for grave faults, especially with those who were seen to be capable of being won by gentleness and reason. He, however, desired this punishment to be used with those who were naturally thoughtless, or hasty-tempered, or who were given to lying or laughing on the most serious occasions.[1] In fine, he did not wish, any more than Saint Benedict, that faults committed in church should be pardoned.

But he said that using chastisement without much previous prayer was to act like a Jew, and not to know that all depended on the blessing and grace of God, which we should endeavour to draw down on them by our patience in bearing with them. He added that sometimes even we should punish and chastise ourselves instead of them, as much because we should always fear that we may have been partly responsible for their faults by our hastiness or negligence as because this duty was a general obligation on all who were entrusted with the conduct of others.[2] He said that it was necessary to oppose a constant watchfulness to that of the devil, who is always seeking an entrance into these tender souls. He recommended also to sustain the prayers of the children of whom they had charge by their own, thus aiding the attention which was not to be expected from them.

He was careful to warn that, in order to guide children well, it was necessary *plus prier que crier*,[3] to ask rather than scold, and to

---

[1] M. Varin makes this sprightly remark: "Saint-Cyran only whipped children for grave faults, but he put bursts of laughter in the number of grave faults." (*La vérité sur les Arnauld*, t. ii. p. 185.) The critic should not have omitted these important words: "On the most serious occasions."

[2] A very wise precept, in which we are not to suppose a refinement of spirituality. It is a very judicious and exact estimation of the responsibility for the faults of the pupils that may often be traced back to the master. May not their inattention, for example, be often explained by facts which are not in the least personal to them? The unprepared lesson is not interesting, it is too long, it is not sufficiently within their capacity, &c.

[3] A very effective conjunction of words. How many young teachers, in the inconsiderate zeal of their first attempts, would derive profit from meditating upon it? It is not only hygiene that recommends it for the wise conservation of energy, it is especially pedagogy, which teaches that the authority of the master has no surer foundation than calmness and self-control.

speak more of them to God than of God to them, for he did not like long speeches on piety to be made to them, or that they should be wearied with instruction. He wished that they should only be spoken to at those opportunities and on those occasions which God called into existence, and according to the impulse that He gave us, and the disposition to receive it well that He showed us in them, because the impulse to give depended on God as well as the gifts, and that what we said to them in this way had a quite different effect from what we might say of ourselves.

In fine, he thought that the chief point in the good education of children was the good example that should be given them,[1] and the perfect regularity of the house in which they were pupils. A Father of the Church once said, speaking of the education of a young girl, "Remember, you who have brought a virgin into the world, that you must teach her more by example than precept . . . . She must hear nothing but what has reference to the fear of God. Keep from her that criminal liberty that children take; do not let the girls or the servants who accompany her frequent the world lest they teach their pupils more evil than they would otherwise have learnt." And this is what M. de Saint-Cyran recommended for the boys as well as the girls, desiring also that they should be careful to limit intercourse with the outside world, from which they might receive some hurtful influence; and he was accustomed to say that communication with the world was infectious, and did no less harm to the soul than the plague did to the body. Neither did he wish that money should be left with them. And one day when he sent some sweetmeats to a little girl he gave this caution to a person who had charge of some children: "*Do not accustom them to the delights of earth, which destroy the taste for those of Heaven.*"

He could not tolerate that the sciences and study should be

---

[1] We feel that Saint-Cyran means here by good example especially the practice of religion, but it is easy to give a wider and more general interpretation to this advice. Pedagogy has no more important precept. The teachers of Port-Royal, with Saint-Cyran at their head, had the right to place in the first rank of maxims that which they practised so well themselves, namely, *example*.

made the principal thing in the education of children as we do now. He regarded this conduct as one of the greatest mistakes which could be committed against the sanctity of this employment, and observed that, besides dissatisfying those who were backward and making others vain, it reacted on the State and the Church, burdening the Spouse of Christ with a number of persons whom she had not called, and the State with a great number of idlers who considered themselves above the rest because they knew a little Latin, and who thought they would be dishonoured in following the calling in which their birth would have placed them. Therefore he said that among the children of whom one should be entirely master, although there might be a great many of them, very few ought to be put to study,[1] and only those in whom great docility and submission had been noticed, with some mark of piety and of assured virtue.

M. de Saint-Cyran, having this conception of the education of youth, and regarding it as one of the most necessary duties of the State and the Church, often said, and he once wrote to me, that he would have been delighted to pass all his life in it. But he did not intend, in saying that, to make himself a slave to the temper and injustice of parents who only burden us with their children in order to relieve themselves at a time when they have only the trouble of them, and take them away as soon as they can to sacrifice them to their interest and vanity; for it may be said in this case that an occupation worthy of the angels and a work of love is turned into meanness and pedantry. And certainly it would be better, if some persons are reduced by necessity to submit to such conditions, to learn a trade or to cultivate the land. They would have at least this consolation, that they were doing penance in the way that God imposed it on the first man, and would be exempt from a great number of bad consequences in which they are often involved either for themselves or for those who are brought

---

[1] Arnauld d'Andilly advises the queen-mother to diminish the number of colleges, and only to have schools to teach reading and writing. (VARIN, *la Vérité sur les Arnauld*, 1847, t. ii. p. 353.) This was also the idea of Richelieu.

up in a thoroughly pagan manner; and besides, the labour a man undergoes in this employment, when it is not governed by the maxims of God, is much greater when he takes some care in discharging it, than that of cultivating the land, and undermines the body more, and very much accelerates the end of our life.[1]

M. de Saint-Cyran never undertook the charge of children unless he had some hopes of being entirely their master, and was certain of the mind and intentions of the parents. Thus, one day, the late duchesse de Guise having sent a person to speak to him about the education of the present M. de Guise (Henri II.), who was then destined for the Church, as he had a great desire to see persons of high rank better educated than others, because he knew its importance, he did not decline the proposal, and even partly pledged his word, but only on condition that this princess should not interfere in it at all, and should entrust the care of her son entirely to him, which Mme. de Guise not being sufficiently disposed to do, he withdrew his promise, and would not hear it spoken of again.

After that we ought to be less astonished that M. de Saint-Cyran was so eager to induce everybody to do charitable offices to children, since he did not decline to do them himself; and that he thought that the merit and rank of private persons did not give them the right to despise them, since God judged them worthy of His angels, according to this saying of Christ, "Their angels do always behold the face of my Father who is in heaven."

But it is perhaps one of the greatest artifices of the devil to have rendered contemptible that method by which he foresaw that very many souls might be rescued from him by preserving the children in innocence. There are means of inducing persons of every condition to undertake all sorts of pious works, but simply to propose this to them would seem to be an error. No one is afraid to expose them to the infectious diseases of prisons in order to visit the prisoners, or to the vitiated air of the

---

[1] Camper, of Berlin, has calculated that out of 100 persons, the age of 70 years is reached by 42 theologians, 29 lawyers, 28 artists, 27 schoolmasters and professors, and 24 doctors. (MICHEL LÉVY, *Traité d'hygiène*, t. ii. p. 872.)

hospitals in order to assist the sick, to serve the poor, and to dress wounds, which are sometimes loathsome; and yet they would think they were lowering themselves and taking too much trouble if they undertook the education of a child. I know very well that everybody is not fitted for it; but if this gift is rare, that is no reason for despising it; and if the lack of this gift excludes many persons, it would seem to me very reasonable that men's fancies should not exclude still more.

I have sometimes wondered why, when the profession of doctors obliges them to see so many foul and disagreeable things, and often exposes them to infected air, so many, nevertheless, are found to adopt it—presumably it is because men's attachment to life makes this profession honourable—and why, at the same time, these same men have so little scruple in despising that profession which can most contribute to the eternal salvation of their children. . . . And I have in the same way been astonished that the apostle St. Paul, having expressly stated that judicial affairs should be the portion of the inferior persons in the Church (1 Cor. vi. 4), we, nevertheless, see no one higher placed now than those who take part in them, and that one of the greatest of the successors of the apostles having assured us that the guidance of the most tender soul is a greater thing than the government of a world,[1] we see no employment so despised as this to which it appertains to lay the foundations of a good character.[2] But it is still more astonishing to see occupations and offices which are base in themselves so highly esteemed in princes' houses, such as those of seneschal and master of the stables, and that what has reference to the care and education of reasonable creatures, who have been redeemed by the blood of God, is considered the lowest employment in nature. Truly we must acknowledge that men's blindness is very great.

---

[1] CHANNING, *De l'education personnelle*, p. 35: "The perfect education of a child requires more reflection, and perhaps more wisdom, than the government of a State, for this simple reason, that political interests and needs are more tangible, material and sensible than the development of thought and feeling, or than the subtle laws of the soul, which should all be studied and understood before education is finished. . . ."

[2] "Lucian has said somewhere that the gods made schoolmasters of those whom they hated; and Melanchthon has written an oration *de miseriis paedagogorum*." (GUI PATIN, *Lettres*, t. iii. p. 140.)

I know very well that most worldly people would laugh at me if they saw this. But let them laugh, if Thou, O my God, dost not laugh at it. . . . Let them say what they will, that the world is ordered thus, that habits cannot be changed, and that men will never be induced to hold in esteem an employment which they have always despised. Let them not pretend, then, to induce us to pity them very much for misfortunes which often happen in their families for want of this esteem; or, rather, let them not prevent us pitying them very much, since the love of Christ constrains us to blame this unfortunate habit. . . .

As M. de Saint-Cyran was very enlightened, he was far removed from these worldly maxims, and knowing the importance of the care and education of the young, he looked upon them in a very different manner. However painful and humiliating these offices were in men's eyes, yet he did not fail to employ in them persons of position without their thinking that they had a right to complain, because they saw with how much zeal and charity he practised what he advised others to do. For I have often seen him give lessons to his nephews, who lived with him, not regarding them as his nephews, as he once told me, but as children whom he was endeavouring to bring up in a Christian manner.

One day, when he went into a shop to buy a pair of stockings, he saw a little boy who seemed to him very promising. He was sorry to learn that he was sent to college, where he ran the risk of being spoilt, and told the shopkeeper to send him to him, and that he would teach him with his nephew. He did so for some time, but the child, not having turned out so well as he wished, he was obliged to dismiss him.

When he was in prison he had three young children whom he took the trouble to instruct; and when he placed M. d'Espinoy[1] and M. de Villeneuve (son of M. d'Andilly) under my care, he was good enough to tell me that he would be their undermaster, and that if God restored him to liberty he would take them with him.

---

[1] M. d'Espinoy, youngest son of M. de Saint-Ange, head steward to the Queen, retired to Port-Royal des Champs on the death of his father in 1651, and died in 1676, under the care of M. de Saci, who had a great affection for him, says a note of Lancelot. (*Mém.* t. i. p. 338.)

Thus M. de Saint-Cyran reduced to practice his ideas of things and his knowledge of virtue, and advised others in this spirit; for when M. Singlin first submitted himself to him he was delighted with the proposition that he made to him to devote himself to children, and destined him for this employment, for which he had told me that God had sent him to him. Long before this he had given his nephew, M. de Barcos, to M. d'Andilly, in order to take charge of his children, at a time when Cardinal Richelieu would have been glad to have him. He entrusted M. de Saci with the instruction of a little boy who had been taken from him when he was in prison, and for whose guidance he wrote him two beautiful letters, in which it is wonderful to see with how much care and precision he descends to the smallest details; and after he had placed this boy with me he wished M. de Saci to take charge of him in the mornings, because I was occupied in the church.[1] When M. Arnauld placed himself under his direction, he proposed to him to undertake the charge of a young marquis who gave signs of wishing to retire from the world. In fine, we know that he set everybody, on every opportunity, to this employment. . . . (Lancelot, *Mémoires touchant la vie de M. de Saint-Cyran*, t. ii. p. 330.)

SAINT-CYRAN'S LITERARY THEORY.

If M. de Saint-Cyran had a great desire to see truth defended, he was not less particular about the manner in which he wished its defence to be conducted. What he has written on the subject in various letters[2] would almost dispense me from speaking of it here if I did not consider this point very important, and had not learnt from him several things on this subject which I should scruple to omit.

The first maxim that M. de Saint-Cyran laid down on that subject was that one should never write unless the impulse came from God, and he said that it was sometimes more difficult to know when a truth should be published or defended than to

---

[1] Lancelot fulfilled the sacristan's duties.
[2] Chiefly in letters addressed to M. Arnauld, bearing on the title-page: *A un ecclésiastique de ses amis.* In vols. ii. and iii., ed. 1679.

know the truth itself. Nevertheless, he thought that it was necessary to do so when it was attacked by its enemies, or there were some persons who desired instruction in it. He said that then God would guide our pen and direct our steps;[1] otherwise there was nothing more dangerous than to advance by oneself, and that nothing led more easily to deception and error than such rashness, whatever natural ability and learning a man might possess. He showed this by the books of Origen,[2] De Principiis, in which he wished to treat of questions more curious than useful. And he always said, *Qui a semetipso loquitur gloriam propriam quaerit.* (He who speaketh of himself seeketh his own glory), paying attention to what is said in the same place that he only who submits to the will of God can know the truth, as he who seeks only this glory is true and free from all unrighteousness.

Nor was it sufficient that the motive should be legitimate. M. de Saint-Cyran still wished that it should not be carried out in too solely human a manner,[3] as if it were only a question of carrying things by force of words, or that God had need of our eloquence, because truth has need of no one; and after having done all we can, and all we think ourselves obliged to do, we must still say, *Servi inutiles sumus* (St. Luke xvii. 10),

---

[1] "I have often seen him," says Lancelot, "after having soared like an eagle while speaking to us, suddenly stop short, 'not because I have nothing to say, on the contrary, because too many things present themselves to my mind; and I look to God to know what is best for me to say to you.' Thus his speech as well as his reading, in a word, his whole life, became a continual oblation to God, neither saying nor doing anything of himself, and always looking to the Holy Spirit with deep humility, in order to act only in and by Him." (*Mémoires*, vol. i. p. 45.)

[2] Origen, of Alexandria (185-254), a doctor of the Church, author of *Commentaries on Holy Scripture*, an *Apology for Christianity against Celsus*, a treatise against heresies, entitled *Philosophumena*. Several of his opinions have been condemned.

[3] The disciples of Saint-Cyran did not always follow this important advice. Lancelot candidly acknowledges it: "Perhaps," said he, "the manner in which we acted in defence of the truth was not pure enough, and the means employed were too hasty or ill-concerted, or even too human . . . Sometimes the things of God are injured by too much action rather than by remaining in humble repose. . . We may also add that we did not confine ourselves within the limits marked out by M. de Saint-Cyran, contenting ourselves (as he wished) by showing that the doctrine that was followed was not that of M. d'Ypres, but of St. Augustine; it was thought safer to insist on the distinction between law and fact, for which we had contended for ten or twelve years.

(*We are unprofitable servants*). Therefore he wished that in such conjunctures a man should rather consult the movements of his heart than those of his mind, in order to listen to God and not be led astray by his own imagination.

Just as in order to derive profit from the sacred books we should read them in the same spirit in which they were written, so, in order usefully to defend sacred truths, we should be animated with the spirit of the saints.

Therefore M. de Saint-Cyran wished men to write as they prayed, that is, with the same respect and submission to the Divine Majesty. He recommended men always to keep their hearts attentively fixed on God, that they might say nothing but what He inspired, so that work becoming as it were a prayer, it might draw down His blessing on their labours. For that reason his maxims were that, in order to write the truth, it was not so much necessary to look to the moments that human wisdom might choose as to those suggested by the Spirit of God, which it was necessary to wait for, and to follow the impulse that it might please Him to give us; and that nothing was more dangerous than to speak of God from memory, or by a mere human effort of our spirit, and it was, in his judgment, far from being permissible to mingle with such matters our own interests or passions.

Thus, as those who are skilful in eloquence remark very justly that it consists almost entirely in vividly representing a picture of the thing they wish to express, so M. de Saint-Cyran, in a much more pointed manner, said that we could only speak usefully of truth, which is God Himself, by following the idea of it that He impressed on us, and accompanying it by the movements that it pleased Him to inspire in us, when we were careful to look to Him with great purity of heart. Hence it was that He did not wish men to waste time over speech,[1] and to take more time

---

[1] "I do not know who that Monsieur de Vaugelas is who writes to you. It seems to me that he has the humour of M. de Balzac, whom I esteem more than his letter, which I intend to read in three days because I am otherwise occupied, and I wish that, following my example, you would moderate the passion you have for words, of which the fine tissue is less estimable than you think." (SAINT-CYRAN, *Lettre à Arnauld d'Andilly*.) Saint-Cyran gave that day very wittily an excellent lesson in literature to the *grand épistolier de France*. But the Discourses of Balzac are worth more than his letters,

in weighing their words than a miser in weighing his gold in his scales, because nothing more retarded the movement of the Holy Spirit, which we ought to follow. He said that this precision of speech was rather fitted for academicians than for defenders of the truth; that it was almost enough that there should be nothing that offended in our style; and that what carried away readers most was the eloquence of the thoughts and the purity of the movements that the Spirit of God impressed on us when we were careful to keep ourselves in that sacred union which we should have with Him. It is certain that there is a secret in writings which it seems we do not sufficiently know. There is a certain transmission on to the paper of the mind and heart of him who writes,[1] which is the cause that we perceive, so to say, his likeness in the picture of the thing that he represents," and that we feel, in a certain way, that mood in which he was when he wrote. The most incomprehensible thing is that this impression remains in the books for ages, so that the devil lives in the books of the wicked as well as in their souls, and in the same way the Holy Spirit lives in good books in proportion to the grace that animated the soul of him who wrote them. And this shows that a man cannot purify his heart too much in order to speak of the things of God and of His sacred truths, and that we should work longer and more seriously to mortify our passions than to acquire knowledge, when we find ourselves called to speak of things that may benefit others.[2]

The slightest cloud that is found in our heart overflows on to

---

and Joubert has estimated him well: "One of our greatest writers, and the first among the good, if we take into account the order of time, useful to read and to meditate and excellent to admire; he is equally fit to instruct and to form, both by his defects and his good qualities. He often overshoots the mark, but he leads to it. It lies in the reader's power to stop there, although the author goes beyond it." (t. ii. p. 181.)

[1] Pascal said with more clearness and force: "When we see a natural style we are astonished and delighted, for we expected to see an author, and we find a man." (*Pensées*.)

[2] "When a man feels himself called upon to compose some work for God," writes Saint-Cyran to Lemaître on a project of Lives of the Saints, "for which, although he may not be very humble, he should always think himself not very fit, he should withdraw into himself, humble himself, lament, and pray. He must think of himself as the tool and the pen of God... You have seen in St. Bernard that he compares God, with

the paper, like a breath that dims the surface of a mirror, and the slightest corruption that we have will be like a gnawing worm, which will pass into this writing and gnaw the heart of those who shall read it till the end of the world. (Lancelot, *Mémoires*, t. ii. p. 127.)

REGULATIONS FOR THE CHILDREN OF THE SCHOOL OF LE CHESNAI.[1]

On Rising.

The elder children rise every day at five o'clock winter and summer, the younger at six.

As they sleep in the same room, each master has no trouble to awaken his own pupils.

They rise quickly, it being very dangerous to accustom them to idling at the first hour of the day.

They kneel immediately they are out of bed to worship God.

After which they finish dressing, comb each other in great silence, it being very reasonable that their first words should be prayers and thanksgiving to God for their preservation during the night.

If, however, anyone had need to leave the room he should ask permission in a low voice.

Of Morning Prayer.

At six o'clock they all kneel before the crucifix which is in

---

respect to men, to a writer or painter who guides the hand of a little child, and only asks the child not to move his hand, but to let it be guided. . . It is, then, the writer and not the child who writes, and it would be ridiculous for the child to be vain of what he had done. . . Holding these sentiments, we grow at once in virtue and knowledge. We acquire wonderful strength, and throw an odour of piety over the work, which first strikes the author and then those who read it." (FONTAINE, *Mém.* t. ii. p. 51.)

[1] A small village a quarter of a league from Versailles. The house belonged to M. de Bernières, one of the most active and generous friends of Port-Royal; he sold his office of maître des requêtes in order to devote his time and fortune to the relief of the poor in the provinces of Normandy, Picardy, and Champagne. His connection with Mme. de Longueville and Port-Royal caused his exile to Issoudun, where he died in 1662. (See notice of him, BESOGNE, *Hist. de Port-Royal*, t. iv. p. 143.)

the room, and repeat the usual prayers, namely, the Veni Creator, the Lord's Prayer, the Ave-Maria, and the Creed.

Then follows *Prime* for the elder scholars, who all remain standing during the repetition of this prayer.

After this is finished each goes to his table to study his lesson and write his composition, and they remain there in great silence until seven o'clock. At seven repetition of lessons, which lasts until breakfast.

Of Breakfast.

They breakfast about eight o'clock.

During this time, which lasts a good half-hour, they are at liberty to converse aloud with one another on what subject they like, or to read some history, or look at maps, &c. They do not, however, leave the room. In winter they are round the fire.

After breakfast, each goes back silently to his table, to work at his second lesson until ten o'clock.

This second lesson consists, for the elder scholars, in repeating their Greek lesson, which they translate into French, or reading their Latin composition. The Greek lesson is usually three pages of Plutarch, in folio, in the morning and as much in the afternoon; for the juniors, translation of Livy, Justin, Severus Sulpicius, &c.

The second lesson lasts until eleven o'clock, which is the dinner hour.

Of Mass.

They do not go to mass every day, especially the juniors, until they are sufficiently advanced for it; for great care is taken that they are well-behaved in church, and do not look about them. Two are usually sent to make the responses, which they do in turn.

As on this occasion they fulfil the office of the angels, they are exhorted to behave with great respect, and to present themselves at this bloodless sacrifice of Jesus Christ in remembrance of that which He offered to His Father for our sins on Mount Calvary.

If the seniors commit any fault they are reprimanded, and especially as, being more advanced in age, they should be wiser, and edify the others by their example.

Of Grace before Meat.

At eleven o'clock they all assemble in one of the rooms, where they make an examination of conscience, after having said the *Confiteor* as far as *Mea Culpa*. After the examination is ended they finish the remainder with the prayer.

One of the seniors repeats by heart a Latin sentence taken from the *Proverbs*. They then go down to wash their hands and go into the refectory.

Of the Dinner.

The children are seated beside and in front of their own master, who distributes to them what has been served up, after they have eaten their soup each in his own porringer.[1]

They endeavour to accustom them not to affect an inconvenient delicacy, and always to eat with propriety.

During dinner all sorts of histories are read, as the History of the Jews by Josephus, Church History by M. Godeau, History of France, Roman History and such like. Nothing has been so useful, and it is surprising that the children who are busy eating lose scarcely anything of what is read.

On feast-days and Sundays books of piety are read, such as some of the fine translations that have been made, the *Christian Instructions*, the *Confessions* of St. Augustine, and others like them.

Of Recreation after Dinner.

One of the masters, who never loses sight of the children, is always present; but his presence does not incommode them in any way, because he gives them entire liberty to play at the games which they like to choose; this is always done with

---

[1] A song of M. de Coulanges teaches us that this custom was quite recent. Advice to Fathers:

> Formerly they ate their soup
> Without ceremony from the dish,
> And often wiped the spoon
> On the boiled fowl;
> Formerly in the fricassee
> They dipped their bread and their fingers,
> Now each one eats
> His soup in his plate.

modesty and good manners, and as the close in which they play is very large, they can choose their walks.

In summer, during the heat of the day, they usually walk in the shade of the woods.

In winter they exercise themselves in running, or retire to a large room, and as there is a good billiard table in it, when they have warmed themselves some stop at it, others like better to play at backgammon, draughts, chess, or cards.

These cards were a certain pack which embraced the history of the first six centuries ;[1] that is to say, the time and place in which the chief councils were held, in which the popes, emperors, eminent saints, and profane authors lived, and in which the most memorable events of the world happened. By constantly playing this little game, the greater number had these things so impressed on their mind, and the circumstances of the different times and places in which these great men lived, that no doctor could speak on them more pertinently. What M. de Sainte-Beuve[2] often wondered at, after having put it to the proof, was what gave these lads, of whom the greater number had not yet reached the age of sixteen or seventeen, such a great and wide knowledge of all things, of all the countries of the world, and of periods of time, that they were able to converse agreeably with all sorts of persons, to study all sorts of affairs, and even to explain them.

No disputes or contentions were ever seen among them upon any matter. They had been so accustomed to respect one another that they never used the familiar "thou," and were never heard to utter the least word that they might think would be disagreeable to any of their companions.

Recreation usually lasted a good hour and a half.

---

[1] The pack was composed of 52 cards. When, for instance, those relating to the popes had been dealt, he who had in his hand the longest pontificate gained, and if he recited correctly the information given on his card he took a counter.

[2] Jacques de Sainte-Beuve (1613-1677), a doctor of the Sorbonne, and a great friend of Port-Royal. He would not subscribe the censure pronounced against Arnauld, was excluded from the Faculty, and lost his chair of theology (1658). Nicole had been his pupil. Sainte-Beuve, however, eagerly signed the formulary in 1661, and refused all intercourse with the nuns of Port-Royal.

On holidays they left the close and went towards Marly, Versailles, and Saint-Cyr (the building of Versailles was not yet commenced[1]).

During these walks the children conversed familiarly and gaily with the masters upon all subjects, which formed their minds in a remarkable manner.

After recreation they repeated alternately what they had read in history or talked about geography.

As children have good memories, they noticed the smallest facts of history, so that when the seniors began to talk first the juniors always said something on the subject, and thus they were accustomed to speak in good terms and to form an opinion on the facts mentioned in the history which had been read. In fine, by making them pass their early years in these kinds of exercises, the teachers endeavoured to put them in a position to render service to God and the public when they should be grown up.

Of the Return to the Class-room in the Afternoon.

On entering they said a short prayer, to ask for the grace of God to pass the rest of the day in a godly manner, and to accustom them to do no action without beginning and ending by prayer.

Each being at his table, they began to work; some wrote their copy, which was always some sentence taken from the Holy Scripture, and the others copied their notes on Virgil.

Others prepared[2] their lessons or read some good book. That lasted until afternoon refreshment, which was regularly brought them at three o'clock; it lasted a good half-hour, during which they were at liberty to converse with one another as they did during breakfast. This refreshment was thought necessary for the juniors on account of their greater natural activity. The others might go without it if they wished.

---

[1] It was not until after 1672 that Louis XIV. passed a large part of the year at Versailles, and only fixed his residence there in 1682. The Court was then at Paris, which it left for Saint-Germain in 1661.

[2] An excellent practice, which involves individual initiative, permits greater benefit to be derived from the lessons, and singularly facilitates the taking of notes.

At half-past three all took their places at their tables to study their lessons, which they repeated from four to six o'clock, when they supped.

Recreation was the same as after dinner.

In summer opportunity was often taken of conversing during this time with the seniors on some points of history or on other useful subjects, while the juniors amused themselves with games.

This recreation lasted till eight o'clock. They then returned to pass a good half-hour in the class-room in preparing what they had to do for the next morning.

Evening Prayer.

Evening prayer was said at half-past eight, when they repeated the *Pater-noster*, *Credo*, and *Confiteor* in Latin, the litanies of the Virgin, *Sub tuum praesidium*, &c.

Then, after examination of conscience, each returned to his room in silence.

Of going to Bed.

After saying his prayers, each undressed and got into bed quickly and in silence.

Thus all were in bed at nine o'clock.

As all the exercises of the day were, in this manner, regulated and diversified, the children had no time to become wearied; and the greatest punishment that could be given to those who sometimes showed a disagreeable humour was to threaten to send them home, as I have already said.

Directions for Sundays and Holy-days.

They rose at five o'clock as usual.

After they were dressed *Prime* was said; after which they read privately some pious books, until they all assembled to go to catechising, which lasted until the bell rang for mass.

They always had to learn by heart two or three articles of the catechism of M. de Saint-Cyran, which is esteemed one of the best that have been written.

The teachers always began by making the juniors repeat what

had been said the last time, in order to impress it well on their memory.

They always had to hear high mass at the parish church; for it is necessary to accustom children of good family early to submit to the order which has been established in the Church, and which has been followed during a long succession of ages.[1] For, thinking only of amusing ourselves, feasting and paying visits after having been to hear low mass, as quickly as possible, is not sanctifying the Sunday .... (*Supplément au Nécrologe*, p. 54.)

A LETTER FROM M. LE MAÎTRE DE SACI TO ONE OF HIS FRIENDS.

PATIENCE AND SILENCE.

It seems to me, Sir, that if I were allowed to choose an employment, I should readily desire yours, so much do I esteem it, and think you happy to have devoted yourself to it. I am convinced that there is no occupation equal to yours, nor one more worthy of a Christian, when it is undertaken from pure love. It is sufficient to say that Jesus Christ has commended it to us, and that, in order to oblige us still more to acquit ourselves well in it, He exhorts us to become as children, and assures us that we must do so in order to enter paradise.

Children whose nature is good and docile render their in-

---

[1] This is one of the grievances of Father Rapin in an interest that he does not conceal: "At Port-Royal they only recommended the worship at the parish church and the spiritual direction of the *curés*, who were called the true pastors because they wished to acknowledge their position in order to obtain their favour. This notion became then so fashionable, that even in the freest and most polite society they laughed at ladies who confessed to the regular clergy as not belonging to the hierarchy .... Nothing so much lowered the esteem in which the religious orders were held, and which it was desired to annihilate in order to destroy the jesuits, and nothing more tended to raise the ecclesiastical spirit and everything that related to the parishes which had been formerly so despised, that even the most important parishes in Paris were abandoned to Picards, Normans, and Manceaux as being posts unworthy of men of position .... It was, properly speaking, the scheming of the jansenists that set in fashion this spirit of parochialism which afterwards dominated Paris, and by which the beneficed clergy became so important, that they made themselves dreaded by the great, respected by the lower classes, and held in honour by everybody." (*Mémoires*, t. i. p. 484.)

truction easier and more agreeable; but the others, who try our patience more, also give reason to deserve more.[1] It is necessary to labour to root out in them the works of the old man, and that is done better by actions and example than by exhortations, which are not of much use to children unless they are few, short, and adapted to their age, and appear to spring from particular circumstances rather than from a general intention to exhort and reprove them. Children are not usually so capable of being taught by reason as by the senses and habit which insensibly impress on them the spirit of modesty and humility, the love of heavenly things and contempt of earthly things, especially when those who guide them are careful to unite the spirit of prayer to their work, and to offer them every day to God, remembering that he who plants and he who waters is nothing, and that it is God alone who, possessing all power, thus produces the result. As the chief end of education should be to save them and ourselves with them, we must also have more trust in Him who is the true Saviour and Master than in all human means and industry, considering ourselves as instruments, which can have no movement except what He gives them, that He may thus shed His blessing on the scholars through the masters. That is all the desire of my heart, for the children as much as for yourself. If you see any good in them, praise God for it, who has put it in them, but let it be in secret, and be careful to speak little of it;[2] if, on the contrary, you find that there is much to do, do not despair, remembering their age.

---

[1] Fontaine, who has reproduced the principal passages of this letter, and commented on them, adds some ideas worthy of note: "M. de Saci always gave this advice, not to undertake the charge of other children than those of respectable parents." Education at Port-Royal, as with Montaigne, Rabelais, Locke, and Rousseau, preserves an aristocratic character. The large heart of Pestalozzi will be devoted to those who have the greatest need of education—the poor and neglected.

[2] It requires, in fact, much tact and discretion to praise without exciting the bad feeling of vanity. De Saci, perhaps, uses too much reserve; we, on the contrary, misuse publicity. Why insert in our scholastic journals that a child found a purse and did not keep it? A simple act of honesty is praised as an act of heroism. Let us reserve our public acknowledgments for acts of courage and devotion.

Every day we see those degenerate who were good in their childhood; and, on the contrary, those in whom we saw nothing good when they were children improve as they grow older. They are like the young wheat, which often produces more or less than was expected. We must not be too uneasy about their faults, or too precise in marking them.[1] If there is any conduct which it is necessary to feign not to notice, it is that of children whom we should be satisfied to reprove for serious faults, closing our eyes to others, although they may not appear small. It is sufficient not to encourage them by too much indulgence in excessive liberty; and, for the rest, we must work little by little, and with reference to one thing at a time, to cure them, having towards them an untiring charity; otherwise we give ourselves great trouble, and do them no good, we even sour their tempers by too frequent and injudicious reproofs. We must endeavour to instil into them some feelings of piety and the fear of God . . . . We must make the most of the confidence that they have in those who guide them, and encourage it, in order to use it for their salvation. When it is necessary to reprove and warn them, it should be well considered, in order not to discourage them. By overlooking some of their faults we correct others which are of more consequence; and we provide against the small irregularities that we wish to prevent in children more by prayer than by words. Then God shows us when it is time to speak to them, and most frequently we find that there was nothing to be said. We can only understand these tender souls by adapting ourselves to them, and conforming ourselves to their inclinations; otherwise they do not understand our words, and this imposes on us the need of continual prayer and attention both for ourselves and them, not telling them all they should do, but only as much as their weakness, for which we should have great regard and consideration, can bear. We should not exercise authority over them untempered by charity, adapting ourselves in such a manner to them, that it is they who draw the conclusion, and

---

[1] This language is truer and more simple than that of Saint-Cyran, who speaks too much of "trembling" and of "tempest of the mind."

do by persuasion what is demanded of them.[1] When we see that they cannot submit, we should retire and feign not to notice, leaving them with a few imperfections for a time, rather than forcing their will, by which we gain nothing, and which might even irritate them.

Above all, they should never be left alone; and whether they are studying, playing, or doing anything else, we should always be witnesses, either by ourselves or by grave persons to whom we entrust this duty, of all their actions.

In fine, there are no virtues that should be more practised with children than patience and silence, avoiding, by patience, hasty reproof, and taking care, by cultivating silence, to say no more than they can bear.

Jesus Christ often withdrew Himself from His disciples to pray to His Father, in order not to be obliged constantly to reprove them, as their imperfect condition often gave Him reason to do. Thus you would do well to take for a motto these two words, *Patience and silence*, and this verse of the Psalmist, *Adhaereat lingua faucibus meis*, desiring that your words should cleave to your mouth rather than that any should drop which might wound the children. (LECLERC, *Vies intéressantes*, t. iv. p. 351.)

PASCAL AT PORT-ROYAL.[2]

M. Pascal came, at that time, to live at Port-Royal des Champs. I do not stop to tell who this man was, whom not only all France but all Europe admired. His active mind, always at work, had a breadth, elevation, firmness, penetration, and clearness beyond anything that can be imagined. There was no adept in mathematics who did not yield to him, as witness the story of the

---

[1] This is, in fact, true education; education from within and not from without, by the association of the pupil with the master, and by his personal influence on himself. Without this condition education is but a very superficial work, without real efficacity.

[2] "I can scarcely believe," observes Sainte-Beuve with reason, "that the fine conversation between Pascal and M. de Saci on Epictetus and Montaigne is not the compilation of M. Lemaître himself." (*Port-Royal*, t. i. p. 395.)

famous roulette,[1] which was then the subject of conversation of all the learned. He could animate copper and put mind into brass. He brought it about that little wheels without reason, on each of which were the first ten figures, should give a reason to the most reasonable persons; and, in a manner, he made dumb machines speak, to solve, in working, the difficulties in numbers which puzzle the learned; and this cost him so much application and effort of mind, that to arrange that machine to the point at which everyone admired it, and which I have seen with my own eyes, his own head was almost deranged during three years. This wonderful man, being at last touched by God, submitted this eminent mind to the yoke of Jesus Christ, and this grand and noble heart humbly submitted to penance. He came to Paris to throw himself into the arms of M. Singlin, resolved to do whatever he ordered him.

M. Singlin thought, on seeing this great genius, that he should do well to send him to Port-Royal des Champs, where M. Arnauld would measure his strength with him in what regarded the other sciences,[2] and M. de Saci would teach him to despise them. He came, then, to live at Port-Royal. M. de Saci could not excuse himself from seeing him, especially as he was requested to do so by M. Singlin; but the sacred light that he found in the Scriptures and the Fathers made him hope that he should not be dazzled with the brilliancy of M. Pascal, which, nevertheless, charmed and carried away everybody. He was strongly impressed with the force of all he said. He admitted with pleasure the strength of his reasonings, but he learnt nothing new from them. All that Pascal told him that was grand he had seen before in St. Augustine; and, doing justice to everybody, he said: "M. Pascal is very estimable in that, not having read the Fathers of the Church, he has of himself, by the penetration of his mind, discovered the same truths that they did. He thinks them

---

[1] The roulette or cycloid is the name given to the curve described by a point in a circumference rolling on a straight line. This problem very much occupied the learned in the seventeenth century. Descartes, Roberval, Father Mersenne, Torricelli, Fermat, Huyghens, &c., made it the object of their studies.

[2] Bossuet calls Arnauld "a man eminent in every kind of knowledge." (*Œuvres*, t. ix. p. 451.)

surprising, because he has not seen them anywhere ; but, for our part, we are accustomed to see them everywhere in our books. . . ."

It was a habit of M. de Saci, in conversing with people, to adapt his conversation to those with whom he was speaking. If, for instance, he saw M. Champagne,[1] he spoke to him of painting. If he saw M. Hamon,[2] he conversed with him about medicine. If he saw the surgeon of the place, he questioned him about surgery. Those who cultivated trees, the vine, or grain, told him what he should observe. He used everything as an occasion to speak of God and to lead others to Him. He thought, then, that he ought to take M. Pascal on his strong point, and to speak to him of the reading of philosophy, in which he was most occupied. He led him to this subject in the first conversations they had together. M. Pascal told him that the two books he usually read had been Epictetus and Montagne, and highly praised these two intellects. M. de Saci, who had always thought he ought to read these authors very little, begged him to make him acquainted with them.

"Epictetus,"[3] said M. Pascal, "is one of the men of the world who has best known the duties of man. He wishes him before all things to look upon God as his chief object, to be persuaded that He does everything with justice, to submit to Him heartily, to follow Him willingly in everything, because He does everything

---

[1] Philippe de Champagne (1602-1674), "this jansenist Poussin," says Théophile Gautier, who points out in the gallery of the Louvre "that singular and characteristic painting in which we see Sister Sainte-Suzanne (the daughter of Ph. de Champagne and a nun of Port-Royal) sitting with her feet stretched out on a stool, her hands joined, while the Mother Catherine Agnes Arnauld, on her knees, implores of heaven the healing of the sick woman, who was, in fact, restored to health, as the inscription on the picture states. When we have seen this picture," he adds, "we know Port-Royal as well as if we had read the voluminous work of Sainte-Beuve." (*Guide de l'amateur au musée du Louvre*, p. 158.) Two *chefs-d'œuvre* of this painter are exhibited in the *salon d'honneur*, namely, Christ lying in His shroud, and a portrait of Richelieu.

[2] See note, p. 243.

[3] Epictetus, a Greek Stoic philosopher of the first century after Christ. Abstain, be resigned, were the two principles of his morality. See the study of M. Martha on *Stoic virtue*, personified in that slave who honours humanity as much as the wise emperor Marcus Aurelius. (*Les moralistes sous l'empire romain*, p. 155.)

with great wisdom; that thus this disposition will stop all his complaints and murmurings, and prepare his heart to support the most painful occurrences. Never say, he said, I have lost that, but rather I have returned it; my wife is dead, but I have given her back; and thus of goods and everything else. But he who takes it from me is a wicked man, you say. Why do you trouble yourself through whom He who lent it to you comes to demand it again?[1] While He allows you the use of it, take care of it as of a good that belongs to another, as a man who is travelling looks upon himself in an inn. You ought not to wish, said he, that things which happen should happen as you desire, but you ought to wish them to happen as they do. Remember, said he, that you are here like an actor, and that you play your part in a comedy, such as it pleases the Master to give you. Remain on the stage as long as He wishes, and appear rich or poor as He commands. Your business is to play the part that He gives you well, but the choice of the part is another's business. Always keep before your eyes death and the ills which seem the most insupportable, and you will never think of anything low, nor desire anything inordinately.

"He shows in a thousand ways what man should do. He wishes him to be humble, to hide his good resolutions, above all in their initial stages, and to accomplish them in secret. Nothing ruins them more than showing them. He never tires of repeating that all the study and desire of man should be to recognize the will of God and to follow it.[2]

"You see here, Sir, the intelligence of this great man who understood so well the duty of man, and I dare to say that he would deserve to be worshipped if he had known equally well his impotence, since it would be necessary to be God to teach both these things to men. Thus, as he was dust and ashes, after having so well comprehended what ought to be done, this is how he loses himself in the presumption of what can be done. He

---

[1] This is really showing too much resignation. Would not this sort of fatalism put at their ease assassins and robbers, transformed into agents of Providence?

[2] "To will what God wills is the only science
That gives us repose."—MALHERBE.

said that God has given to every man the means of fulfilling all his obligations; that these means are always in our power; that we must only seek happiness through the things which are always in our power, since God has given them to us for this end; that we must consider what is free in us; that goods, life, and esteem are not in our power and do not lead to God, but that the mind cannot be forced to believe what it knows to be false, nor the will to love what it knows must make it unhappy; that these two powers are entirely free, and that by them alone we can make ourselves perfect; that man, by these powers, can thoroughly know God, love Him, obey Him, please Him, cure himself of all his vices, acquire all virtues and thus make himself holy and a companion of God. These principles, which spring from a diabolical pride, lead him to other errors; for example, that the soul is a part of the divine substance, that pain and death are not evils, that we may kill ourselves when we are so persecuted that we may believe God summons us, &c.

"As to Montagne, Sir, of whom you wish me to speak to you, being born in a Christian state, he professed the Catholic religion, and in that there is nothing peculiar. But as he wished to find a morality founded on reason without the light of faith, he took his principles on this supposition; and thus considering man deprived of all revelation, he discourses in this manner. He puts everything in universal doubt, and so general that this doubt doubts of itself, and that man doubting even whether he does doubt, his uncertainty rolls on itself in a perpetual circle without ceasing, opposing itself equally to those who say that everything is uncertain and to those who assert that all is not so, because it will assert nothing. It is in this doubt which doubts of itself, and in this ignorance which is ignorant of itself, that the essence of his opinion lies, which he has not been able to express by any positive term. For if he says that he doubts he betrays himself by asserting at least that he does doubt; which, being expressly contrary to his intention, he has only been able to explain himself by interrogation, so that not wishing to say *I do not know*, he says *what do I know?* And this he takes for his motto, under a pair of scales, which, weighing contradictories, are in perfect equilibrium, that is to say, he is a pure Pyrrhonist. All his discourses

and *Essays* move on this principle, and this is the only thing that
he pretends to thoroughly establish, although he does not always
let his intention be seen. He insensibly destroys by it all that
passes among men as most certain, not in order to establish the
contrary with a certainty of which by itself he is the enemy, but
simply to show that appearances being equal on both sides, a man
does not know on what to found his belief.

"In this spirit he laughs at all assertions. For example, he
combats those who have wished to provide in France a great
remedy for lawsuits by the number and so-called precision of the
laws, as if the root of the doubt whence lawsuits spring could be
cut and there were dams that could stop the torrent of uncertainty
and fix conjectures. In this, however, when he says that it would
be just as well to submit the case to the first passer-by as to judges
armed with this number of laws, he does not mean that the order
of the State should be changed, he has not so much ambition; nor
that his opinion is the best, he does not think any opinion good;
it is solely to prove the vanity of the most generally received
opinions showing that the exclusion of all law would rather
diminish the number of disputes than that multitude of laws,
which only serves to augment it, because obscurities increase in
proportion as it is hoped to remove them, that these obscurities
increase by the commentaries, and that the surest means of understanding the sense of a discourse is not to examine it, but to take it
as it appears at first, for if it is examined ever so little all its clearness disappears. Thus he judges at random all the actions of men
and all the points of history, sometimes in one manner and sometimes in another, freely following his first view, and without
submitting his thought to the rules of reason, which has only
false standards, delighted to show by his example the contradictions of the same mind. As a result of this wholly independent
attitude, it is the same to him either to get angry or not in
disputes, having always by one example or the other a means
of showing the weakness of opinions, being led with so much
advantage into universal doubt that he fortifies himself in it
equally by his triumph or defeat. It is on this foundation, all
floating and tottering as it is, that he combats with invincible
firmness the heretics of his time upon this that they are certain

that they alone know the true meaning of Scripture, and it is from there also that he most rigorously strikes down the horrible impiety of those who assert that there is no God.

"He takes them in hand especially in the apology of Raymond of Sabunde,[1] and finding them voluntarily deprived of all revelation and left to their natural reason, which is nevertheless put on one side, he questions them by what authority they who really know not one of the least things in nature undertake to judge of that sovereign Being who is infinite by His own definition. He asks them on what principles they rely, and presses them to point them out to him. He examines all those that they can produce, and goes so far by the talent in which he excels that he shows the self-conceit of all those who pass for the most enlightened and the most firm. He asks if the soul knows anything, if it knows itself, if it is substance or accident, body or spirit; what each of these things is, and if there is anything that is not of either of these orders, if it knows its own body, if it knows what matter is, and if it can distinguish bodies in the vast variety in which they are produced; how it can reason if it is material, and how it can be united to a particular body and feel its passions if it is spiritual. When did it begin to exist—with the body or before? and if it ends with it or not, if it is never deceived, if it knows when it errs, considering that the essence of error consists in not knowing it, if in obscurities it does not as firmly believe that two and three are six as it believes afterwards that they are five; if animals reason, think, and speak, who can decide what time is, what space or extension is, what movement is, what unity is, all which things surround us and are entirely inexplicable; what health is, or death, life, sickness, good, evil, righteousness, sin, of which we are constantly talking; if we have in ourselves the principles of the true, and if those that we believe and which are called axioms or notions common to all men are conformable to essential truth. And since we know by faith alone that an infinitely good Being has given them to us true, creating us to know the truth, who will know without this light if, being formed

---

[1] Raymond of Sabunde professed, about the middle of the XVth century, at Toulouse, medicine, theology, and philosophy. Montaigne translated his *Théologie naturelle* into French.

by chance, our notions are not uncertain? or if, being formed by a false and wicked being, he has not given them to us false in order to mislead us, thus showing that God and the true are inseparable, and that if the one is or is not, if it is certain or uncertain, the other is necessarily the same? Who knows if common sense, which we usually take for the judge of the true, was destined for this office by Him who created it? And more, who knows what truth is, and how we can be assured of having it without knowing it? Who knows even what a being is? Since it is impossible to define it, there is nothing more universal, and to explain it we should have to start by making use of the word being itself, saying it is such or such a thing. And since we do not know what the soul, body, time, space, motion, truth, good, nor even being are, nor how to explain the idea that we form of them, how can we assure ourselves that it is the same in every man, seeing that we have no other marks than uniformity of consequences, which is not always a sign of uniformity of principles? For they may be different and yet lead to the same conclusions, everybody knowing that the true is often deduced from the false.

"Then he examines profoundly all the sciences: geometry, of which he endeavours to show the uncertainty in its axioms, and in the terms which it does not define, as extension, motion, &c.; natural science and medicine, which he depreciates in many ways; history, politics, ethics, jurisprudence, and the rest; so that, without revelation, we might believe, according to him, that life is a dream from which we shall only awake at death, and during which we possess the principles of truth as little as during natural sleep. Thus he depreciates so strongly and cruelly reason devoid of faith, that, making it doubt if it is reasonable, and if animals are so or not, or more or less so than man, he brings it down from the excellence it has attributed to itself, putting it as a favour on a level with the brutes, without permitting it to leave this order until it be informed by its Creator Himself of its true rank, of which it is ignorant; threatening, if it complains, to put it below all, which appears to him as easy as the contrary, and in the meanwhile only acknowledging its power to act so far as to recognize its weakness with sincere humility, instead of exalting itself by a foolish vanity."

M. de Saci thought himself in a new country, and listening to a strange language; and repeated to himself these words of St. Augustine: "O God of truth! are those who know these subtleties of reasoning more pleasing to thee on that account?" He pitied this philosopher, who pricked and tore himself everywhere with the thorns that he himself made, as St. Augustine says of himself, when he was in that state. After having patiently heard all, he said to M. Pascal, "I am much obliged to you, Sir; I am sure that if I had read Montagne for a long time I should not know him so well as I know him through the conversation that I have just had with you. This man should wish to be known only by the account that you give of his writings, and he might say with St. Augustine, *Ibi me vides, attende.* I certainly think that this man had talent, but I am not sure that you do not lend him a little more than he had by that exact concatenation that you make of his principles. You may judge that, having passed my life as I have done, I have seldom been advised to read this author, all whose works contain nothing that we ought especially to seek in our reading, according to the rule of St. Augustine, because his words do not spring from humility and Christian charity, and because they overturn the foundations of all knowledge, and consequently of religion itself. This is what this pious doctor blamed in those philosophers of former times, who were called academicians, and who wished to throw doubt upon everything.

"But what need had Montagne to divert his mind by reviving a theory which rightly passes among Christians for folly? If it is alleged in his excuse that, in what he says, he puts faith on one side, we who have faith ought to put on one side all that Montagne says. I do not find fault with the talent of this author, which is a great gift of God; but he ought to make a better use of it, and rather offer it to God than to the devil. Of what use is a good thing when it is used so ill? You, Sir, are happy in having raised yourself above these doctors who are plunged in the intoxication of science, and whose hearts are void of the truth. God has poured into your heart other sweetness and attractions than those you found in Montagne. He has recalled you from that dangerous pleasure, as St. Augustine says, who gives thanks to

God that He has pardoned him the sins he had committed in loving these vanities too much. St. Augustine is to be believed in this so much the more as formerly he held those opinions; and, as you say of Montagne, that he combats the heretics of his time by this universal doubt, it was also by this same doubt of the academicians that St. Augustine forsook the heresy of the Manichæans. After he devoted himself to God, he renounced this vanity, which he calls sacrilegious. He acknowledged the wisdom of St. Paul in warning us not to be led away by eloquent arguments. For he admits that there is a certain pleasure in them that carries us away. We sometimes think that things are true because they are said eloquently. They are dangerous viands, said he, that are served up on fine dishes; but these viands, instead of nourishing the heart, leave it empty. We are then like men who are asleep, and who think they are eating while they are sleeping."

M. de Saci added several similar things; upon which M. Pascal said that if he complimented him on knowing Montagne so thoroughly, and knowing how to turn him so well, he might say, without compliment, that he knew St. Augustine more thoroughly and knew how to turn him better, although not very much to the advantage of poor Montagne. M. Pascal appeared to be very much edified by the solidity of all that M. de Saci had just put before him. However, being still full of his author, he could not avoid saying, "I admit, Sir, that I cannot see without pleasure, in this author, haughty reason so irresistibly attacked with its own weapons, and this sanguinary revolt of man against himself, which casts him down to the condition of the brutes, from that intercourse with God to which he raised himself by the principles of his feeble reason. I should, with all my heart, have loved this instrument of a great punishment, if, being a humble disciple of the Church through faith, he had followed the rules of morality by inducing these same men, whom he had so profitably humbled, not to irritate by new crimes Him who alone can draw them from those which he has proved to them that they cannot even understand. But he acts, on the contrary, like a pagan. From this principle, says he, that apart from faith everything is uncertain, and considering how long we have been seeking the true and the good without making any progress towards tranquillity, he concludes that we ought to leave the search for these to others and to remain in repose, passing lightly over these subjects, lest by bearing on them we sink into them; and to take the true and the good as they first present themselves without insisting upon them, because they have so little solidity that, however slightly we close our hand on them, they run through the fingers and leave it empty. For this reason he follows the impressions of the senses and common feelings, because he would have to do violence to himself to ignore them, and does not know whether he would gain by doing so, being ignorant as to where the truth lies. Thus he flies from pain and death because his instinct drives him to do so, and because he will not resist this instinct. He does not, however, decide whether they are true evils, as he does not altogether trust these natural feelings of fear, seeing that we have other feelings of pleasure which are censured as being bad, although nature, he says, asserts the contrary. Thus, he adds, there is nothing irrational in my conduct. I act like others, and all that they do, with the silly idea that they are following the true good, I do in accordance with another principle, which is that, appearances being equal on both sides, example and convenience are the influences which should determine me.

"He follows, then, the manners of his country, because custom governs him. He mounts his horse because the horse allows him to do so, like any ordinary man who is not a philosopher; he does not conceive that he has any moral right to do this, inasmuch as he does not know whether the animal has not, on the contrary, just as good a right to make use of him. He also does some violence to himself in order to avoid certain vices, and even keeps his marriage vow because of the trouble that follows disregard of it, his rule of action in everything being his own convenience and tranquillity. He casts far from him that Stoic Virtue that is painted with a severe countenance, a fierce look, dishevelled hair, a wrinkled and perspiring forehead, in a strained and painful attitude, far from men, in gloomy silence and alone on the top of a rock, a phantom, as he says, to frighten children, and which does nothing but seek repose, which she never finds, by constant toil. His science is artless, familiar, humorous, sportive, and frolicsome. She follows what pleases her, and jests about things that happen whether good or bad, lying softly in the lap of an idle tranquillity whence she shows men who are so painfully seeking happiness, that it is only to be found there where she is reposing, and that ignorance and absence of curiosity are two soft pillows for a sound head, as he says himself.

"I cannot conceal from you," added M. Pascal, "that in reading this author and comparing him with Epictetus, I have thought that they were most certainly the two greatest defenders of the two most celebrated schools of the infidel world, which alone, among those of men destitute of the light of religion, have judgments which are in some measure connected and consistent. For what could they do but follow one or other of these two systems? The first, there is a God; hence, it is He who created man. He made him for Himself. He created him such as he should be in order to be just and to become happy. Man can, then, know the truth, and is in a position to raise himself by wisdom up to God, who is his highest good. Second system, man cannot raise himself up to God. His inclinations contradict the law. He is prone to seek his happiness in visible good things, and even in those which are most disgraceful. Everything appears then uncertain, and the true good is so also; and this seems to reduce us to a state in which we have neither a fixed rule for morals nor certainty in the sciences. I have had great pleasure in remarking, in these various reasonings, in what points both have perceived something of the truth that they have essayed to learn. For if it is agreeable to observe in nature her desire to paint God in all her works, in which indeed we see some mark of Him, because they are images of Him, how much more just is it to consider in the productions of men's minds the efforts that they make to arrive at the truth, even while flying from it, and to note in what points they touch it and in what points they depart from it, as I have endeavoured to do in this study?

"It is true, Sir, that you have just shown me, in an admirable manner, the little need that Christians have of these philosophical readings. I will, nevertheless, with your permission tell you my thoughts on the subject, being ready notwithstanding to give up all knowledge that does not come from God, from whom alone we can receive the truth with confidence. It seems to me that the source of the errors of the Stoics on the one hand, and of the Epicureans on the other, is that they did not recognize that man's present state differs from that at his creation; so that the one sect, noting some traces of his primitive dignity and ignorant of his corruption, has considered nature as sound and without need of a restorer, which leads it to the most extreme pride; while those who belong to the other, feeling man's present misery, and ignorant of his primitive dignity, consider nature as necessarily unsound and incapable of improvement; this makes them despair of attaining a true good, and hence throws them into extreme sloth. These two states, which it is necessary to see together in order to perceive the whole truth, being seen separately, necessarily lead to one of these two vices, pride or sloth, in which all men are infallibly plunged before grace, since, if they do not continue in their disorders through sloth, they emerge from them through pride. Thus they are always slaves of the spirits of evil, to whom, as St. Augustine remarks, men sacrifice in many fashions. From this imperfect knowledge, then, it happens that the one, knowing his impotence and not his duty, sinks into sloth; and that the other, knowing his duty without knowing his impotence, rises up in his pride; whence it seems that by combining them we should form a perfect morality. But instead of this peace, there would only result from their junction war and general destruction. For, the one establishing certainty and the other doubt, the one the dignity of man and the other his weakness, they cannot unite and agree; so that they can neither exist separately by reason of their defects, nor unite because of their opinions, and thus they must necessarily be shattered and annihilated in order to give place to the truth of the Gospel. This truth, by a divine art, reconciles contradictories. Uniting all that is true, and rejecting all that is false, it teaches a truly heavenly wisdom, in which the opposing principles, which were incompatible in those human doctrines, agree. And the reason of this is that those wise men of the world have placed the contraries in the same object. For one attributes strength to nature, the other weakness to this same nature, which cannot be; whereas faith teaches us to put them in different objects, all that is weak appertaining to nature, and all that is powerful appertaining to grace. This is a new and astonishing union, which a God alone could teach, which He alone could make, and which is but an image and effect of the ineffable union of two natures in the sole person of a God-man.

"I beg your pardon, Sir, for transporting myself before you into theology instead of remaining in philosophy. But my subject led me to it insensibly; and it is difficult to avoid entering into it, whatever truth is treated of, because it is the centre of all truths; and this is very plain here, since it so visibly contains all those which are found in these opinions. Moreover, I do not see how any one of them can refuse to follow it. For, if they are full of the idea of the dignity of man, what have they imagined in it that does not give way before the promises of the Gospel, which are nothing else than the worthy reward of the death of a God? And if they take pleasure in seeing the infirmity of nature, their idea does not equal that of the real weakness of sin, of which the same death was the remedy. Thus all find in it more than they wished; and, what is wonderful, they find themselves united in it, they who could not unite in an infinitely lower grade."

M. de Saci could not avoid showing M. Pascal his surprise at the manner in which he turned things. He acknowledged at the same time that everybody had not the secret, like him, of making such wise and elevated reflections on their reading. He told him he was like those clever doctors, who by their skilful manner of preparing the most powerful poisons could draw from them the most powerful remedies. He added that, although he saw very well, by all he had just told him, that this reading was useful to him, nevertheless he could not think that it was advantageous to many people, whose minds would not have sufficient elevation to read and weigh these authors, and be able to pick up some pearls from the dunghill, whence a black smoke arose, which might obscure the tottering faith of those who read them; that, for this reason, he always advised those persons not to expose themselves lightly to this reading, for fear of losing themselves with those philosophers, and becoming the prey of demons, and food for worms, according to the language of Scripture, as those philosophers had been.

"As to the utility of this reading," said M. Pascal, "I will tell you very simply my opinion. I find in Epictetus an incomparable art to trouble the repose of those who seek it in exterior things, and to compel them to acknowledge that they are veritable slaves and miserable blind men; that it is impossible for them to find anything else than the error and pain that they shun if they do not give themselves unreservedly to God. Montagne is incomparable for confounding the pride of those who, without-faith, boast of true righteousness; for disabusing those who cling to their opinions, and who think they find in the sciences unshaken truths, independently of the existence and perfections of God; for so thoroughly convicting reason of its small intelligence and of its aberrations, that it is difficult, after that, to be tempted to reject the mysteries because we think we find contradictions in them; for the mind is so beaten by them that it is far from being willing to consider whether the Incarnation and the mystery of the Eucharist are possible, which ordinary men do only too often. But if Epictetus opposes idleness, he leads to pride, and may be very hurtful to those who are not persuaded of the corruption of all righteousness that does not spring from faith.

"Montagne is absolutely pernicious for those who have a leaning towards impiety and vice. Therefore this reading should be regulated with much care, discretion, and regard for the position and morals of those to whom it is recommended.[1] It seems to me even that by combining them they would not succeed entirely ill because one opposes the evil of the other. They cannot give virtue to man, but only disturb him in his vices; man finding himself opposed by contraries, one of which chases away pride and the other idleness, and not being able to rest in any of these vices, although he cannot flee them all."

In this manner these two large-minded men agreed on the subject of the reading those philosophers, and arrived at the same

---

[1] Mme. de Sévigné recommends Mme. de Grignan not to let her daughter Pauline "dip her little nose into Montaigne, nor Charron . . . There is time yet for her." (1690.) But how she felt the charm of the author of the *Essays!* "Ah! what an amiable man! What good company he is! He is my old friend; but, by force of being old, he is new to me." (6 Oct., 1679.)

result, although they did so by slightly different means; M. de Saci arriving at once by solely regarding Christianity, and M. Pascal only arriving after many deviations by following the principles of these Philosophers. (Fontaine, *Mémoires*, t. iii. p. 77.)

OF A NEW METHOD OF EASILY LEARNING TO READ IN ANY LANGUAGE.[1]

This method chiefly concerns those who cannot yet read. Simply learning the letters is not much trouble to beginners; there is more in putting them together.

Now what makes this more difficult at present is that, each letter having its name, it is pronounced alone differently than when it is joined with others. For example, if we make a child put together *f r y*, we make him pronounce *ef, ar, wy;* which infallibly confuses him when he wishes to join these three sounds together to make the sound of the syllable *fry*.

It seems then, that the most natural way, as some intelligent persons have already remarked, would be, that those who are teaching to read should, at first, only teach the children to know their letters by their value in pronunciation; and that thus, to teach to read in Latin, for example, they should give the same name *e* to simple *e, æ* and *œ,* because they are pronounced in the same way; and the same to *i* and *y;* and also to *o* and *au,* as

---

[1] M. Cousin has edited an unpublished letter of Jacqueline Pascal (26 Oct., 1655), from which it results that the method of reading styled of Port-Royal must be attributed to Pascal. ". . . Our mothers have commanded me to write to you to send me all the particulars of *your method* of learning by the B, C, D, E, in which it is not necessary for the children to know the names of the letters; for I see very well how they can be taught to read, for example, Jesu, making them pronounce *Je e, ze u ;* but I do not see how they can easily be made to understand that final letters must not add *e ;* for naturally, following this method, they will say Jesuse, unless they are told that they must not pronounce *e* at the end unless it is really there ; nor do I see how to teach them to pronounce the consonants which follow the vowels, for instance *en ;* for they will say *ene,* instead of pronouncing *an* as the French often requires. In the same way, for *on* they will say *one,* and even by making them slur over the *e* they will not pronounce it with a good accent if they are not taught separately the pronunciation of the *o* with the *n.*" (*Jacqueline Pascal*, p. 265.) Jan. 31, 1656, Arnauld writes to the mother Angélique to have Pascal's method of reading, in order to try it on a boy of twelve years of age.

they are now pronounced in France, for the Italians make *au* a diphthong.

Let the consonants also only be named by their natural sound, simply adding *e* mute, which is necessary in order to pronounce them. For example, let the name given to *b* be what is pronounced in the last syllable of the French word *tombe;* to *d* that of the last syllable of *ronde;* and thus to the others which have only a simple sound.

Let those which have several sounds, as *c, g, t, s,* be named by the most natural and usual sound, which is for *c* the sound of *k*,[1] and for *g* the sound *g* hard, for *t* the sound of the last syllable of *forte*, and for *s* that of the last syllable of *bourse.*

And then they would be taught to pronounce separately, and without spelling, the syllables *ce, ci, ge, gi, tia, tie, tii.* And they would be taught that *s* between two vowels is pronounced like *z;* *miseria, misère,* as if it were mizeria, mizère, &c.

These are the most general observations on this new method of teaching to read which would certainly be very useful to children. But to set it out in full would require a small separate treatise, in which the observations necessary to fit it for any language might be made.[2]

OF THE VERB.

Men have not had less need to invent words which should mark affirmation, which is the principal mode of our thought, than to invent those which should mark the objects of our thought.

---

[1] Duclos proposed to employ *k* instead of *c*, keeping *c* for the sound *ch*, for which there is no character in the alphabet. *Charles-Quint* would be written *Carle-Kint.*

[2] "The whole of this chapter is excellent," writes Duclos, "and admits of no exception or reply. It is astonishing that the authority of Port-Royal, especially at that time, and supported as it has since been by experience, has not yet caused reason to triumph over the absurdities of the ordinary method. Following the reasoning of Port-Royal, the Typographic Table gave their most natural denomination to the letters *fe, he, ke, le, me, ne, re, se, ze, ve, je,* and the abbreviation *cse, gse;* and not *èfe, ache, ka, èle, ème, ène, esse, zède, i* and *u* consonants, *icse.* This method, already admitted in the last edition of the Dictionary of the Academy, and practised in the best schools, will prevail sooner or later over the former system by the advantage that cannot fail to be eventually acknowledged; but it will require time, because that is reasonable." (*Commentaire sur la grammaire générale.*) The victory is not yet complete. See note on p. 255.

And it is in this properly that what we call the verb consists, which is nothing else than *a word whose chief use is to signify affirmation*, that is to say, to mark that the discourse in which this word is used is the discourse of a man who not only conceives of things, but judges of them and affirms something of them. And in this the verb is distinguished from some words which also signify affirmation, as *affirmans, affirmatio*, because they signify it only in so far as, by a reflection of the mind, it has become the object of our thought, and thus they do not mark that he who uses these words affirms, but simply that he conceives an affirmation.

I have said that the principal office of the verb was to signify affirmation,[1] because we shall show further on that it is also used to signify other movements of the mind, as to desire, to ask, to command, &c., but it is only by changing inflection and mood, and thus we only consider the verb in the whole of this chapter according to its principal signification, which is that which it has in the indicative mood. According to this idea we may say that the verb in itself ought to have no other office than to mark the connection that we make in our mind between the two terms of a proposition. But it is only the verb *to be*, which is called substantive, that has preserved this simplicity; and also, properly speaking, it has only preserved it in the third person of the present tense, *is*, and in certain connections; for, as men are naturally led to shorten their expressions, they have almost always added other significations to the affirmation in the same word.

1. They have joined to it that of some attribute, so that then two words form a proposition; as when I say, *Petrus vivit*, Peter lives, because the word *vivit* contains in itself the affirmation, and also the attribute *to be living;* and thus it is the same thing to say, *Peter lives*, as to say, *Peter is living*. Hence has come the great diversity of verbs in every language; whereas if men had been content to give the verb the general signification of affirmation, without adding to it any particular attribute, a single verb only would have been necessary in any language, namely, that which is called substantive.

---

[1] *To affirm* would be more exact than *to signify affirmation*.

2. They have also joined to it in certain circumstances the subject of the proposition, so that then two words, and even one word, may form a complete proposition. Two words, as when I say, *sum homo*, because *sum* not only signifies affirmation, but includes the signification of the pronoun *ego*, which is the subject of this proposition, and which is always expressed in our language, I am a man. One word, as when I say, *vivo, sedeo;* for these verbs include in themselves both the affirmation and the attribute, as we have already said; and being in the first person, they include also the subject: I am living, I am sitting. Hence has arisen the difference of persons which is usually found in all verbs.

3. They have also joined a reference to the time with respect to which they affirm, so that a single word, as *cœnasti*, signifies that I affirm of him to whom I speak the action of supping, not for the present time, but for the past, and hence has come the diversity of tenses, which is also usually common to all verbs.

The diversity of these significations joined to the same word has prevented many persons, otherwise very intelligent, from thoroughly understanding the nature of the verb, because they have not considered it in its essential part, which is *affirmation*, but in its other relations, which are accidental to it in so far as it is a verb.

Thus Aristotle,[1] having stopped at the third of the significations added to that which is essential in the verb, has defined it as *a word that signifies with time.*[2]

---

[1] M. Egger very justly blames the author for not taking the trouble to refer to the original texts, and for giving as Aristotle's an incomplete definition of the verb from a quotation of Boxhorn's: "This idea of affirmation is very clearly expressed in the second part of Aristotle's phrase, which has been omitted in the quotation: *It is always the sign of what is affirmed of some other thing.* This is precisely what the Port-Royal logician wished to show. In no edition that I know of the work of Port-Royal has this omission been noticed." (*De l'hellénisme en France,* t. ii. p. 61.)

[2] Beauzée remarks the same mistake in Scaliger. "The verb," says he, "is the only kind of word which appears susceptible of distinction of tense. Julius Cæsar Scaliger thought it so essential to this part of speech that he took it for the specific character which distinguishes it from all the rest." (*Grammaire générale,* t. i. p. 422.) "The German grammarians," he adds, "have given to the verb, in their language, the name of *Zeit wort,* composed

Others, as Buxtorf,[1] having added the second to it, have defined it as *a word which has different inflexions with times and persons*.

Others having stopped at the first of these added significations, that of the attribute, and having considered that the attributes which men have joined to the affirmation in a word are usually those of actions or passions, have thought that the essence of the verb consisted in *signifying actions or passions*.

And, in fine, Julius Cæsar Scaliger[2] thought that he had found a mystery in his book on the *Principles of the Latin Tongue*, by saying that the distinction of things *in permanentes et fluentes*, into those which remain and those which pass, was the real origin of the distinction between nouns and verbs, the nouns signifying what remains and the verbs what passes.

But it is easy to see that all these definitions are false, and do not explain the true nature of the verb.

The manner in which the first two are conceived shows this sufficiently; since it is not said what the verb signifies, but only that with which it signifies, *with times and persons*.

The last two are still worse; for they have the two greatest defects of a definition, that they do not include the whole of the thing defined, nor only the thing defined.

For there are verbs which signify neither actions nor passions, nor that which passes, as *existit, quiescit, friget, alget, tepet, calet, albet, viret, claret,* &c.

And there are words which are not verbs, which signify actions and passions, and even things which pass, according to the definition of Scaliger; for it is certain that participles are true nouns, and that, nevertheless, those of active verbs do not the less signify actions, and those of the passive verbs passions, than the verbs from which they come; and there is no reason to assert that *fluens* does not signify a thing which passes as well as *fluit*.

---

of *Zeit*, time, and *Wort*, word; so that *das Zeit wort* signifies literally the *word of the time*." Beauzée would only accept it by interpreting, by metonymy, the name time by that of existence.

[1] Buxtorf, a celebrated professor of Hebrew at Bâle, died 1629.

[2] Julius Cæsar Scaliger, a celebrated philologer (1484–1558). His work, *De causis linguae latinae*, libri xiii., appeared at Lyons in 1540. We see even by Arnauld's criticism that Scaliger had endeavoured to introduce the philosophical spirit into grammatical studies.

To which may be added, in opposition to the first two definitions of the verb, that the participles also signify with time, since there are present, past, and future, especially in Greek; and those who think, and not without reason, that a vocative is a true second person, above all when it has a different termination from the nominative, will find that there will only be, on that point, a difference of more or less between the vocative and the verb.[1]

Thus the essential reason why a participle is not a verb is that it does not signify affirmation;[2] whence it comes that it cannot make a proposition, which is the property of the verb, unless by restoring what has been taken from it in changing the verb into a participle. For why is *Petrus vivit, Peter lives*, a proposition, and *Petrus vivens, Peter living*, not one, unless you add *est, is*, to it, *Petrus est vivens, Peter is living*, unless, because the affirmation contained in *vivit* has been taken away to make the participle *vivens?* Whence it appears that the affirmation which is or which is not in a word makes it a verb or not a verb.

On which it may be remarked, in passing, that the infinitive which is very often a noun, as we shall state, as when we say *le boire, le manger, to drink, to eat*, is then different from participles in this, that the participles are nouns adjective, and that the infinitive is a noun substantive, made by the abstraction of this adjective, as from *candidus* is made *candor*, and from *white whiteness*. Thus the verb *rubet* signifies *is red*, including the affirmation and the attribute; the participle *rubens* signifies simply *red*, without any affirmation; and *rubere*, taken as a noun, signifies *redness*.

It must, then, be regarded as certain, considering only what is essential in the verb, that its only true definition is, *vox significans affirmationem, a word signifying affirmation*. For no word denoting affirmation can be found which is not a verb, nor a verb which does not denote it, at least in the indicative. And it is undoubted that, if we had one, as *is* would be, which should always mark

---

[1] The nominative is the case that indicates the subject; *Dominus*, the Lord, the vocative is used to call *Domine*, O Lord.

[2] Certain grammarians admit, however, and not without reason, the participial proposition. In this phrase, *the parts being made*, the lion spoke thus, the words in italics are exactly equivalent to this proposition, *when the parts were made*.

affirmation without any difference of person or tense, so that the difference of person should be marked only by nouns and pronouns, and the difference of tense by adverbs, there would still be one real verb. As, in fact, there is in the propositions that philosophers call eternal truths, as, God is infinite; every body is divisible; the whole is greater than its part; the word *is* signifies simple affirmation only, without any regard to time, because it is true for all times, and without our mind taking into consideration any difference of persons.

Thus the verb, according to what is essential to it, is a word which signifies affirmation; but if we wish to put into the definition of the verb its principal accidents, we may define it thus: *vox significans affirmationem, cum designatione personae, numeri et temporis; a word which signifies affirmation, with designation of person, number, and tense*, which exactly agrees with the verb substantive.

For, in so far as the other verbs differ from the verb substantive by the union which men have made of the affirmation with certain attributes, they may be thus defined: *vox significans affirmationem alicujus attributi ; cum designatione personae, numeri et temporis ; a word which marks the affirmation of some attribute, with designation of the person, number, and tense*.[1]

And it may be remarked, in passing, that the affirmation, in so far as it is conceived, being able to be the attribute of the verb, as in the verb *affirmo*, this verb signifies two affirmations, of which one regards the person speaking, and the other the person spoken of, whether it be oneself or another. For, when I say *Petrus affirmat, affirmat* is the same thing as *est affirmans*,[2] and then *est* marks my affirmation, or the judgment that I form concerning Peter; and *affirmans* the affirmation that I conceive and attribute to Peter. The verb *nego*, on the contrary, contains an affirmation and a negation for the same reason.

For it must still be remarked that although all our judgments

---

[1] There is room to complete this definition by adding to the mention of time that of *mood*.

[2] In English these two forms are not equivalent; the present participle with the auxiliary *to be* expresses more precisely that the affirmation is relative to the moment in which the person is speaking.

are not affirmative, but some are negative, the verbs, nevertheless, never signify by themselves anything but affirmations, the negation being marked by the particles *no, not,* or by words which include it, *nullus, nemo, none, no one,* which, being joined to verbs, change the affirmation into negation, as *no man is immortal; nullum corpus est indivisibile,*[1] *no body is indivisible.* (Grammaire générale et raisonnée.)

QUESTIONS OF GRAMMAR.

MADAM,[2]—Nothing could be more obliging than the reply of the Academy. But as you would have reason to take it amiss if I did not speak to you with all sincerity, I will tell you frankly than I expected something more from such a celebrated society. For of the five questions proposed to them, the last only regarding French grammar in particular, and the first four regarding general grammar, and being some of those which M. de la Chambre[3] admits can only be resolved by the deepest meditations of philosophy, it would have been desirable that they should rather have attended to them than to the last, which they might with more reason refer to French grammar than the former; since it is not usual to treat in special grammars what is common to every language. . . . After all, Madam, it would be an ill return for the obligation we are under to them for the information they have given us to stop and make complaints that they have not thought proper to give us more.

---

[1] Beauzée (*Grammaire générale*, t. i. p. 395) does not accept the theory of Port-Royal. But his objections do not appear to me to be sound, and the definition that he proposes to substitute has not been received very favourably: *Verbs are words which express indeterminate beings, pointing them out by the precise idea of intellectual existence with relation to an attribute.* The least defect in this phrase is its abstractness and want of clearness.

Lancelot would, in my opinion, be inattackable if he had more clearly laid it down that the essential and not only the principal office of the verb is to affirm, and that it is by that that it has deserved to be called the *word par excellence*, for it is the soul of the sentence. The moods, which he has forgotten to mention, are only *different manners of affirming*. A negation is still an affirmation contrary to another.

[2] Letter of Arnauld to a lady on the subject of the reply of the French Academicians to five questions that M. Arnauld had proposed to them on general grammar, &c.

[3] De la Chambre (1594–1660), physician to Louis XIV., member of the French Academy and of the Academy of Sciences.

The manner in which they have answered the question which specially referred to the French language shows such a strict investigation into all the modes of expression in our language, that there is nothing perfect and finished which may not be expected from this society, if they give to the public, as we are led to hope, their meditations and remarks. You will, nevertheless, Madam, allow me to lay before you a few small doubts.

I have some difficulty with the examples they bring forward at the beginning, *ville qui parlemente, eau qui dort*, &c. For our language should be regulated by present and not by former usage. Now I do not think that these modes of speaking, *ville qui parlemente, eau qui dort*, &c., are in the present use, but are proverbs which have survived from the ancient language in which the articles were almost always omitted.[1] To speak as we do now we must no doubt say, *une ville qui parlemente, une eau qui dort*, &c. And reason itself requires it thus, because, excepting proper names, I think that it is a general rule that when a noun is the subject of a proposition it should have an article or some word standing in place of it, as *tout, plusieurs*, and names of number *deux, trois*, &c.; *l'homme est raisonnable, tout homme est raisonnable, deux hommes l'ont attaqué*, &c. But these gentlemen have well remarked that vocatives must be excepted, because it is the having no article[2] that distinguishes them from the nominative. And besides, in our language they are only the subject of a proposition when the pronoun *vous* is added, *Ciel, vous voyez mes maux; Soleil, vous éclairez toutes choses*. It is true that the pronoun is not used when they are joined to the imperative; *Ciel, voyez ce que je souffre; Seigneur, écoutez ma voix*. But then they are not the subject of a proposition. I may easily be mistaken, never having paid much attention to these things which depend on usage. Nevertheless I think that this rule, that *in our language a common noun should always have an article when it is the subject of a proposition*, is true; and that it should not be thought false because the contrary is seen in many proverbial modes of speaking, which have survived from the old language,

---

[1] Latin, whence French is derived, has no article.
[2] See note, p. 115.

and which it is proper to notice, but not to take as rules of usage at the present time.

I am not sure, Madam, that we cannot say as much for the greater number of the phrases that are given in the five remarks that these gentlemen make to show in what circumstances *qui* may be put after nouns without the article. For *homme qui vive, âme qui vive, vie qui dure* are the remains of the old style, which continue to pass because usage permits it, especially in popular style, but upon which, as I have already said, I do not think we should regulate our language.

I also think that, to speak correctly according to present usage, we should rather say, *j'ai un homme en main qui fera ; je connais des gens qui disent*, &c., than *j'ai homme en main, je connais gens qui disent*, &c. And I doubt, Madam, if you would use this last, or if you ever said, *Prenez racines de bétoine qui aient été séchées au soleil*, or *prenez eau-de-vie qui ait été rectifiée*, instead of saying, as you no doubt have always done, *prenez des racines de bétoine*, &c. ; *prenez de l'eau-de-vie*, &c. If doctors and apothecaries speak thus we should value their remedies without imitating their style.

Nor do I think that you would agree that it would be speaking correctly to say, *c'est grêle qui tombe, c'est poison qu'il a pris, c'est vin que vous buvez*. But I think that you would always say, *c'est de la grêle*, &c. ; *c'est du poison*, &c. ; *c'est du vin*, &c.

Their remarks on these expressions, *il vit en philosophe*, &c., which are used sometimes absolutely and sometimes with *qui*, as, *il vit en philosophe qui suit Épicure*, appeared to me very good ; but I find a difficulty in the reason they give for them. They say that some of these expressions are indeterminate and others determinate ; that the indeterminate do not take the *qui*, and that the others do. But it seems to me that this is giving for a reason the thing itself for which we are seeking the reason. For it is incontestable that the *qui* which is joined to a word without the article determines its signification ; and thus it is the *qui* itself which determines the expressions in which it is found, and which without it would not be determined. So that it must not be said that it is because they are determined that they take the *qui*, since, on the contrary, they are only determined because they have a *qui*.

And, in fact, if this rule were good, the rule would never be broken by putting *qui* after a noun without the article; since, the *qui* making the expression determinate, we should always be making an exception to the rule.

Thus, if we could say, *c'est un effet d'avarice, qui est la plus injuste des passions,* or *qui le possède depuis longtemps,* we might say, *il a été enlevé par violence, qui est tout à fait cruelle.* For we might always give this reason, that these expressions are good because they are determinate, whereas, what makes them bad is that they are determined by the *qui*, the noun not being determined by the article. Therefore, as far as possible, the article should be used with the noun, when we wish it to be followed by *qui*. I say as far as possible, because there are combinations in which the article cannot be used. And then, in such a case of necessity, we can put the *qui* or an adjective, when we wish to determine the general noun that we are using. Now I think that one of these combinations is when the particle *en* is used in the sense of the Latin *ut*, and not in that of *in*. For when it is taken for *in* the article may be used; *il est allé en un pays étranger; il est en la ville d'Amiens.* But in the sense of *ut*, usage does not allow us to use the article; *vivit ut philosophus, il vit en philosophe,* and not *il vit en un philosophe; il donne en roi, il agit en politique.* Thus, when we wish to determine these expressions it is done with *qui; il agit en politique qui sait gouverner;* because on the one hand it was necessary to be able to determine them, and on the other the article could not be used, as it always should be when it is possible. And thus I can say without determining, *il lui a gagné son argent par fourberie.* But if I wish to determine this *fourberie* I cannot do so simply by adding *qui, il a gagné son argent par fourberie, qui est horrible,* but must also add the article to *fourberie, par une fourberie qui est horrible.* Whence it seems that we should conclude that, if we use *qui* in the other expressions, *en philosophe, en roi,* although the noun has no article, it is not because they are determined, for they are so only by the *qui* itself, and they are no more so than this one, *par fourberie qui est horrible;* but it is by a necessity that dispenses with the rule, because they are not capable of taking the article.

There remains, Madam, a word to say on the question which was the object of this resolution of the Academy. It was not on the general rule; but, on the contrary, taking that for granted, it was asked why this expression is not contrary to it, *Il est accusé de crimes qui méritent la mort.*

These gentlemen answer, as they had done in the preceding difficulty, that it is not contrary to it, *because it is only used to specify the nature of the crimes, which is done by adding* qui, *or an epithet which virtually contains it.* But, besides what I have already said against this reason, I do not see, if it is true, why it does not take place in the singular as well as in the plural. Those persons, however, who wish to speak correctly will not say, *il a été accusé de crime qui mérite la mort;* but *il a été accusé d'un crime qui mérite la mort.* There is an intention to specify the nature of the crime in the singular as well as in the plural. Why does not this reason, then, dispense from putting in the singular the *qui* without the article, as is done in the plural, according to the opinion of these gentlemen? This difficulty, Madam, gave me an idea which I submit to the judgment of this illustrious society. I think that the article *un* has a plural, not formed from itself, for we do not say *uns, unes,* but taken from another word, which is *des* before substantives, and *de* when the adjective precedes. What inclines me to think so is that in every case, except the genitive, for the reason that we shall give afterwards, wherever *un* is put in the singular *des* is put in the plural, or *de* before adjectives, as I have already said, and it should always be put in all those cases where a *qui* is added.

Nominative.—*Un crime qui est si horrible mérite la mort, des crimes qui sont si horribles,* &c.

Dative.—*Il a eu recours à un crime qui mérite la mort, il a eu recours à des crimes qui méritent,* &c.

Accusative.—*Il a commis un crime qui mérite la mort, il a commis des crimes qui méritent la mort.*

Ablative.—*Il est puni pour un crime qui mérite la mort, il est puni pour des crimes qui méritent la mort.*

According to this analogy, as *à*, which is the dative particle, is added to form the dative of this article, as well in the singular *à un* as in the plural *d des ; il a eu recours à un crime, il a eu recours à des crimes ;* and as the genitive particle *de* is also added to form the genitive singular *d'un ; il est accusé d'un crime*, it is evident that the genitive plural should be formed in the same manner by adding *de* to *des*, or *de ;* but this has not been done, for a reason which causes the greater number of the irregularities of languages, namely, disagreeable sound. For *de des*, and still more *de de*, would have grated on the ear, which would scarcely have supported *il est accusé de des crimes*, or *il est accusé de de grands crimes ;* whereas it is not offended by hearing in the dative, *il a pardonné à des criminels, il a pardonné à de méchants hommes*. Thus, Madam, if you will kindly pardon me this little Latin sentence, which M. Valant will explain to you, *impetratum est a ratione ut peccare suavitatis causa liceret*.[1] If that is well founded, there is no longer any difficulty in the question proposed. For either it is resolved, as in the preceding, by the impossibility of putting the article, which gives liberty to use the *qui*, although the noun has no article; or, indeed, we may say that the mere difficulty of pronunciation preventing the use of the articles with nouns in these combinations, the article is in the sense, although it is not expressed.

If I had not the honour, Madam, of knowing you as well as I do I should offer you many excuses for having importuned you by so long a letter upon things which appear very small. But I know that you will not judge of them like ordinary people, and that you consider nothing small that has reference to the mind and reason. And, indeed, since speech is one of the greatest endowments of man, the possession of this endowment in the greatest possible perfection must not be despised, namely, not only to have the use of it, but also to know the reason.

I am, &c.
(Arnauld, *Œuvres*, t. iv. p. 125.)

---

[1] Reason allows a fault to be made for the satisfaction of the ear.

MEMOIR OF ARNAULD ON THE REGULATION OF STUDIES IN THE HUMANITIES.[1]

The regulation of the order of studies should be considered both from the end proposed and from the means employed to attain it; for among the various ends that might be proposed, it is necessary to choose those which are of the greatest, most general, and most lasting utility. And among the different means that may be adopted, those which lead the most directly and easily to it should be employed.

After having censured exercises in versification, amplification, and declamation, themes and "empty phrases void of sense, in order to make them learn rules which might be taught vivâ voce," theatrical representations, dictated lectures, and the infrequent reading of authors, he proposes the following remedies :—

"1. The examination of scholars, in order to promote them from one class to another, should only consist in seeing if they thoroughly understand the authors they have been reading in the class from which they wish to remove; without which they should be retained in it with inflexible rigour, unless they are found to be incapable of doing more or better.

"2. An entire hour should be given to the explanation of an author every time the class meets, morning and afternoon; and this exercise should always be preferred to every other, and never omitted.

"3. It is, above all, very important to divide this explanation into different portions, and oblige the scholars to give an account in Latin and in French of what has been explained to them. They would be accustomed without trouble to take the turn of good Latinity by always making them speak like the best authors, and they would acquire that spirit of analysis so necessary in all positions. . . .

"4. The scholars should question themselves mutually, and correct one another with politeness; firstly, on the substance of what has been translated during the week ; secondly, on the most

---

[1] Although this memoir treats of classical studies, judicious advice on teaching will be found in it, of which our teachers can make good use in primary instruction.

remarkable thoughts and the finest turns of language; thirdly, on the explanation of certain passages that the teacher may have thought necessary to give in a few words.

"5. The regent should be careful to make them mark in the margin, in different ways, the sentences and the fine thoughts, and generally all that is noticeable in the authors, then to review them after the reading is finished, and then to sum up the whole at the end of each week.

"6. Places should only be awarded every month, or every fortnight, by the examination of those who have succeeded best in all the exercises, either *vivâ voce* or by written translation, not of French into Latin, but of Latin into French, at least in the four lower classes; for what sort of Latin can really be expected from those who do not yet know that language?

"7. Without excluding compositions for which prizes are offered, the chief prizes will be distributed to those who have most distinguished themselves during the first six months, or the whole year, if they are given only once; and by this means the hopes of all the scholars will be excited. It must not be forgotten to publish the names of those who nearly succeeded in gaining them; but the first prizes should be given to those who have shown most religion and whose morals are irreproachable. Those who have made efforts to imitate these should also be mentioned. The heart should be rewarded before the head. Besides books that will be explained in class, a book should be given to the scholars to read privately, prescribing the same book to the whole class; and they should be compelled, as far as possible, to give to it every day an hour of their private study.

"8. In order to induce them to give more attention to it, one day in the week should be set apart to review this particular book, when the regent, who will have read and annotated the book, will question the scholars on the difficult expressions and fine thoughts which they ought to have remarked in it, in order to make them accurate and judicious.

"9. In order to teach elocution, beginning from the lower classes, it is useful to make two scholars tell a short story every day, which they may take from Valerius Maximus, or Plutarch, or any book they like, leaving them the choice; and those must be judged the best who make the recital in the most free and natural manner, and most in the spirit of the author, without confining themselves to the same terms and expressions. This story should be told in French in the three lower classes, setting them French books. A very short piece of these authors will be given them to recite, and all will be required to read every day a certain portion of the history of France, and to be ready to recite it as well as they can.[1]

"10. A short time only should be given to the recitation of the lessons that have been set, and which should be very short; a quarter of an hour is sufficient, because this is one of the things that cause much loss of time. When the regent explains the lessons he should confine himself to making them well understood without many words.

"11. The regents will never teach any verse or declamation of their own making, nor dictate any rhetoric that they have composed. They should explain especially Aristotle and Quintilian . . . with the books of Cicero . . . the best part of the time is lost in dictating.

"13. It would be still better[2] to read out distinctly the Latin of what has been dictated to them in French, and to make them compose at once from the Latin they have just heard. The model is correct, their time is spared, and, repeating this short exercise, they are led by use to speak Latin well, without much hesitation.[3]

"14. Useless methods, for the most part ill-conceived, ill-digested, and wearisome for the young, should not be set to be learnt by heart. They should be taught *vivâ voce* and by

---

[1] Rollin, the recognized inheritor of the traditions of Port-Royal, ought to have thoroughly assimilated this formal recommendation of Arnauld, and not have permitted himself to write this phrase, a strange one in the mouth of an ex-rector of the University of Paris: " Young people have no time to learn the History of France !"

[2] Instead of giving a translation to be put into Latin.

[3] Franklin declares that he had no other master for composition. About the age of fifteen, when he was a printer's apprentice, he procured an odd volume of Addison's *Spectator*, read an article in it, noted the principal ideas, then, a few days after, in the evening or the morning, before work or on Sundays, he tried to reproduce the original, which served him for a key. This exercise may safely be recommended in primary schools, and in classes for adults.

practice what are called rules, and only set in the lower classes to bring them up as a small history; and according as a noun or a verb is met with out of the general rule, the attention of the scholars should be called to it, and they should be required to give a reason for it, as we have just explained, on the next meeting of the class.

"18. Lessons and translations should only be given to the juniors and composition to the seniors in so far as it may be reasonably calculated that they will have time remaining after reading the prescribed authors. This article is more important than may be thought, for we may be easily misled in it. Much is thought to be gained by overloading the children with lessons and compositions. There is no greater mistake.[1] They do not know the value of the time sufficiently to make good use of it when they are left to themselves. They are in no hurry, time flies, the clock strikes; hence punishments, all is sadness, and disgust finally spoils the whole. Those who learn more easily, and have better memories, will be set to do more than the others, by attaching rewards for it.

"19. It is usually lost time to set them to compose verses at home. There may be two or three scholars out of seventy or eighty from whom something may be drawn. The rest lose heart, or torment themselves to do nothing of any value. A subject may be prescribed to those who show taste and facility, and the others may be set something according to their ability. It may, however, be proposed to all to compose then and there a small piece of verse of which the subject is given, each having the liberty of saying how he will turn the matter of each line. An epithet then comes from one corner, a more appropriate one from another; with permission to speak, which is asked and obtained by a sign only, in order to avoid confusion, they judge, criticise, and give a reason for their choice. Those who have the least energy try their utmost, and all strive at least to distinguish themselves. This is one of the most useful exercises to please them, and to form at least those who have some talent."

---

[1] An excellent observation. We are always too much inclined to think that the child is a vase that cannot be sufficiently filled. It is a soul that must be formed.

Art. 22. *He inscribes the History of France among the conditions for the degree of Master of Arts.*

". . . what is gained by the exclusion of verses in the upper classes, of themes in the lower, and, in fact, of lessons which produce nothing of any value, will give time which will be much more agreeably employed in reading for repetition and in learning set passages by heart, and for private preparation of what has been set in Latin grammar and rhetoric, according to the classes to which one or two rules of grammar have been set, on which the class will be questioned at their next meeting, in the evening or morning, without compelling anyone to learn them word for word.[1] They will the more readily give themselves up to this study, which will even be useful in teaching them the art of reasoning in a small way; and more will be gained in this manner than would have been from the other.

"*Objection.*—By making fewer compositions they neither learn to write nor speak Latin.

"*Reply.*—We answer that the scholars will most certainly learn much more by reading much, and speaking frequently after the best authors, than by writing many dictations and incorrect expressions to which they become accustomed, and which must be corrected. Not being in a position to produce solid thoughts, they do nothing else in all these school compositions but contract the habit of bad speaking and bad thinking. On the contrary, by filling their minds with good models their judgment is formed.

"*Objection.*—The regents do not acquire practice if the liberty of speaking is taken from them.

"*Reply.*—We answer, they may speak as much as they like, provided that it be not in the class time set apart for the instruction of the scholars. So much talk is not necessary to point out the beauties of an author." (Arnauld, *Œuvres*, t. xli. p. 85.)

---

[1] The definitions and rules, however, require great accuracy. When they are well understood, it is very easy to retain the exact formula, which is preferable, and is not useless to intellectual education.

PORT-ROYAL LOGIC.

FIRST DISCOURSE, SETTING FORTH THE DESIGN
OF THIS NEW LOGIC.

Nothing is more estimable than good sense and accuracy of mind in discriminating the true from the false. All other mental qualities have limited uses; but accuracy of reasoning is useful generally in all parts and employments of life. It is not alone in the sciences that it is difficult to distinguish truth from error; but also in the greater number of the subjects on which men speak, and the affairs of which they treat. Almost everywhere there are different courses, some true, some false; and it is the part of reason to make choice between them. Those who choose well are those who have sound minds, those who take the wrong course are those whose minds are unsound; and this is the chief and most important distinction that can be made between the qualities of men's minds.

Thus we should set ourselves principally to form our judgment, and make it as accurate as possible; and the greater part of our studies should tend to this. We use reason as an instrument to acquire the sciences, but we should, on the contrary, use the sciences as an instrument for perfecting the reason;[1] accuracy of mind being infinitely more important than all speculative knowledge, which we may attain by means of the most accurate and solid sciences. And this should lead sensible persons to take them up only in so far as they can serve to this end, and to make an essay of them simply, and not employ the whole strength of their minds. . . .

This care and study are so much the more necessary, that it is strange how rare a quality this accuracy of judgment is. We meet everywhere with unsound minds which have scarcely any

---

[1] This pedagogic point of view is excellent; but, without neglecting it, we must attach more value to the acquisition of the sciences than Port-Royal does; they are not only an instrument and means of culture, they are also an aim and an end. To learn the truth is the most legitimate employment of the intellect. They are besides, as Bacon says, the only source of man's power over nature, and the most effective agents of civilization and progress.

clear perception of the truth; who take everything the wrong way; who are satisfied with bad reasons, and wish to satisfy others with them; who are carried away by slight appearances; who are always in excess and extremes; who have no firm hold on the truths which they know, because it is rather by chance than real knowledge that they are attached to them; or who stop short, on the contrary, at the evidence of their senses, with so much obstinacy, that they will hear nothing that may undeceive them; who rashly decide on what they are ignorant of, what they do not understand, and what no one, perhaps, has ever understood; who make no difference between one way of speaking and another,[1] or who judge of the truth of things only by the tone of voice: he who speaks fluently and gravely is right; he who has some difficulty in explaining himself, or who shows some warmth, is wrong; they know no more about it than this.

Therefore there are no absurdities so gross as not to find supporters. Whoever means to deceive the world is certain to find persons very willing to be deceived; and the most ridiculous nonsense always finds congenial minds. After seeing so many persons infatuated with the follies of judicial astrology,[2] and even grave persons treating this matter seriously, we need be astonished at nothing. There is a constellation in the heavens which it has pleased some persons to name the Balance, and which resembles a balance as much as it does a wind-mill; the balance is the symbol of justice, hence those who are born under this constellation will be just and equitable.[3] There are three other signs of the Zodiac, which are named, one the Ram, another the Bull, another the Goat, and which might just as well have been called Elephant, Crocodile, and Rhinoceros. The ram, the bull, and the goat are ruminating animals, hence those who take

---

[1] The opposition is still clearer in that very sensible judgment that Molière puts in the mouth of Chrysale, who is laughing at Trissotin:
We seek what he *said* after he has *spoken*.
(*Les Femmes savantes*, act ii. sc. 7.)
[2] "This is," said Bailly, "the longest malady that has afflicted human reason; it is known to have lasted fifty centuries." (*Hist. de l'astronomie.*)
[3] Louis XIII. was surnamed the Just, not by the gratitude of his people, but from the day of his birth, because he was born under the sign of the Balance!

K

medicine when the moon is in these constellations run the risk of vomiting it again. However extravagant these reasonings may be, there are persons who promulgate them, and others who suffer themselves to be persuaded by them.[1]

This unsoundness of mind is not only the cause of the errors that are mixed up in the sciences, but also of the greater part of the faults that are committed in civil life, unjust quarrels, ill-founded lawsuits, rash advice, and ill-concerted enterprises. There are few of these things which have not their source in some error or fault of judgment, so that there is no defect which we have more interest in correcting.

But it is as difficult to succeed in this correction as it is desirable, because it depends very much on the measure of intelligence we have at birth. Common sense is not so common a quality as is supposed.[2] There is an infinite number of coarse and stupid minds[3] that cannot be amended by giving them a knowledge of the truth, but only by keeping them to the things that are within their capacity, and preventing them passing judgment on what they are not capable of understanding. It is true, nevertheless, that many of the false judgments of men do not

---

[1] La Fontaine protested against this popular error in the fable of the *Horoscope*:—

> I do not think that Nature
> Has tied her hands, and ties ours still
> So far as to write our fate in the skies:
> It depends on a conjuncture
> Of places, persons and times;
> Not of conjunctions of all the mountebanks.
> This shepherd and this king are under the same planet;
> The one bears the sceptre, the other the crook.
> Jupiter willed it so.
> What is Jupiter? An inanimate body.
> Whence comes it then that his influence
> Acts differently on these two men?
> Then, how can it penetrate to our world?
> How pass the deep regions of the air,
> Mars, the Sun and the infinite void?
> An atom may turn it aside in its course:
> Where will the casters of horoscopes find it again? . . .
>
> (LA FONTAINE, *Fables*, viii. 16.)

[2] In spite of its name, common sense is rare. (ANDRIEUX.)

[3] Here we recognize Nicole, the author of the *Traité de la faiblesse de l'homme*, who indulges himself too much in painting the mass of his fellow-creatures as "steeped in stupidity." (Chap. x.)

spring from this principle, and are only caused by hastiness of mind and want of attention, which cause men to judge rashly what they only know in a confused and obscure manner. The little love that men have for truth is the reason that they take no trouble, for the most part, to distinguish the true from the false. They allow all sorts of reasonings and maxims to enter their minds; they prefer to consider them as true rather than to examine them. If they do not understand them they are willing to believe that others understand them well; and thus they load their memories with a host of things false, obscure, and not understood, and then reason from these principles, scarcely paying attention to what they say or what they think.

Vanity and presumption contribute still more to this defect. They think there is some disgrace in doubt and ignorance, and prefer to speak and decide at a venture rather than to acknowledge that they are not sufficiently informed on the matter to give a decision. We are all of us full of ignorance and errors; yet, nevertheless, it is the greatest trouble in life to draw from men this confession so true and so conformable to their natural state: I am wrong, and know nothing about the matter.

There are others, on the contrary, who, having sufficient intelligence to know that there are very many things obscure and uncertain, and wishing, by another sort of vanity, to show that they do not allow themselves to be carried away by popular credulity, pride themselves on maintaining that nothing is certain. They thus relieve themselves of the trouble of examining them; and, on this vicious principle, they throw doubt on the most certain truths and on religion itself. This is the source of Pyrrhonism, another extravagance of the human mind, which, appearing contrary to the rashness of those who believe and decide on everything, nevertheless springs from the same source, namely, want of attention. For if the one set will not take the trouble to discriminate errors, the other will not be at the pains to examine the truth with the care necessary to discover the evidence for it. The slightest glimmer suffices to persuade one set of things very false, and to make the other doubt of the most certain things; but the same defect of application produces in both such very different results.

True reason sets all things in their proper rank; it causes the doubtful to be doubted, rejects those which are false, and honestly recognizes those which are evident, without pausing over the empty reasonings of the Pyrrhonists, which do not destroy, even in the minds of those who propose them, the reasonable assurance we have of things that are certain. No one ever seriously doubted that there is an earth, a sun, and a moon, nor that the whole is greater than its part. We can say outwardly, with our mouth, that we doubt of these things, because we may lie; but we cannot say so to our heart. Thus the Pyrrhonists are not a sect of men who are convinced of what they say, but are a sect of liars.[1] Moreover, in speaking of their opinions, they often contradict themselves, their reason not being able to agree with their words, as may be seen in Montaigne, who endeavoured to revive this sect in the last century. . . .

SECOND DISCOURSE, CONTAINING A REPLY TO THE PRINCIPAL OBJECTIONS MADE AGAINST THIS LOGIC.

Some persons have objected to the title *The Art of Thinking*, instead of which they would have written, *The Art of Reasoning well;* but we beg them to consider that, the end of logic being to give rules for all the operations of the mind, as well for simple ideas as for judgments and arguments, there was scarcely any other word that included all these different operations; and certainly the word *thought* includes them all; for simple ideas are thoughts, judgments are thoughts, and arguments are thoughts. We might, indeed, have said, *The Art of Thinking well;* but this addition was unnecessary, being sufficiently indicated by the word *art*, which in itself signifies a method of doing something well, as Aristotle himself remarks. Hence it suffices to say the art of painting, the art of reckoning, because it is supposed that no art is required to paint badly or to reckon badly.

---

[1] This, in a work on the art of thinking, is a very bad example of reasoning. Insults are never reasons, and the good faith of opponents should never be doubted. Some years later Nicole will give the sage advice "to put our mind in a condition to calmly support the opinions of others, which appear to us to be wrong, in order to oppose them only with a desire of being useful to them." See p. 185.

A much more important objection has been made against the great number of examples drawn from different sciences that are found in this logic; and since it attacks its whole design and thus gives us an opportunity of explaining it, we will examine it with more care. Of what use, they say, is this medley of rhetoric, ethics, physics, metaphysics, and geometry? When we expect to find the rules of logic we are suddenly carried off to the highest sciences, without the authors knowing if we have learnt them. Ought they not to suppose, on the contrary, that if we already had this knowledge we should not want this logic? And would it not have been better to give us one quite simple and plain, in which the rules were explained by examples taken from common things, than to load them with so much matter as to deaden them?

But those who reason in this way have not sufficiently considered that a book can scarcely have a greater defect than not to be read, since it is only of use to those who read it; and thus everything that contributes to make a book read contributes also to make it useful. Now it is certain that, if we had followed their opinion, and only written a dry logic with the usual examples of animal and horse, however accurate and methodical it might have been, it would only have added to the great number of others, of which the world is full, that are not read. Whereas it is precisely that collection of different things that has given some reputation to this one, and caused it to be read with a little less tedium than the others.

But, nevertheless, our principal aim was not to attract people to read it by making it more amusing than the ordinary books on logic. We claim, in addition, to have followed the most natural and advantageous mode of treating this art by remedying, as far as possible, an inconvenience which rendered its study almost useless.

For experience shows that of a thousand young men who learn logic there are not ten who know anything of it six months after they have finished their course. Now the real cause of this forgetfulness, or this negligence, which is so common, seems to be that all the matters treated of in logic being of themselves very abstract and far removed from ordinary usage, they are illustrated by uninteresting examples, such as are never spoken of elsewhere. Thus the mind, which has some difficulty in attending to it, has nothing to fix its attention, and easily loses all the ideas that it had acquired, because they are never renewed by practice.

Besides, as these ordinary examples do not clearly show how this art can be applied to anything useful, they are accustomed to confine logic to itself, without extending it further;[1] whereas it is only made to be an instrument for the other sciences; so that as they have never seen its real use they never use it, and are very glad to get rid of it as a trivial and useless knowledge.

We have thought, then, that the best remedy for this disadvantage was not to separate logic so much as is usually done from the other sciences for which it is intended, but to join it in such a way, by means of examples, to solid knowledge, that the rules and their application may be seen at the same time, in order that we may learn to judge of the sciences by logic and retain logic by means of these sciences.

Thus, so far from this diversity suppressing the rules, nothing can more contribute to the understanding of them and cause their retention, because they are too subtle by themselves to make an impression on the mind, if they are not attached to something more agreeable and more obvious.

In order to render this diversity more useful, the examples have not been taken at random from these sciences; but the most important points have been chosen, and those which might best serve as rules and principles for discovering the truth in other matters which we have not been able to treat of. . . .

It only remains to answer a more unworthy complaint that some persons make, namely, that examples of defective definitions and bad arguments have been extracted from Aristotle, which appears to them to arise from a secret desire to depreciate this philosopher.

But they would never have formed so inequitable a judgment

---

[1] Ramus had already complained of the little practical utility of the exercises: "They have never regarded their rules but under the shadow of scholastic disputations; they have never brought logic into the dust and sunshine of every-day use; they have never called it into the conflict of human examples."

if they had sufficiently considered the true rules that should be followed in quoting examples of errors, and which we have had in view in quoting Aristotle.

Firstly, experience shows that the majority of examples that are usually given are not very useful, and make little impression on the mind, because they are formed at pleasure, and are so plain and palpable that it is thought impossible to fall into them. It is, then, advantageous, in order to cause what is said of these faults to be remembered and the faults to be avoided, to choose real examples taken from some eminent author, whose reputation excites us the more to beware of this kind of mistakes to which we see that the greatest men are liable.

Besides, as our aim should be to make all we write as useful as possible, we must endeavour to choose examples of faults of which it is proper not to be ignorant, for it would be very useless to load the memory with all the reveries of Flud,[1] Van-Helmont,[2] and Paracelsus.[3] It is better, therefore, to seek these examples in authors so celebrated, that we are obliged in some sort to know them, even to their faults.

Now all this is met with in Aristotle; for nothing can more powerfully lead us to avoid an error than showing that such a great mind fell into it; and his philosophy has become so celebrated through the great number of meritorious persons who have embraced it, that it is necessary to know what defects it might have. Thus, as it was judged to be very useful that those who read this book should learn, in passing, various points of this

---

[1] Robert Fludd, an English physician and philosopher (1574-1637), fell into the errors of Alchemy. Gassendi, Mersenne, and Kepler did him the honour of refuting him.

[2] Van-Helmont (1577-1644), born at Brussels, chemist and physician. Gui-Patin is never tired of calling him a wretch, ignorant, a mountebank, a public impostor, and a sorry rogue. "He passes at the present day," says Dr. Réveillé-Parise, "for one of the greatest physicians that ever lived, for the boldness, depth, and originality of his conceptions, in spite of the oddity of his language and a certain affectation of mystical obscurity."

[3] Paracelsus (1493-1541), a Swiss physician. "This prince of mountebanks," exclaims again the irascible Gui-Patin, "and shameless impostor." While a professor at Bâle, he publicly burned the works of Avicenna and Galen. His shoe-strings knew more than these authors, he impudently asserted, and all the universities knew less than the hairs of his beard! He boasted of being able to prolong life and cure incurable diseases.

philosophy, and that, nevertheless, it is never useful to be deceived, they have been brought forward in order to explain them, and the error that has been found has been noted in passing in order to prevent anyone being deceived.

It is not, then, to disparage Aristotle, but, on the contrary, to honour him as much as possible in those things in which we are not of his opinion, that we have taken examples from his books; and it is plain, besides, that the points on which he has been criticised are of very slight importance, and do not touch the foundation of his philosophy, which no one had any intention of attacking.

If several excellent things which are found throughout Aristotle's books have not been quoted, the reason is that they did not enter into the subject of the discourse; but if there had been occasion to do so, it would have been taken with pleasure, and we should not have failed to award the just praise due to him. For it is certain that Aristotle had a vast and comprehensive mind, which discovers in the subjects of which he treats a great number of connections and consequences; and for this reason he has succeeded so well in what he has said on the passions in the second book of his *Rhetoric*.

There are, besides, several beautiful things in his books on Politics and Ethics, in his Problems and in the History of Animals. And although there may be some confusion in his Analytics, it must, nevertheless, be acknowledged that almost all that is known of the rules of logic is taken from it; so that, in fact, there is no author from whom more things in this logic have been borrowed than from Aristotle, since the whole body of rules belongs to him.

It is true that his Physics appears to be his least perfect work, as it is also that which has been the longest condemned and forbidden by the Church, as a learned author has shown in a book written expressly for this purpose;[1] but yet its principal defect is not that it is false, but, on the contrary, that it is too true, and teaches us only things of which it is impossible to be

---

[1] M. de Launoi, a doctor of the Sorbonne (1603-1678). *De varia Aristotelis in Academia Parisiensi fortuna*.

ignorant. For who can doubt that all things are composed of matter and of a certain form of that matter? Who can doubt that matter, in order to acquire a new manner and form, must not have had it before, that is to say, that it had the privation of it? Who can doubt, in fine, those other metaphysical principles, that everything depends on form, that matter alone does nothing, that there are place, motion, qualities, and faculties? But after having learnt all these things, it does not seem that we have learned anything new, or that we are in a position to give a reason for any of the effects in nature.

If there are persons who assert that it is by no means allowable for a man to say that he is not of Aristotle's opinion, it would be easy to show them that this scrupulousness is unreasonable.

For if any deference is due to certain philosophers, this can only be for two reasons: either on account of the truth that they have followed, or of the opinion of the men who support them.

In regard to the truth, respect is due to them when they are right, but the truth cannot oblige us to respect falsehood in any man, whoever he be.

The general consent of men in their estimation of a philosopher certainly deserves some respect, and it would be imprudent to run counter to it without using great precautions, and for this reason, that by attacking what is generally accepted, a man renders himself suspected of presumption in supposing that he has more intelligence than others.

But when men are divided touching the opinions of an author, and there are persons of eminence on either side, a man is not obliged to show this reserve, but may freely declare what he approves or disapproves in those books with regard to which men of letters are divided, because this is not so much preferring his own opinion to that of this author and his supporters, as taking the side of those who are against him on this point.

This is exactly the position in which Aristotle's philosophy is at the present time. As it has had various fortunes, having been at one time generally rejected and at another generally received, it is now reduced to a position that holds the mean between these extremes; it is upheld by many learned men and is opposed by others of no less reputation, and every day men write freely for and against Aristotle's philosophy in France, Flanders, England, Germany, and Holland.

The conferences at Paris are divided, as well as the books, and no one offends by opposing him. The most celebrated professors no longer submit to the servitude of blindly accepting all that they find in his books, and some of his opinions even are generally abandoned. For what physician would now maintain that the nerves spring from the heart, as Aristotle thought, since anatomy clearly shows that they originate in the brain? . . . And what philosopher persists in saying that the velocity of falling bodies increases in the same ratio as their weight, since there is no one now who cannot refute this opinion of Aristotle by letting fall from a height two things of very unequal weight in which, nevertheless, a very small inequality of velocity will be perceived?

Violent states are not usually lasting, and all extremes are violent. To condemn Aristotle generally, as was formerly done, is too severe; and it is a great constraint to be obliged to approve him in everything, and to take him as the standard of the truth of philosophical opinions, as it seems men wished to do afterwards.

The world cannot long submit to this constraint, and is insensibly regaining possession of natural and reasonable liberty, which consists in approving what we think true and rejecting what we think false.[1]

For it is not strange that reason should be subjected to authority in those sciences which, treating of things that are above the reason, must follow some other guidance, which cannot be other than divine authority; but it seems to be very just that in human sciences, which profess to be founded only upon reason, it should not be subjected to authority against reason.[2]

---

[1] "In every nation," Luís Vives had already written in the early part of the sixteenth century, "great and free spirits, impatient of servitude, arise; they courageously shake off the yoke of the most dull and hard servitude, and call their fellow-citizens to liberty."

[2] Pascal has eloquently claimed the rights of reason in scientific matters. See the preface to his *Traité du Vide*.

Of bad reasoning employed in civil life and in ordinary discourse.

.... In considering generally the causes of our errors, it appears that they may be referred chiefly to two; the one internal, namely, the uncertainty of the will, which troubles and disorders the judgment; the other external, which lies in the objects on which we form a judgment, and which deceive our minds by a false appearance. Now, although these causes are almost always conjoined, there are, nevertheless, certain errors in which one is more apparent than the other, and therefore we treat of them separately.

Of the sophisms of self-love, interest, and passion.

1. If we carefully examine that which usually attaches men to one opinion rather than to another, it will be found that it is not the penetrating power of the truth and the force of reasons, but some bond of self-love, interest, or passion. This is the weight which inclines the balance and which decides the majority of our doubts; it is this which gives the greatest impulse to our judgments, and attaches us to them the most firmly. We judge of things, not by what they are in themselves, but by what they are with respect to us, and truth and utility are, in our opinion, one and the same thing.

No other proofs are needed than those which we see every day, that things held everywhere else as doubtful, or even false, are held to be very true by all those of some one nation, profession, or institution. For it not being possible that what is true in Spain should be false in France,[1] nor that the minds of all Spaniards should be formed so differently from those of Frenchmen, as that, judging things only by the rules of the reason, what appears generally true to the former should appear generally false to the latter, it is plain that this diversity of judgment can proceed from no other cause than that it pleases some to hold as

---

[1] "Truth on this side the Pyrenees, error on the other," said Pascal ironically in his *Pensées*.

true what is advantageous to themselves, and that the others, not having any interest in it, judge of it in another manner.

Nevertheless, what is less reasonable than to take our interest as the motive for believing a thing? All that it can do at most is to induce us to examine more attentively the reasons that may lead us to discover the truth of that which we wish to be true; but it is only this truth which must be found in the thing, even independently of our wish, which ought to persuade us. I belong to such a country, therefore I must believe that such a saint preached the Gospel there. I belong to a given order, therefore I believe that a given privilege is right. These are no reasons. Whatever country you may belong to you ought to believe only what is true, and what you would be inclined to believe if you were of another country, another order, or another profession.

2. But this illusion is still more apparent when some change takes place in the passions; for although all things have remained in their places, it seems, nevertheless, to those who are stirred by some new passion that the change which has only taken place in their hearts has transformed all external things which had any connection with them. How often do we see persons who cannot recognize any good quality, either natural or acquired, in those against whom they have conceived an aversion, or who have been opposed in some way to their opinions, their wishes, or their interests! That suffices to make them become at once, in their eyes, rash, proud, and ignorant, without faith, without honour, and without conscience. Their affections and desires are not more just nor moderate than their hatred. If they love anyone, he is free from all defects; everything he wishes is just and easy, all that he does not desire is unjust and impossible, without their being able to allege any other reason for all these judgments than the passion itself that possesses them; so that, although they do not make this formal reasoning in their mind, I love him, therefore he is the most clever man in the world; I hate him, therefore he is worthless, they do so, in a certain way, in their hearts; and for this reason we may call this kind of aberration sophisms and illusions of the heart, which consist in transporting our passions into the objects of our passions, and in judging that they are what we wish or desire they should be;

which is, doubtless, very unreasonable, since our wishes change nothing in the existence of what is outside ourselves, and that it is God alone whose will is so efficacious that things are what He wills them to be.

3. We may refer to the same illusion of self-love that of those who decide everything by a very general and convenient principle, which is, that they are right, that they know the truth; whence it is not difficult for them to conclude that those who are not of their opinion are wrong; in fact, the conclusion is necessary.

The fault in these persons springs only from this, that the favourable opinion they have of their own sagacity makes them consider all their thoughts as so clear and evident, that they imagine it to be sufficient to state them in order to oblige all the world to assent to them. They therefore give themselves little trouble to advance proofs; they scarcely listen to others' reasons; they wish to carry everything by their authority, because they never distinguish their authority from reason. All those who are not of their opinion they call rash, without considering that, if others are not of their opinion, neither are they of the opinion of others, and that it is not just to suppose, without proof, that we are right, when it is a question of convincing others who are of another opinion than ourselves simply because they are persuaded that we are not right.

4. There are others, also, who have no other ground for rejecting certain opinions than this humorous reasoning : If that were so, I should not be a clever man ; now I am a clever man, therefore it is not so. This is the principal reason which has caused certain very useful remedies and some very decisive experiments to be so long rejected, because those who had not yet known them thought that they must have been in error up till that time. "What!" said they, "if the blood circulates in the body,[1] if the food is not carried to the liver by the mesaraic veins, if the pulmonary vein carries the blood to the heart, if the blood rises by the descending vena cava; if nature does not abhor a vacuum; if the air has weight and a downward motion,

---

[1] The discovery of the circulation of the blood is due to Harvey, an English physician, in 1628.

I have been ignorant of important things in anatomy and physics! All this then cannot be." But, in order to cure them of this fancy, it is only necessary to show them that it is a very small disadvantage for a man to be mistaken, and that they may be very clever in other things although they have not been so in those which have been newly discovered.

5. Nothing is more usual than to see people blame one another, and call each other obstinate, passionate, and captious when they are of different opinions. There are very few litigants who do not accuse each other of lengthening the suit and concealing the truth by subtle speeches; and thus those who are right and those who are wrong use very nearly the same language, make the same complaints, and attribute to each other the same faults. This is one of the most mischievous things in men's lives, and one which throws truth and error, justice and injustice, into such obscurity that ordinary people are incapable of distinguishing them; and thus it happens that some attach themselves, by chance and without knowledge, to one of these parties, and others condemn both as being equally wrong.

All this oddness springs from the same malady which makes each man assume as a principle that he is right; for from that it is not difficult to conclude that all who oppose us are obstinate, since obstinacy is not giving way to reason.

But, although it be true that these reproaches of passion, blindness, and captiousness, which are very unjust on the part of those who are mistaken, are just and legitimate on the part of those who are not mistaken, nevertheless, because they suppose that truth is on the side of him who makes them, wise and judicious persons, who treat on any disputed matter, ought to avoid using them before thoroughly establishing the truth and justice of the cause which they uphold. They will never then accuse their opponents of obstinacy, rashness, and want of common sense before they have clearly proved it. They will not say, if they have not previously shown it, that they fall into gross absurdities and extravagances, for the others will say as much on their side, which advances nothing . . . and they will be satisfied with defending the truth by arms which are appropriate to it and which falsehood cannot borrow, namely, by plain and solid reasons. . . ..

Of False Reasonings which Spring from the Objects Themselves.

. . . It is a false and impious opinion that truth is so like falsehood and virtue so like vice that it is impossible to discriminate between them; but it is true that in the majority of things there is a mixture of error and truth, of vice and virtue, of perfection and imperfection, and that this medley is one of the most ordinary sources of the false judgments of men.

The reason of this is that men seldom consider things in detail; they judge only by their strongest impression, and appreciate only what strikes them most; thus, when they perceive many truths in a discourse, they do not notice the errors that are mingled with them; and, on the contrary, if there are truths mixed with many errors, they pay attention only to the errors; the strong carrying off the weak, and the clearer impression effacing the more obscure.

Nevertheless, it is a manifest injustice to judge in this manner; there cannot be a just reason for rejecting reason, and truth is none the less truth through being mixed with error. . . .

Therefore justice and reason requires that in all things that are thus made up of good and bad a discrimination should be made, and it is especially in this judicious separation that accuracy of mind appears. . . .

And reason obliges us to this when we can make this distinction; but since we have not always the time to examine in detail how much good and bad there is in each thing, it is fitting, in these circumstances, to give them the name they deserve according to their most considerable part; thus we should call a man a good philosopher when he reasons well generally, and a book good when it has markedly more good than bad in it.

And it is in this again that men are often mistaken, for they often only appreciate or blame things from their least important parts, their small understanding making them unable to grasp the most important part when it is not the most striking.

Thus, although those persons who are judges of painting value drawing very much more than colouring or lightness of touch, nevertheless, the ignorant are more impressed by a picture whose colours are bright and striking than by another more sombre, of which the drawing might be admirable.

It must, however, be admitted that false judgments are not so usual in the arts, because those who know nothing of them more readily defer to the opinion of those who are skilled in them; but they are very frequent in things which are in the jurisdiction of the people, and of which the world takes the liberty of judging, as, for example, eloquence.

A preacher, for instance, is called eloquent when his periods are just, and he does not make use of inappropriate words; and, on this ground, Vaugelas says in one passage that an inappropriate word does more harm to a preacher or an advocate than a bad reason. We must believe that it is an actual truth that he states and not an opinion that he sanctions. It is true that persons are found who judge in this manner, but it is also true that nothing is less reasonable than these judgments; for purity of language and the number of rhetorical figures are, at most, to eloquence what the colouring is to the picture, that is to say, its least important and most materialistic part; but the principal part consists in strongly conceiving and expressing the subjects, so that a bright and lively image is impressed on the minds of the hearers,[1] which presents not only the things themselves but also the emotions with which they are conceived; and this may be met

---

[1] Fénelon, who reduces all eloquence to three points, namely, to prove, *to paint*, and to move, thus develops the second: "To paint is not only to describe things, but to represent their surroundings in such a lively and impressive manner that the hearer may almost imagine he sees them. For example, a cold historian relating the death of Dido would be satisfied with saying she was so overcome with grief after the departure of Æneas that she could not bear her life; she went up to the top of her palace, threw herself on a funeral pyre, and killed herself. In listening to these words you learn the fact, but you do not see it. Listen to Virgil, he will set it before your eyes. Is it not true that when he brings together all the circumstances of this despair, when he shows you Dido furious, with a face in which death is already painted, when he makes her speak at the sight of that portrait and sword, your imagination transports you to Carthage; you think you see the Trojan fleet retiring from the coast, and the queen whom nothing is able to console; you have all the feelings that the actual spectators would have had. You no longer listen to Virgil; you are too attentive to the last words of the unhappy Dido to think of him. The poet disappears, and we see nothing but what he shows, and only hear those whom he makes speak. Here is the power of imitation and painting." (2ᵉ *Dialogue sur l'éloquence.*)

with in persons who are not very precise in language nor exact in harmony, and which is seldom met with in those who give too much attention to words and embellishments, because this turns them from the things and weakens the vigour of their thoughts, as painters remark that those who excel in colouring do not usually excel in drawing, the mind being incapable of this divided attention, the one part injuring the other.

It may be said generally that in the world the majority of things are judged only by the outside, because there is scarcely anybody who examines the interior and foundation of them; everything is judged by the label, and woe to those who have not a favourable one! He is clever, intelligent, sound, what you will; but he does not speak fluently and cannot turn a compliment neatly; let him make up his mind to be held in small esteem all his life by ordinary people, and to see a multitude of little minds preferred to himself. Not to have the reputation we deserve is not a very great evil, but to follow these erroneous judgments, and only to look at things from the outside is so, and is what we should endeavour to avoid.

2. Among the things which entangle us in error by a false brilliancy, which prevents our recognizing it, we may rightly put a certain sonorous and copious eloquence; for it is strange how a false reasoning glides gently from a period that satisfies the ear, or from a figure that surprises us, and which it amuses us to consider.

Not only do these ornaments conceal from us the falsehoods that are mixed up in the discourse, but they insensibly form part of them, because they are often necessary to the accuracy of the period or the figure. Thus, when we hear an orator begin a long climax or an antithesis with several clauses, we have a motive for being on our guard, since it seldom happens that he extricates himself without giving a wrench to the truth in order to fit it to the figure.[1] He usually arranges it as a man would the stones of a building or the metal of a statue; he cuts it, spreads it out, shortens it, and disguises it at need, in order to place it in that useless work of words that he wishes to form.

---

[1] Pascal compares these forced antitheses to "sham windows for symmetry." (*Pensées.*)

L

How often has the desire to make a point produced unsound thoughts! How often has rime invited men to lie! How often has the affectation of using only Ciceronian words and what is called pure Latinity made certain Italian authors write nonsense! Who would not laugh to hear Bembo[1] say that a pope had been elected *by the favour of the immortal gods!* There are indeed poets who imagine that it is the essence of poetry to introduce the pagan divinities; and a German poet, as good a versifier as he is an injudicious writer, having been properly censured by Francis Picus Mirandola for having introduced all the divinities of paganism into a poem in which he describes the wars of Christians against Christians, and for having mixed up Apollo, Diana, and Mercury with the pope, the electors, and the emperor, boldly maintained that without that he would not have been a poet, employing this strange reason, in order to prove it, that the verses of Hesiod, Homer, and Virgil are filled with the names and fables of these gods, whence he concludes that it is allowable for him to do the same.

This unsound reasoning is often unperceived by those who use it, and deceives them first; they are stunned by the sound of their own words, dazzled by the brilliancy of their figures, and the grandeur of certain words draws them on, without their perceiving it, to thoughts of little solidity, which they would no doubt regret if they reflected on them at all.

It is probable, for example, that it was the word vestal which pleased an author of the present time and led him to say to a lady, to prevent her being ashamed of knowing Latin, that she need not blush to speak a language that the Vestals spoke; for if he had considered this idea, he would have seen that he might have said to the lady, with as much reason, that she ought to blush to speak a language that the courtezans of Rome formerly spoke, who were much more numerous than the Vestals;[2] or that she ought to blush to speak any other language than that of her

---

[1] Pierre Bembo (1470-1547), secretary to Leo X., was so enamoured with Cicero's style as to imitate him even in his pagan expressions; he was elected cardinal, and took orders in 1539.
[2] The Vestals were virgins appointed to keep up the sacred fire on the altar of the goddess Vesta; there were only six.

own country, since the ancient Vestals spoke only their native language. All these arguments, which are worth nothing, are as good as that of this author, and the truth is that the Vestals can serve neither to justify nor condemn girls who learn Latin.[1]

False reasonings of this sort, which are constantly met with in the writings of those who most affect eloquence, show how the majority of persons who speak or write would need to be persuaded of this excellent rule that *nothing is beautiful but what is true*,[2] which would remove a vast number of worthless ornaments and false thoughts from discourse. Certainly this precision renders the style drier and less sonorous, but it also renders it more lively, serious, clear, and worthy of a cultivated man; its impression is stronger and more durable, whereas that which simply springs from these nicely-balanced periods is so superficial, that it vanishes almost as soon as it is heard.[3]

3. It is a very common failing among men to judge rashly of the actions and intentions of others, but they seldom fall into it except through bad reasoning, by which, through not recognizing with sufficient clearness all the causes that may produce a certain effect, they attribute this effect to one cause alone, when it may have been produced by several others; or again, they suppose that a cause which, by accident, has had a certain effect on one occasion, when it was united with several other circumstances, ought to have it under all conditions.

---

[1] Malebranche quizzes good-naturedly the pretended reasons alleged by Tertullian to justify himself for wearing the philosopher's mantle instead of the ordinary robe. This mantle was formerly in use at Carthage, but "is it allowable at the present time to wear the cap and ruff because our fathers wore them?" How could the phases of the moon, the variations of the seasons, the renewing of the serpent's skin, &c., serve to justify his change? (*Recherche de la vérité*, liv. ii.)

[2] Boileau will make it the rule of literature: *Rien n'est beau que le vrai; le vrai seul est aimable.* (*Épitre* ix.)
"Nothing is beautiful but the true; the true alone is pleasing."

[3] Fénelon very happily puts this criticism in the mouth of one of his characters, the admirer of the sermon for Ash-Wednesday. He cannot give an account of it. "The thoughts are so delicate, and depend so much on the tone and shades of expression, that after having charmed for the moment they are not easily remembered afterwards, and even if they should be, say them in other terms and it is no longer the same thing, they lose their grace and force. They are very fragile beauties then, Sir; on endeavouring to touch them they disappear. I should much prefer a discourse with more body and less spirit." (1er *Dialogue sur l'éloquence*.)

A man of letters holds the same opinion as a heretic on a matter of criticism, independent of religious controversies; an ill-natured opponent will conclude from this that he has some leaning towards the heretics; but he will conclude rashly and maliciously, since it is perhaps reason and truth which lead him to this opinion.

If a writer speak with some force against an opinion that he thinks dangerous, he may be accused upon that of hatred and animosity against the authors who have advanced it, but it would be rashly and unjustly, for this force might spring from zeal for truth quite as well as from hatred to persons.

A man is the friend of a bad man, hence it is concluded he is allied with him by interest, and is a partaker in his crimes. This does not follow; perhaps he is ignorant of them, and perhaps he has had no share in them.

A man fails to pay a compliment to those to whom it is due; he is called proud and insolent, but perhaps it is only inadvertence or simply forgetfulness.

All these exterior things are only equivocal signs, that is to say, signs which may signify several things, and it is judging rashly to limit this sign to a particular thing without having any special reason for doing so. Silence is sometimes a sign of modesty and judgment, and sometimes of stupidity. Slowness sometimes indicates prudence and sometimes dulness of mind. Change is sometimes a sign of inconstancy and sometimes of sincerity; thus it is bad reasoning to conclude that a man is inconstant simply because he has changed his opinion, for he may have had good reason to change it. . . .

It is a weakness and an injustice, which is often condemned but seldom avoided, to judge advice by the results, and to blame those who have taken a prudent resolution according to the circumstances that they could then see, for all the bad results that have followed,[1] either through a simple casualty or through the malice

---

[1] Compared with this lagging prose how brilliant and striking is the eloquence of Demosthenes, crushing that sophism in the mouth of Æschines! Accused of being the author of the disaster at Chæronea, he haughtily accepts the responsibility: "Athenians, I am going to say a strange thing. . . . If all of us had clearly seen the future, if you, Æschines, had

of those who have thwarted it, or through some other circumstances which it was impossible for them to foresee.

Not only do men like to be fortunate as much as to be wise, but they make no distinction between the fortunate and the wise or between the unfortunate and the culpable. This distinction appears to them too subtle. They are ingenious in finding out the faults that they imagine have led to the ill-success, and as the astrologers, when they know a certain event, never fail to discover the aspect of the stars which produced it, they also never fail to find, after disgraces and misfortunes, that those who have fallen into them deserved them by some imprudence. He has not succeeded, therefore he is wrong. Thus men of the world reason, and have always reasoned, because there has always been little equity in men's judgments, and because, not knowing the real causes of things, they substitute others according to the event, praising those who succeed and blaming those who do not.

If there are pardonable errors, they are certainly those that are committed through excessive deference to the opinions of those who are considered good men. But there is an illusion much more absurd in itself, but which is, nevertheless, very common, namely, thinking that a man speaks the truth because he is a man of birth, wealth, or of high dignity.

Persons do not formally reason in this manner: he has a hundred thousand livres a year, therefore he is right; he is of high birth, hence we ought to believe what he advances to be true; he is a poor man, therefore he is wrong. Nevertheless, something of the kind passes through the minds of the majority of men, and unconsciously carries away their judgment.

If the same thing be suggested by a person of quality and by a man of no position, it will often be approved in the mouth of the person of quality, while people will not deign to listen to it from a man of the lower classes. Scripture intended to

---

announced it to us with your voice of thunder, you who did not even open your mouth, even then Athens ought not to have renounced her principles, if she had at heart her dignity, the glory of her ancestors, and the judgment of posterity. . . . No, Athenians, you have not erred in throwing yourselves into the midst of dangers for the liberty and the safety of all, I swear it by your ancestors who braved the dangers of Marathon, by those who fought at Platæa, at Salamis, at Artemisium," &c.

teach us this disposition of man, representing it exactly in the book of Ecclesiasticus : " When a rich man speaketh, every man holdeth his tongue, and look, what he saith, they extol it to the clouds ; but if the poor man speak, they say, What fellow is this ?"

It is certain that complaisance and flattery have a large share in the approbation that men give to the words and actions of persons of good birth, and these often attract it by a certain outward grace, and a noble, free, and natural manner, which is sometimes so peculiar to them that it is almost inimitable by those of low birth; but it is also certain that many approve all that the great do and say from a poverty of spirit which bends under the weight of grandeur, and has not a sufficiently strong sight to support its brilliancy, and that this external pomp which surrounds them always imposes a little, and makes some impression on the strongest minds.

The cause of this deception is in the corruption of the human heart, which, having an ardent desire for honours and pleasures, necessarily conceives a great love for riches and the other qualities by means of which these honours and pleasures are obtained. Now, the love that we have for all these things that the world values causes us to think those fortunate who possess them, and, judging them fortunate, we place them above ourselves, and look upon them as exalted and eminent persons. This habit of looking upon them with esteem passes insensibly from their fortune to their mind. Men do not usually do things by halves. They attribute to them, then, a mind as exalted as their rank, and yield to their opinions, and this is the reason of the credit they usually have in the affairs of which they treat.

But this illusion is still stronger in the great themselves, who have not been careful to correct the impression that their fortune naturally makes on their own minds, than it is in their inferiors. There are few of them who do not make a reason of their rank and wealth, and do not think that their opinions ought to prevail over the opinions of those who are below them. They cannot bear that people upon whom they look down should lay claim to as much judgment and reason as themselves, and this makes them impatient of the least contradiction.

All this springs from the same source, that is to say, from the false ideas they have of their grandeur, nobility, and wealth. Instead of considering these as things entirely extraneous to their existence, which do not prevent them being on a perfect equality with the rest of mankind as to soul and body, nor having the judgment as feeble and as capable of being deceived as that of everybody else, they incorporate, in a certain way, in their very essence all these qualities of great, noble, rich, master, lord, and prince; they magnify their idea of them, and never think of themselves without all their titles, their equipage, and their train.[1]

They are accustomed to look upon themselves from their childhood as a separate species from other men; they are never mixed up in imagination with the crowd of mankind; they are always counts or dukes in their own eyes, and never simply men; thus they cut out for themselves a mind and a judgment in proportion to their fortune, and think themselves placed as far above others in mind as they are in rank and wealth.

The folly of the human mind is such that there is nothing that does not help it to aggrandize its idea of itself. A fine house, a splendid coat, a long beard, make a man think himself more clever; and if we take notice, he thinks more of himself on horseback or in a coach than on foot. It is easy to persuade everybody that nothing is more ridiculous than these judgments, but it is very difficult to protect ourselves entirely against the secret impression that all these things make on the mind. All that we can do is to accustom ourselves, as far as possible, to give no weight to those qualities which can in no way contribute to the discovery of the truth, and to give to those that do contribute to it only as much as they do really contribute. Age, knowledge, study, experience, mind, activity, caution, accuracy, and labour serve to discover the truth of hidden things, and therefore these qualities deserve respect; but, nevertheless, they must be carefully weighed, and then compared with

---

[1] You are deceived, Philemon, if you think you are more esteemed for this brilliant carriage, this great number of knaves that follow you, and these six animals that draw you. Men put aside all this outward show to penetrate to you, who are nothing but a fop. (LA BRUYÈRE, *Caractères*, ch. ii.)

the opposite reasons, for we can decide nothing with certainty from each of these things by itself, since very erroneous opinions have been maintained by men of great intellect who had many of these qualities. (*Logique*, part iii. ch. xx.)

RULES OF THE METHOD IN THE SCIENCES.

Analysis consists more in the judgment and mental skill than in particular rules. These four, nevertheless, that Descartes lays down in his Method, may be useful in avoiding error in the pursuit of truth in human sciences, although, to say the truth, they are general for all kinds of methods and not peculiar to analysis.

The first is, *never to accept anything as true which we do not plainly recognize as such ; that is to say, to carefully avoid hastiness and prejudice, and not to include in our judgments anything that is not presented so clearly to the mind that there is no room for doubt.*

The second, *to divide each of the difficulties that we are examining into as many parts as possible, or as are requisite to resolve it.*

The third, *to conduct our thoughts in order, beginning with the simplest and most easily understood objects, in order to rise by degrees to the knowledge of the more complex, and even to suppose an order among those that do not naturally precede one another.*

The fourth, *to make throughout such complete enumerations and general reviews that we may be certain of having omitted nothing.*

It is true that there is much difficulty in observing these rules; but it is always useful to bear them in mind and to observe them, as far as possible, when we wish to discover the truth by means of the reason and as far as our mind is capable of knowing it.

The Method of the Sciences reduced to eight principal rules.

TWO RULES TOUCHING DEFINITIONS.

1. To leave no term in the least obscure or equivocal without defining it.
2. To employ in the definitions only terms which are perfectly known or already explained.

TWO RULES FOR THE AXIOMS.

3. To demand as axioms only things perfectly evident.
4. To accept as evident that which needs only a little attention in order to be recognized as true.

TWO RULES FOR THE DEMONSTRATIONS.

5. To prove all propositions, which are in the least obscure, by employing in proof of them only preceding definitions, accepted axioms, or propositions already demonstrated.
6. Never to abuse what is equivocal in terms by failing to substitute for them mentally the definitions which restrict and explain them.

TWO RULES FOR THE METHOD.

7. To treat of things as far as possible in their natural order, commencing with the simplest and most general, explaining everything that belongs to the nature of the genus before passing to its particular species.
8. To divide, as far as possible, every genus into all its species, every whole into all its parts, and every difficulty into all its cases.

I have added to these two rules, *as far as possible*, because it often happens that we cannot observe them rigorously, either on account of the limits of the human understanding or of those we have been obliged to set to every science.

This often causes us to treat of a species when we are not able to treat of all that belongs to its genus; as we treat of the circle in common geometry without saying anything specially of the curved line, which is its genus, and which we are satisfied with simply defining.

We cannot either say all that can be said of a whole genus, because that would often be too long; but it is sufficient to say all we wish to say of it before passing to the species.

But I think that a science can only be treated perfectly by observing these two last rules as well as the others, and only resolving to dispense with them from necessity or for some special advantage. (*Logique*, part iv. ch. ii. and iii.)

ON TEACHING READING AND WRITING; EXERCISES IN TRANSLATION, ELOCUTION, AND COMPOSITION.

"DEAR READER,—Some of my friends having desired me to speak more at length on the subject of teaching children Latin than I have done in the different prefaces to translations that I have given to the public, in which I have been satisfied with representing chiefly that the system now followed is long, difficult, and unnatural, and that I thought that there might be another shorter, easier, and more conformable to nature, that is, to reason, I will endeavour to satisfy them here as succinctly as possible, labouring to build up, after having laboured in my other writings to destroy. . . .

"In the first place, then, I say that it is a grave error to begin, as is usually done, to teach children to read through Latin and not through French.

"This road is so long and difficult, that it not only repels the scholars from all other learning, by prejudicing their minds from their earliest childhood with a distaste and an almost invincible hatred for books and study, but it also makes the teachers impatient and peevish, because both are equally wearied with the trouble and time they give to it, which extends to three or four years; but the masters must consider that, if they have difficulty in teaching, the children have incomparably more in learning, which should be a motive for making them gentler and more patient with them by making them sympathize with the weakness of childhood. For they must not imagine that what they find pleasure in knowing children can learn without trouble; but they should rather remember their own childhood, and the difficulties they had in becoming learned. Thus they will adapt themselves to the weakness of their scholars, and not give them more trouble than they can help. . . .

"There will always be difficulties enough, either from things or from their minds, or, in fact, from their natural inclinations or aversions, without our adding others ourselves by the bad method we follow in instructing them.[1]

---

[1] This justification of the method is full of good sense and clearness.

"How, then, can children be expected to learn in a short time and with pleasure, or, at least, without very great trouble, by commencing to make them read in Latin, which is a tongue they do not understand in the least, and which they never hear spoken (for that would be of great use to them, at least for the pronunciation) except while they are being taught it? Is it not more natural to make use of what they know already, in order to teach them what they do not know, since the very definition of the method of teaching tells us to act in this manner? . . .

"Now French boys already know French, of which they are acquainted with a large number of words; why not, then, teach them first to read in French, since this method would be shorter and less tedious? for they would only have to retain in their minds the shape of the letters and their combinations; in which the memory of the things and the words that they already know, with what they are constantly hearing in every-day life, would aid them little by little in remembering them again; whereas in Latin they are not helped in any way, everything is strange and new, and they can only fix their attention on the characters and combinations which are shown them; and this is the cause that they only retain them with much trouble and time, during which they must be dinned into their ears over and over again, before they can remember them once, having nothing to hold by, neither words, nor things, nor what they hear said every day.

"Since, then, we must use what the children already know to teach them what they do not know, which is a general rule, without exception, for everything we wish to teach them, it would be proper to make them read at first detached words only, of which they know the things they represent, as those which they commonly use, as bread, a bed, a room, &c. But they should have been shown beforehand the shapes and characters of these words in an alphabet, making them pronounce the vowels and diphthongs only, and not the consonants, which they should be taught to pronounce only in the different combinations that they form with the same vowels or diphthongs in the syllables and words.

"For yet another fault is committed in the ordinary method of teaching children to read, which is the manner in which they are taught *to name the letters separately*, both consonants and vowels.

Now the consonants are called consonants only because they have no sound by themselves, but they must be joined with vowels and sound with them.[1] We are, then, contradicting ourselves in teaching to pronounce alone letters which can only be pronounced when they are joined with others; for in pronouncing the consonants separately, and making the children name them, we always add a vowel, namely, *e*, which, belonging neither to the syllable nor to the word, makes the sound of the letters named different from their sound when joined with others; thus, after the children have spelled all the letters of a word one by one, they cannot pronounce them altogether in the same word, because the medley of different sounds confuses their ears and imagination. For example, a child is made to spell the word *bon*, which is composed of three letter *b, o, n*, which they are made to pronounce one after the other. Now *b*, pronounced by itself, makes *bê*; *o*, pronounced alone, is still *o*, for it is a vowel; but *n*, pronounced alone, makes *enne*. How, then, can this child understand that all these sounds that he has pronounced separately in spelling these three letters one after the other can only make this single sound, *bon?* He can never understand this, and he only learns to put them together because his teacher himself puts them together, and shouts in his ear over and over again this single sound, *bon*.

"Again, the poor child is made to spell this other word, *jamais*, and it is done in this way, *j–a–m–a–i–s, jamais*. How can this child imagine that the six sounds which he has pronounced in spelling these six letters make only these two, *jamais?* For, when we spell the letters of this word we pronounce separately *j–a–em–a–i–esse*. Here are six or seven sounds, of which, they say, he ought to make these two, *ja-mais*. Would they not have done it sooner by making him pronounce these two syllables only, *ja–mais*, and not all the consonants and vowels separately, which only confuses his mind by this multitude of different sounds, which he can never put together as you wish him to do if you do not do it yourself and pronounce it to him several times? The same thing

---

[1] The definition is not quite exact, since there are consonants which have really a sound by themselves, for example, *f, s,* and even *r*.

may be said of a great number of difficult words, as *aimoient faisoient, disoient*, &c.[1]

"Besides, you may make a child spell his letters as much as you like, but he will never learn by this means to pronounce the syllables and words; it is only the use and habit that he has of hearing the same sound pronounced many times when they point out to him the letters which make him learn them. But this is because we always want to reason with children and teach them by rules what depends on usage alone, which is the only rule of language. And if you will pay attention to what I say you will see that the syllables and words together are repeated to them so many times that at last they retain them, and remember that such and such letters joined together have such a pronunciation, which they would never otherwise have imagined by spelling the letters one after another. Therefore it is very useless to make them lose so much time and pains by this way of spelling, whereas they would have learnt the combinations of letters very much sooner than this multitude of sounds from which they are desired to compose one or two syllables. Thus the knowledge of reading, which the children acquire at length, is attributed, without reason, to this manner of spelling the letters, but it is only an effect of the habit they have of hearing the syllables and entire words pronounced very often. And for a similar reason it is thought that the rules of Despautère[2] are the cause of the correctness with which a child composes in Latin, although in composing he had not even thought of them, having only followed in that the usage of the Latin, which he has only learnt by reading and writing and by making many mistakes which have been corrected.

"After having shown to the children and pronounced the five

---

[1] The pronunciation of *oi* of the imperfect was not then fixed. Father Chiflet wrote in 1677: "It is softer and more common among the upper classes who speak well to pronounce *je parlais*. Nevertheless, it is not a fault to say *je parlois*, since at Paris, at the bar and in the pulpit, many eloquent speakers do not condemn this pronunciation." (*Nouvelle et parfaite grammaire française*, p. 203.)

[2] Van Pauteren, in French Despautère (1460-1520), a professor at Louvain and Bois-le-Duc. His Latin grammar was long in vogue in schools.

vowels *a, e, i, o, u,* and the diphthongs *ae, oe, au, eu, ei,*[1] and making them only look at the shapes of the consonants without letting them pronounce them except in combination in entire syllables, of which they have drawn up and learnt a list, it will be well to make them read first entire words detached from one another, of which they should make a list in which they would only insert the most common words that they hear most often and whose meaning they know. And as they are taught to pray to God from the age of four or five years (I suppose it is done in French), we must begin by their prayers and the catechism,[2] which they already know by heart, to make them read a connected narrative, then break the thread of it to see if they read from a knowledge of the words, or by heart and rote; in order that, when they can read their prayers and their catechism equally well anywhere they are asked, we may then begin to give them French books.

"Being, then, in a position to be able to learn to read in French books, they must be given those in which the matter is adapted to their intelligence. The small colloquies of Mathurin Cordier[3] would be very proper for this use, if they were translated into better French; for the purity of their native language must not be corrupted from this early age; but the fables of Phaedrus, the *Captivi* of Plautus, the *Bucolics* of Virgil, the three comedies

---

[1] It is an error to call "diphthong" (two sounds) *ae, oe, au, eu, ei,* since there is only one sound represented by two letters, which lose their proper sound to form a new one. The *Grammaire générale* of Port-Royal did not commit this error: "*Eu,* as it is in *feu, peu,* is only a simple sound, although we write it with two vowels." (Part i. ch. i.) However, in chapter iii. the authors call "diphthong" the sound of *eau,* which is, however, simple.

[2] Even if the law had not taken its religious character from the school, we do not think that these are books to interest young children. The subjects are too serious and beyond their capacity.

[3] "Cordier, Mathurin, a priest (1479–1564), was one of the best class regents that could be desired; he understood Latin well, was a man of much virtue, and devoted himself to his office, being as careful to instruct his pupils in good behaviour as in good Latinity. He employed his life in teaching *children at Paris, Nevers, Bourdeaux, Geneva, Neufchâtel, Lausanne, and, lastly, again at Geneva, where he died on Sept.* 8, 1564, *aged* 85, *teaching the young in the sixth class three or four days before his death.* There is scarcely a book that has served more than that to accustom children to speak Latin." (BAYLE.)

of Terence, these letters and the collection of Cicero's letters might be very useful to them; for, by this means, they will learn at the same time to read and speak their own language with purity, as accomplished men talk in society, which is the principal style in which it is necessary to bring them up, and they will know in advance the subjects contained in the first Latin books that they will read or learn by heart, which will make the understanding of them easy, of which the beginning is so painful. And, in this way, what they already know may be usefully employed to teach them what they do not know.[1]

" With regard to *writing*, great care should be taken to teach children to write well, because, besides its usefulness, it is a very good means of occupying them and driving away tedium; for when they can write well, they like to do so, because we naturally like to do what we do well, and even desire to excel in it. The best teachers should be chosen for this, provided they will take the trouble and be careful that they hold the pen right, for that is most important. They must not, then, be allowed to write by themselves at the commencement, but before their teachers, until they have acquired a good habit of holding the pen, and when they have done that they should often pass the dry pen over the lines of their copy, in order that the muscles, nerves, and the whole hand should acquire the knack and movement necessary for good writing.[2] And I should also wish that they should not be given copies without rime or reason, but some beautiful sentences in French or Latin verse, which might serve to regulate their mind and their manners.[3] They would

---

[1] There is an ingenious foresight in making the children read in French what they will study later in Latin. But, looking closely into the matter, are the proposed works well chosen ? The Fables of Phaedrus are perfectly suitable. But the Comedies of Terence and Plautus and Cicero's Letters ? It is a question of children "of tender years," who have just overcome the first difficulties of reading ; this nutriment is much too strong.

[2] This is a very judicious recommendation, and more simple in practice than the use of those tablets over which the pupil moves his pencil in letters formed of sunken lines.

[3] At the time that Guyot was giving this wise advice Mme. de Maintenon wrote with her own hand in the copy-books of her pupils at Saint-Cyr these maxims as writing copies: " *Seek the truth in everything.—Love to give pleasure and never lie.—There is nothing disgraceful but ill-doing.—Submit to reason as soon as you know it.—Be severe towards yourselves and indulgent to others.*

unconsciously learn a great number of them, which would be so much good seed whose fruit would be seen in due season. It would be well to let them continue this exercise for several years, and not to allow them to write either their themes or translations badly; for, besides that everything that we do should be well done,[1] as far as possible, they would soon unlearn what they have learnt with much time and pains.

"I come now to the Latin, and I suppose, as everybody agrees, that as native and living languages should be chiefly learnt by use and intercourse with persons who speak them well, so the dead languages should be learnt by reading the authors who formerly spoke them well, and who live and speak to us now, in a manner, in their works. But as the life and speech of these dead authors is dying, not to say quite dead, and the tone of their voice is so low and difficult to hear that it scarcely differs from silence, it would be an incomparable advantage to resuscitate, in some sort, these dead authors, and re-animate them with our spirit, voice, and action, that they may teach us in a vivid and natural manner.[2] And this may be done by translating their works *vivâ voce* to the children, or reading the translation to them, in this way serving them as a living and animated interpreter, who speaks to them in their own tongue, as the dead would speak to them in theirs if they were still living. And this shows that, translation being the means that most nearly approaches the natural manner of learning living languages, it is also the most natural and useful means of learning the dead languages.

For is it not an inverted order, and quite contrary to nature, to begin by writing in a language which they not only cannot speak but do not even understand? Children who are beginning to learn their native language begin by hearing it before speaking

---

—*If you feel pleasure when you are reproved, believe that you will have merit.*
—*Let your conscience be simple and sincere.—Never go to rest without having learnt something,"* &c.

[1] An excellent precept to recommend. Of what use is an hour's application to the writing lesson, if they scribble the rest of the time? Good teachers have, from the same motive, suppressed the rough copy.

[2] There is in all this page a very clear perception of the value of oral teaching, of the living word of the teacher. Guyot returns to the subject a little further on with a praiseworthy persistence.

it, and speaking it before writing it. Why, then, reverse this order that nature prescribes in order to make children begin to write in a language they do not understand? And this shows that the method which is so common of making children write Latin themes before teaching them to understand Latin, to say nothing of speaking it, is a method entirely opposed to nature, of which art should be the imitator. It is, then, certain that we must begin by teaching the children Latin in order that they may understand it before they speak or write it, and that there is no other means than translation of making them understand it.

"Now there are two sorts of translation, one *vivâ voce*, the other written. There is no doubt that the first is incomparably more useful and more natural than the second; for the voice in this matter is like a faithful interpreter, who conducts us in a living manner into the country of the dead, and makes us speak and converse with them, or, at least, makes us listen to them speaking and conversing with us, as he would make us speak and converse with Turks or Germans, first letting us hear their language, then speak with them, and finally write to them.

"But the better to understand the advantage that *vivâ voce* translation has over written, it must be remarked that words have a double signification, one natural, the other artificial; for, as words are arbitrary signs of things or of mental ideas, they are also natural signs of the emotions of the heart; and this natural signification is lost, in a manner, in writings, at least for those who are only commencing to learn a dead langnage, for they only understand the artificial signification of the things according to the ideas that it awakens in their mind, which ideas are usually rather obscure and confused in children; but the *vivâ voce* translation better preserves this signification of the emotions of the heart, for voice was given to man, not only to make known things or the ideas they have of them, but also to express the various emotions of their heart with respect to these same things, or the ideas they have of them. And this they do in many other ways, as by gesture and action, by the movements of their hands, eyes, head, or shoulders, in fine, by the mute language of the whole body. It is this language of the heart that must be heard in order to understand a language well, because it is, as it were, its spirit and life. For it is the passions and emotions of the heart which make all the various beauties and figures of the discourse, and which give it that omnipotence which is attributed to eloquence and the distinct air or character which is remarked in it, and which is found, not only in the particular language of each individual man, but even in that of whole tribes and nations. For some speak in a very gentle and others in a rough manner, some in a modest, others in a haughty and boastful manner, some in a simple and artless style, others in a figurative and embellished style, some affect brevity, others a great flow of words, some speak uncivilly, others with politeness, some with amorous and tender air, others in a dry and harsh tone; all these differences spring from the emotions of the heart.

"Thus, in order to bring out this natural signification of the movements of the soul which accompanies the artificial signification of the thoughts, the teacher must brighten the lesson by his tone of voice and his gestures in reading it to them, first in French and then in Latin, with all the appropriate inflections and accents. They will then understand and retain it much sooner, because it will appeal to them more; whereas a simple reading which they do themselves or which is done by the teacher makes little impression on their minds. Thus an orator or an actor makes us understand the subject of a piece much better than a simple reading of it, because, adding his voice and action to the matter, he makes the ideas strike the mind, and the emotions move the heart more vividly. This is how we breathe life into a dead language, and give a double life to a language yet living. This opens and even elevates the children's minds, by stirring up and agitating them powerfully, and thus renders them capable of imitating, by art, the natural passions, which they can only understand and imitate by these means, not being yet able to be touched by them. . . .

"Since, then, French is to serve us as introducer to and interpreter in the Latin country, it must take a step in advance, I mean, French must be taught before Latin; and the children should be so well grounded in the ordinary and familiar French style by reading the books that I have mentioned, making them learn them by heart, that the Latin which they will afterwards learn shall not be able to injure or corrupt the purity of their French. Now the younger children are more fitted to learn French in this way than the elder, because, having an imperfect idea of things, they cannot detach them from the words by which they entered their minds, being, so to say, clothed with the terms and expressions which have made them conceive them; whereas the elder children, conceiving things in their own way, and according to opinions which they have previously formed, express them also in their own way, without confining themselves to the words of their author. The younger children, then, must, as I have said, be first grounded in the ordinary and familiar French, in order that the Latin, which they will learn afterwards, and which is so contrry to the French in its construction, may not injure their native language, as usually happens. For we see that children who have been taught in a different manner have often unlearnt French, or rather have not learnt it at all, in learning Latin, and have even rendered themselves more incapable of learning it, as may be perceived by setting them to write in French. . . . And this is the cause that at the present time the most learned persons, and those who best understand the authors, having neglected their native language in order to learn foreign tongues, and having given up intercourse with the living in order to converse only with the dead, can only translate their works in a lifeless and foreign manner, and thus render themselves less capable of filling the higher posts in the church and at the bar. . . .

"The children, then, must acquire, through these French translations, a moderate usage of their native language, which consists in the correctness of the words and their combinations, and in clearness of style even in ordinary and familiar expressions. They should not, therefore, read many French books of various styles, and especially those of a bad style, for that would make them incapable of distinguishing the good from the bad, as persons who habituate themselves to all kinds of wines can no longer appreciate nor distinguish their differences; and their minds should only be fed on delicate and intellectual things if we wish to give them a delicate and intellectual taste. For this reason it is a great error to make them read indifferently all sorts of authors, whether Latin or French, and those who guide them in this way show that they themselves have had the misfortune not to be better guided, so that the fault that was committed in their education is perpetuated indefinitely by their instructing others as they themselves were instructed; and very few are found who rise above custom to follow reason. . . .

"Since, then, our intention is to form the children to an ordinary and familiar style, we must choose books proper for this object, both in matter and style[1]. . . . Add to them, for Sundays and Holy-days, the *Lives of the Fathers of the Desert*, the last *Lives of the Saints*, written by M. d'Andilly, his *History of Josephus*, the *Confessions of St. Augustine*, the *Imitation of Christ*, the *Homilies of St. Chrysostom*, and a few other books or histories well written in French. This will fortify them in purity of morals as well as in French, and furnish them with many good things, of which they should lay up a store in good time. . . . We may add a few of the most chaste poets, full of lively descriptions, rich comparisons, and good moral teaching; for the sweetness of the verses will charm their ears, and their harmonious cadence will accustom them to a better pronunciation, and even elevate their minds above ordinary thoughts and expressions.

"Children should read a little at a time and often, in a loud and clear voice, because that will exercise the voice and chest, and give an opportunity of teaching them to pronounce well, by giving them the necessary accent to mark the different shades which are appropriate to the subjects, and correct the false cadences or inflections of voice into which they fall; thus they will be habituated to fineness of ear, to the arrangement of the words, and the harmony of the periods, and, in addition, by reading a little at a time and often, their attention will not be fatigued. For children are usually very inattentive, and too long application deadens their mind and extinguishes its fire. It will be well also to read aloud before them, enlivening what is read by the tone and accent proper to the subject, and to make them attend to it; that will do much to form them, for they have a natural inclination to imitate and to learn by imitation. And

---

[1] He repeats here the list already given above.

this is noticed even in animals, so that tones, gestures, and movements make a natural impression on their intelligence, and even on their bodily organs, which turns and disposes them to imitate what they see and hear, as those who dance make others dance, and those who make grimaces cause others to do the same, without their intending or perceiving it. . . .

"It would also be very useful to make the children repeat, then and there, what they have retained of their reading;[1] for that makes them more attentive, and the reflection that they make then will fix the subjects more firmly in their minds, on which the images of the words have just been impressed, following the order of their reading, especially when the subjects are new to them, and they want terms and other expressions to speak of them; for their discourse still retains all the arrangement of the words, without a break, and if they happen to miss or hesitate they must be prompted from the book, if only in order not to change or misplace anything in their minds; and this arrangement of the words is extremely important, because they fail in that more than in the correctness of the words themselves; this is a common fault in those who do not speak or write well, whether in French or Latin.

"But care must be taken, in exercising them in speaking or writing, that they do it with clearness and precision, and as they can only do so by the clear and accurate knowledge they have of things, and according to the construction of each language, the same things should be explained to them clearly in a few words; for the multitude and diversity of words, generally springing from indistinctness and confusion of thought, will cause the same indistinctness and confusion in the minds of the children.[2] And for this reason they should usually be set to speak or write only

---

[1] A very good and useful practice, applicable even to elementary classes, with children who cannot yet write; it fixes their attention, develops their intelligence, teaches them to speak correctly, and prepares them for composition.

[2] The only means of avoiding this capital fault in teaching is a conscientious preparation of every lesson, in addition to the general preparation that a teacher should never neglect by keeping himself abreast of methods and books, and in deepening and completing his knowledge by extensive reading.

on the subjects that they know best, and in the style and terms in which they have had most exercise; otherwise they speak confusedly as their thoughts are, and habituate themselves so to speak, and to be satisfied with what they do not understand, which is the cause of a very common fault among men, that is, of speaking much on what they understand very little. It is necessary, then, to explain to the children what they do not understand, and to question them frequently, because we often imagine that they understand very well what in fact they do not understand, judging of their capacity by our own. They should even be required to ask about what they do not understand, and when they ask of their own accord, although the subject may be above their capacity, we must not fail to instruct them with so much the more care, as they are more disposed to profit by it, since the curiosity which made them ask has opened their minds and rendered them capable of understanding what will be said to them then. Children should be kept for a long time to the same style; for, in that, time will make more impression than all the observations that may be made to them on the language, as water hollows out the stone more by falling drop by drop than by falling all at once with great force.

"They may begin to write in French before they write in Latin, by setting them to write short dialogues, narratives, or stories, little descriptions or short letters, leaving them the choice of subjects from their reading, that they may not be accustomed to write obscurely and to be satisfied with what they do not understand, which makes them lose the power of distinguishing light from darkness, makes them take the false for the true, the doubtful for the certain, in fine, evil for good. . . .

"I say nothing about synonyms and such expressions, about the order and arrangement of the words, their natural or figurative meaning, their connection and combinations, figures and transitions, the turn of the discourse, or how to break it off, take it up again and continue it. This must be reserved for practice,[1]

---

[1] It is evidently in the reading of a passage, or the explanation of a text, that all these details should be taken up, much more usefully than in a dry and barren nomenclature.

and when they are more advanced in intelligence and judgment; it is better to tell the scholars these things than to demand them of them, since any rules that may be given them do not so much prevent faults as serve to correct them when they have been made.

"It is not desirable that whole books should be set to be learnt by heart, but only the finest passages; for the memory of children, which has its limits, should only be charged with what is most excellent in books; it must, nevertheless, be well exercised. . . ." (Guyot, *Billets de Cicéron*, 1668. *Préface*.)

GENERAL VIEWS ON THE EDUCATION OF A PRINCE.[1]

. . . . The most essential quality in the preceptor of a prince is a certain nameless one which does not belong to any special profession; it is not simply the being qualified in history, mathematics, languages, politics, philosophy, ceremonies, and the interests of princes; all that may be made up for. It is not necessary for him who is charged with the instruction of a prince to teach him everything; it suffices that he teach him the use of everything. He must necessarily be assisted sometimes, and while he is preparing for certain things be only a witness of what is taught by others. But that essential quality which renders him fit for this employment cannot be made up for, it cannot be borrowed from another, nor can it be prepared for. Nature implants it, and it is improved by long exercise and much reflexion. And thus those who have it not when they are a little advanced in age will never have it.

— It cannot be better explained than by saying that it is that quality which makes a man always blame what is blameworthy, praise what is praiseworthy, disparage what is low, impress with a sense of what is great, judge everything wisely and equitably,

---

[1] It is a sign of the times, and very honourable to our age, that the advice given by Nicole on the education of a prince may be recommended without exaggeration to the teachers of the people. A very slight change is necessary to adapt it to the needs of elementary education, both to the training of the teaching staff in the normal schools, and to the proper direction of elementary studies.

and express his judgments in an agreeable manner, suitable to those to whom he speaks, and, in fine, makes him direct the mind of his pupil to the truth in everything.

— It must not be imagined that he always does this from special reflection, or that he stops every moment to give rules on good and evil, the true and the false. On the contrary, he almost always does it imperceptibly, by an ingenious turn that he gives to the subject, which exposes to view what is grand and deserves to be considered, and hides that which ought not to be seen, which makes vice ridiculous and virtue pleasing, which forms the mind imperceptibly to like and appreciate good things, and to have a dislike and aversion for bad things. So that it often happens that the same story or maxim which aids in forming the mind when it is used by an able and judicious man only serves to injure it when it is used by a man who is not so.

— Ordinary preceptors only think themselves obliged to instruct the princes at certain hours, when they give them what they call a lesson; but the man of whom we are speaking has no fixed hour for lessons, or, rather, he gives his pupils a lesson at all hours; for he often instructs him as much during play-time and visits, or by conversations and table-talk, as when he is setting him to read books. For his principal aim being to form his judgment, the different subjects which offer themselves are often more appropriate for this end than studied speeches, there being nothing which sinks into the mind less than what enters it under the not very agreeable form of a lesson and of teaching.

— As this mode of instructing is unperceived, the advantage drawn from it is so too, in a certain degree, that is to say, it is not perceived by outward and visible signs; and this deceives persons of small intelligence, who imagine that a child instructed in this manner is not more advanced than another, because, perhaps, he cannot make a better translation from Latin into French, or does not repeat a lesson of Virgil better; and thus, judging of the instruction of their children only by these trifles, they often make less account of a really able man than of one who has but small knowledge and an unintelligent mind.

Not that common things should be neglected in the instruction of princes, and that they should not be taught languages, history, chronology, geography, mathematics, and even jurisprudence up to a certain point. Their studies must be regulated as those of other persons are. The aim should be to make them industrious. They should pass from one occupation to another without leaving any vacant or unoccupied time. Every opportunity of teaching them something useful should be cleverly turned to account. If possible, they should not be ignorant of anything that is celebrated in the world. All this is good, useful, and necessary in itself, provided that a stand is not made there as if it were the end of their instruction, but it should be used to form their habits and their judgment.

— To form the judgment is to give to the mind the taste for and perception of what is true, to render it acute in recognizing rather obscure false reasonings, to teach it not to allow itself to be dazzled by the false glitter of words void of sense, nor to be satisfied with indefinite words or principles, and never to be contented until it has probed things to the bottom; it is to render it quick to seize the point in intricate matters, and to distinguish those which depart from it; it is to furnish it with the principles of truth, which help to discover it in all things, and especially in those of which it has most need. . . .

— Although the study of morality should be the principal and most constant of those to which princes are set, nevertheless it should be carried on in a manner suited to their age and the quality of their mind, so that not only they should not be burdened with it, but should not even be aware of it. The aim should be for them to know all morality almost without knowing that there is a morality,[1] or that there was a design to teach it to them; so that when they come to study it in the course of their lessons, they will be astonished at knowing beforehand much more than is taught in them.

---

[1] Bain equally recommends this indirect but only effective method of moral instruction: "Every man who is able to maintain the order and discipline necessary to good intellectual teaching is sure to leave on the children's minds impressions of true morality, even without intending to do so. If, besides, the teacher possesses sufficient tact to make his pupils like their work, and submit freely and willingly to the restraint that study imposes, so that they have, in sum, only good feelings towards their schoolfellows and himself, he may be called an excellent teacher of morals, whether he has wished to earn this title or not." (*La science de l'éducation*, p. 292.)

— Nothing is more difficult than to adapt ourselves thus to children's minds; and a man of the world rightly said that this power of adaptation to these childish ways was the result of a well-educated mind. It is easy to speak on morality for an hour; but to refer everything to it without a child perceiving it and becoming disgusted demands a tact which few persons possess.

— There are two things in vices: their unlawfulness, which makes them displeasing to God; and their folly, which makes them despicable to men. Children, usually, are not very sensible of the first, but they can be made to feel the second in many ingenious ways that opportunities offer. Thus, by making them hate vices as ridiculous,[1] they will be led to hate them as contrary to the laws of God, and at the same time the impression they make on their minds will be weakened. . . .

— It is necessary to know the failings of the child whom we instruct; that is to say, to notice the bent of his desires, in order to use all our tact to diminish it by removing all that strengthens it, always carefully distinguishing passing faults that age will remove from those which increase with age.

— The aim should be not only to preserve him from failings, but to scatter in his mind some seeds that will aid him to rise if he should be so unfortunate as to let himself fall into them. . . .

— It is not only necessary to form their minds to virtue as far as possible, but it is also necessary to adapt their bodies to it; that is to say, to prevent the body being an obstacle to their leading a regular life, leading them, by its natural instincts, into irregularities and disorders.[2]

For it must be known that, men being composed of mind and body, the bad direction given to the body in youth is often, in the sequel, a great obstacle to piety. There are some who habituate

---

[1] This is one of the favourite themes of Mme. de Maintenon: "Consider that the best of your girls are those who appear the most vain . . . . with a certain vanity that makes them afraid to be thought children, which renders them sensitive to a public mortification. . . . They must die to this sensitiveness when they are more advanced in piety; but before dying to it they must have lived in it."

[2] One of the advantages of gymnastics is to usefully expend the strength of the young, to maintain the equilibrium of body and mind, to secure a refreshing sleep, and thus remove dangerous temptations. I think this moral action of physical exercises needs to be better understood than it is.

themselves to be so restless, so impatient, and so hasty as to become incapable of uniform and tranquil occupations; others become so delicate, that they cannot bear anything that is in the least painful. Some become subject to a mortal tedium that torments them all their lives.

It will be said that these are defects of the mind, but they have a permanent cause in the body, and therefore they continue even when the mind contributes nothing to them. . . .

— Love of books and reading is a general preservative against a great number of irregularities to which the great are subject when they have nothing to occupy them, and therefore it cannot be too much instilled into young princes. They should be accustomed to read much and to hear much read, and to awaken their minds that they may find amusement in it. They should even be attracted to it by the character of the books, as by books of history, voyages, and geography, which would be of no little use to them if they would acquire the habit of passing a considerable time in it without tedium and without ill-humour.[1]

SPECIAL ADVICE CONCERNING STUDIES.

The aim of instruction is to carry our minds to the highest point they are capable of attaining.[2]

It does not give memory, imagination, nor intelligence, but it cultivates them all. By strengthening them one by another the judgment is aided by the memory, and the memory is assisted by the imagination and the judgment.

When some of these parts are absent they should be supplied by others. Thus the tact of a master is shown in setting his scholars to things for which they have a natural liking.[3] Some

---

[1] It was one of Mme. de Sévigné's great troubles to see her daughter and grand-daughter appreciate so little the study of history. "What a misfortune," she says gaily, "if Pauline is obliged to pinch her nose to take it," as if it were a medicine! To grow weary of history! why it is the support of all the world!

[2] The writers of Port-Royal have nowhere found a broader and more admirable formula.

[3] This tact, which bears fruit in competitive examinations, does not in the least deserve encouragement. It is no doubt necessary to cultivate natural aptitudes, but chiefly to endeavour to maintain the equilibrium of the faculties, as lands are improved in which there is an excess of such or such a constituent element of the soil.

children should be instructed almost solely in what depends on memory, because their memories are strong but their judgment weak, and others should at first be set to things requiring judgment, because they have more judgment than memory.

It is not properly the teachers nor extraneous instruction that cause things to be understood, at most they only expose them to the interior light of the mind, by which alone they are comprehended;[1] so that when this light is not found instruction is as useless as wishing to show pictures during the night.

The greatest minds have but a limited capacity, and have always some dark and shady places in it; but children's minds are almost always full of darkness, and only catch a glimpse of small rays of light. Thus everything consists in making the most of these rays, in augmenting them, and exposing to them what we wish to be understood.

For this reason it is difficult to give general rules for the instruction of anyone whatever, because it is necessary to adapt it to this mixture of light and shade which is different in different minds, and especially in children. We must seek the light and bring to it what we wish to be understood, and for that we must often try different ways to enter into their minds and fix upon those which succeed the best.

We may, nevertheless, say generally that as the intelligence of children depends very much on the senses, instruction must, as far as possible, be given through the senses, and be made to enter, not through the mind alone, but through the eye,[2] there being no other sense that makes a more vivid impression on the mind and forms more clear and distinct ideas.

From these observations it may be inferred that geography[3] is a very suitable study for children, because it depends very much

---

[1] An accurate and profound idea, in the development of which Nicole gives a proof of great acuteness in analysis.

[2] An excellent recommendation still to be insisted on. Two gates permit access to the child's intelligence, hearing and sight. Why do so many teachers fail to think of opening them both? It should be a main point in the preparation of lessons to exercise ingenuity in procuring or fabricating everything that might render the objects of the lesson visible to the eyes.

[3] The object lesson, still more than geography, lends itself to this teaching through the sight. A great number of objects may be shown and handled, for others we must be content with pictures.

on the senses, and through them are shown the situations of towns and provinces, and in addition it is very entertaining, which is also necessary in order not to repel them at first, and has little need of reasoning, which they lack most at that age.

But to render this study more useful and pleasant at the same time it is not sufficient to point out the names of towns and provinces on a map, many artifices must be used to aid them to remember them.

Books may be had in which there are paintings of the largest towns,[1] and may be shown to them. Children like this sort of amusement. They may be told some remarkable story about the principal towns to fix them in their memory, battles which have been fought there, councils which have been held in them, or great men who have come from them may be noted, and something may be said upon their natural history if there is anything remarkable, or on the government, size, and trade of these towns. . . .

To this special study of geography should be joined a small exercise which is only an amusement, but which does not fail to contribute much to fix it in their minds. If some story is told them, its place should always be pointed out to them on the map. If, for instance, the *Gazette* is read, all the towns named should be pointed out on the map. In fine, they should mark on their maps every place they hear spoken of, that they may serve them as an artificial memory to retain the stories, and the stories should help them to remember the places where they happened.

There are several other useful subjects besides geography that may enter children's minds through their eyes.

The machines of the Romans, their punishments, dress, arms, and several other things of the same kind are represented in the books of Lipsius, and may be usefully shown to children;[2] they may be shown, for instance, what a battering-ram was, how they made a testudo, how the Roman armies were organized, the number of their cohorts and legions, their officers, and a number

---

[1] We may add views of mountains, of the courses of rivers, and of other geographical prospects. The pictures of M. Félix Hément are a beginning of the application of this mode of teaching through the eye.

[2] Our editors have not failed to put in practice these sensible hints, and our children have in their hands books usefully illustrated for the study of natural history, geography, and common subjects, &c.

of other pleasing and curious things, omitting those that are more intricate. Very nearly the same advantage may be drawn from a book entitled *Roma Subterranea*, and others in which have been engraved what remains of the antiquities of this chief city of the world, to which may be added the plates that are found in certain voyages to India and China, in which the sacrifices and pagodas of these wretched people are described, pointing out to them at the same time to what excess of folly men are capable of going when they follow only their own imagination and the light of their own minds.

The book of Aldrovandus,[1] or rather the abridgment of it made by Jonston, may also usefully serve to amuse them, provided that he who shows it to them has taken pains to learn something of the nature of animals, and to tell it to them not as a formal lesson but in conversation. This book may also be used to show them the pictures of the animals they hear spoken of either in books or conversation.

An intelligent man has shown, at the present time, by a trial that he made on one of his children, that at that age they are quite capable of learning anatomy; and no doubt they might be usefully taught some general principles, if it were only to make them retain the Latin names of the parts of the human body,[2] avoiding, however, certain objectionable points on this matter.

It is useful, for the same reason, to show them the portraits of the kings of France, the Roman emperors, the sultans, the great captains and illustrious men of various nations. It is good that they should amuse themselves by looking at them, and refer to them whenever they are spoken of in their presence, for all this serves to fix the ideas in their memories.

Teachers should try and cultivate a healthy curiosity in the children to see strange and curious things, and lead them to enquire the reasons of everything. This curiosity is not a vice

---

[1] Aldrovandus, of Bologna (1520–1605), the author of a large *Natural History*, comprising no less than 13 vols. in folio. We have nothing to learn now from this immense and undigested compilation, in which poetry, legends, and popular prejudices hold a larger place than real observation.

[2] This is a very secondary consideration in comparison with the advantage we might draw from it for the teaching of hygiene and gymnastics; but then they were more taken up with writing and even speaking Latin.

at their age, since it serves to open their minds, and may divert them from some irregularities.

History may be placed among the acquirements that are gained through the eyes, since various books of pictures and figures may be used to help them to remember it. But even if none should be found, it is in itself very suitable to children's minds. And though it only exercises the memory, it is very useful in forming the judgment. Every artifice, then, should be used to give them a taste for it.

At first they may be given a general idea of universal history, of the various monarchies, and the principal changes that have taken place since the beginning of the world, by dividing the course of time into different ages; as, from the creation to the deluge, from the deluge to Abraham, from Abraham to Moses, from Moses to Solomon, from Solomon to the return from the Babylonish captivity, from the return from captivity to Christ, from Christ to our own times, thus joining general chronology to general history.[1] . . .

Besides these histories, which will form part of their studies and occupations, it would be of advantage to relate to them every day a detached episode, which would have no place in their regular exercises, but would rather serve to amuse them. It might be called *the story of the day*, and they might be practised in reciting it in order to teach them to converse.

This story should contain some great event, some extraordinary meeting, some striking example of vice, virtue, misfortune,

---

[1] The present programmes of secondary classical instruction (decree of 2 Aug., 1880) are inspired by more correct ideas; in the eighth class (the lowest), History of France to Henri IV.; seventh, from Henri IV. to the present time; sixth, History of the East; fifth, History of Ancient Greece; fourth, Roman History; third, History of Europe, and especially of France, from 395 to 1270; second, from 1270 to 1610; in the class of rhetoric (first), from 1610 to 1789; and in the class of philosophy, Contemporary History from 1789 to 1875.

They have been less successful for primary instruction, where the short time allowed for studies has compelled too great a condensation in the upper forms. Where are the teachers to be found who are able to give properly, in a year, notions on ancient history, Greek and Roman, the History of Europe and of France to 1875? I regret, for my part, the old programme, which made the pupils in the three courses review the History of France with new developments.

prosperity, or singularity. It might include uncommon incidents, prodigies, earthquakes, which have sometimes engulphed entire cities, shipwrecks, battles, and foreign laws and customs. By making the most of this practice they might be taught what is finest in all histories; but, for that, it is necessary to be regular, and not to pass a day without relating a story and referring every day to what has been told them before.

They should be taught to connect in their memory similar stories that one may serve to recall another. For example, it is proper for them to know some examples of all the greatest armies that are spoken of in books, of great battles and slaughters, of great cruelties, of great pestilences, of great prosperity and adversity, of great riches, of great conquerors and captains, of fortunate and unfortunate favourites, of the longest lives, of the signal follies of men, of great vices and great virtues.[1] . . .

The idea of those who will have no grammar [2] is only the idea of idle persons who wish to spare themselves the trouble of teaching it; but, far from relieving the children, it burdens them much more than the rules, since it deprives them of knowledge that would facilitate the understanding of the books, and obliges them to learn a hundred times what it would have sufficed to learn only once.

It cannot be denied that the book *Janua linguarum* [3] may have some utility; but it is, nevertheless, irksome to load the memory of children with a book in which there are only words to be learnt, since one of the most useful rules that can be followed in their instruction is to join several useful things, and to act so that the books they read in order to learn the language may also be of use to form their mind, judgment, and morals, to which this book cannot contribute. . . .

It is a general opinion, and one of great importance to teachers, that they should have in their mind all that they should teach

---

[1] Add to this list the much more important history of great inventions and discoveries. Nicole would have heartily approved of the creation of the *Bibliothèque des merveilles*, whose plan, happily enlarged, responds to his indications.

[2] Nicole is here concerned with teaching Latin. His observations are none the less accurate and useful.

[3] See Lancelot's opinion on the book of Comenius. (Introduction, p. 15.)

the children, and not be satisfied with simply finding it in their memory when it is recalled to them. For we find many favourable opportunities of teaching children what we know well, and make them when we will, and adapt ourselves better to their capacity when the mind makes no effort to find what ought to be read. . . .

Children should never be allowed to learn by heart anything that is not excellent. For this reason it is a very bad method to make them learn whole books by heart, because everything is not equally good in books. . . .

This opinion is more important than is thought; its aim is not only to relieve the memory of children, but also to form their mind and their style; for things that are learnt by heart impress themselves deeper on the memory, and are like moulds and forms that the thoughts take when they wish to express them; so that if they only have good and excellent ones, they must necessarily express themselves in a noble and elevated manner.

With respect to the study of rhetoric, Nicole makes this remark:—
All those names of figures, all those subjects of arguments, all those enthymemes and epicheremes will never be of use to anybody; and if they are taught to children, they should at least be taught at the same time that they are very useless things.[1]

Everything in the instruction of the elder scholars should be referred to ethics, and it is easy to apply this rule to what they should be taught in rhetoric; for true rhetoric is founded to true ethics, since it should always leave a pleasing impression of the speaker and make him pass for an honest man, which presupposes that we know what honesty is, and which makes us liked. We are speaking badly if we make ourselves disliked or despised by speaking. And this rule obliges us to avoid all that savours of vanity, levity, malignity, baseness, brutality, or effrontery, and generally everything that gives an idea of any vice or defect of mind.

---

[1] It would be a signal service to the art of teaching to impress this upon the masters and mistresses of our normal schools, who are still too much in bondage to this old rhetoric. All these Greek names, that the children so easily mispronounce, teach them nothing really useful. The secrets of the art of writing should be taught by the explanation of good authors.

There is, for example, in Pliny the Younger, an air of vanity
and a sensitive love of reputation which spoil his letters, however
full of wit they may be, and give them a bad style, because we
can only imagine him as a vain and superficial man. The same
defect makes the person of Cicero despicable at the same time
that we admire his eloquence, because this air appears in almost
all his works.[1] No man of honour would wish to resemble
Horace or Martial in their malignity and impudence. Now,
to give these ideas of oneself is to offend against true rhetoric as
well as against true morality.

There are two kinds of beauty in eloquence of which we should
endeavour to render children sensible. One consists of good and
solid, but extraordinary and surprising thoughts. Lucan, Seneca,
and Tacitus are full of this kind of beauties.

The other, on the contrary, does not at all consist in rare
thoughts, but in a certain natural air, an easy, elegant, and
delicate simplicity, which does not strain the mind, which only
presents to it common, but lively and pleasing images, and
which can follow it in its movements so well, that it never fails to
put before it, on every subject, objects by which it may be
touched, and to express all the passions and emotions that the
things it represents ought to produce on it. This is the beauty
of Terence and Virgil. And we see by this that it is still more
difficult than the other, since there are no authors who have been
less nearly approached than these two.

It is this beauty, however, that causes the pleasure and charm

[1] M. Legouvé has warmly taken up the defence of Cicero in his eloquent
reply to the address of reception of M. G. Boissier: "One day the Emperor
Augustus surprised his grandson reading a book that he made haste to hide;
the Emperor took the volume, it was a work of Cicero. After having read a
few lines he returned it to the child, and added in an agitated voice, in which
perhaps there was some remorse: 'My son, that man deeply loved his
country!' This was Cicero's dominant trait, this effaces all his faults,
this nourishes and immortalises his genius. . . What matters that this
great man had some small weaknesses, some passing vanity? As soon
as the interest of Rome appeared, vanity, fears, hesitation, all disappeared;
he saw but one thing, his country; he had but one aim, the safety of Rome,
and he went straight, not only to duty, but to heroism, so that it may be said
that in those terrible civil commotions he had many small fears and great
courage. . . Ah! believe me, sir, when we meet with such men in history we
must not diminish their greatness by their weaknesses, but sink their weaknesses in their greatness!" (Académie française, séance du 21 déc., 1876.)

of polite conversation; and thus it is more important to make it appreciated by those whom we instruct than that other beauty of thoughts, which is much less in use.

If we do not know how to mingle this natural and simple beauty with that of great thoughts, we run the risk of writing and speaking badly in proportion to our endeavour to write and speak well; and the more intelligence we have the more we fall into this vicious style. For this throws us into the antithetic style, which is a very bad one. Even if thoughts are good and solid in themselves, they nevertheless weary and overwhelm the mind if they are in too great numbers, and if they are employed on subjects which do not require them. Seneca, who is admirable when taken in parts, wearies the mind when read consecutively, and I think that if Quintilian rightly said of him that he was full of agreeable defects, we may say with as much reason that he is full of disagreeable beauties— disagreeable by their number and by the design that he appears to have had of saying nothing simply, but putting everything in antithetical form. There is no fault that it is more necessary to point out to children when they are a little advanced than that, because there is none which more destroys the fruit of studies in what regards language and eloquence.

Everything should tend to form the judgment of the children, and impress on their minds and hearts the rules of true morality. Every occasion should be taken to teach it to them; but, nevertheless, certain exercises may be practised which tend to it more directly. And, firstly, we must endeavour to confirm them in the faith, and strengthen them against the maxims of free-thinking and impiety, which spread only too much in courts. . . .

A book has just been published which may be one of the most useful that can be put into the hands of intelligent princes. It is the collection of *Pensées* of M. Pascal. In addition to the incomparable advantage that may be drawn from it to confirm them in the true religion by reasons which will appear to them so much the more solid the deeper they go into them, and which leave this most useful impression that nothing is more ridiculous than to make a boast of free-thinking and irreligion, a thing that is more important than can be believed for the great, there is, besides, an air so grand, so elevated, and at the same time so simple and so far removed from affectation in everything that he writes, that nothing is fitter to form their minds and to give them the taste for and the idea of a noble and natural manner of writing and speaking.[1] . . .

Saint Basil advises to teach children sentences taken from the *Proverbs* and the other books of Solomon, to sanctify their memory by the word of God, and to instruct them in the principles of morality. . . .

To these sentences from the *Proverbs* might be added others drawn from pagan authors, setting them to learn only one a day.[2] This practice would suffice in the course of a few years to make them retain the finest thoughts of the poets, historians, and philosophers, and would even give an opportunity by choosing some suitable to their faults, which would serve to point them out and set them before their eyes in a gentle and less unpleasant manner.

It would be too severe to absolutely forbid the children to use pagan books, since they contain a great number of useful things; but the teacher should know how to render them Christian by the manner in which he explains them. There are very true maxims in these books, and these are Christian in themselves, since all truth comes from God and appertains to God![3] It remains, then, either to approve of them simply, or to show that the Christian religion carries them farther, and makes the truth penetrate them deeper. There are others that are false in the mouth of pagans,

---

[1] Nicole no longer holds this language in his strange letter on the subject of the *Pensées* of Pascal. (See Introduction, p. 24.)

[2] Seneca, in his *Letters to Lucilius*, recommends his friend to gather in his reading a maxim and to make of it "the food for the day." The suggestion of Nicole is excellent, and deserves to be taken into consideration. Teachers would find it a wonderful help in teaching morality.

[3] These broader and sounder views soften what Nicole, led away by an unreasoning piety, has said elsewhere of pagan literature, in which he sees only the inspiration of the devil. (See Introduction, p. 23.) Minucius Felix says in his *Octavius*: "It seems to me that at times the ancient philosophers agree so well with the Christians, that it might be said, either that the present Christians are philosophers, or that the former philosophers were Christians.

but very sound and true in that of Christians.[1] And this is what a teacher should distinguish, by pointing out the hollowness of the pagan philosophy and opposing to it the solidity of the principles of Christianity.

In fine, there are some absolutely false, and he must show their falseness by clear and solid reasons. By this means everything in these books will be useful, and they will become books of piety,[2] since the very errors they contain will be used to make known the truths which are contrary to them. . . .

(Nicole, *Traité de l'éducation d'un prince.*)

OF THE MEANS OF PRESERVING PEACE WITH MEN.

. . . This agreement of faith and reason appears nowhere so well as in the duty of preserving peace with those who are united with us, and of avoiding all occasions to disturb it. And if religion prescribes this to us as one of the most essential duties of Christian piety, reason leads us to it also as one of the most important for our own interest.

For we cannot consider with any attention the source of the greater part of the disquiet and opposition from which we suffer, or from which we see others suffer, without recognizing that they usually come from the fact that we do not sufficiently give way to each other. And if we will do justice to ourselves, we shall find that we are seldom spoken ill of without reason, or that men take pleasure in hurting and offending us for their amusement; we always contribute something to it. If there are no approximate causes there are distant ones. And we fall unconsciously into a number of small faults, with respect to those with whom we live, which dispose them to take in bad part what they would

---

[1] A singular and inadmissible assertion! Truth is truth. What difference, for example, can be found, without the spirit of system, between these words of Plato, "There is no other means of making ourselves loved by God than to labour with all our strength to resemble Him" (*Lois*, liv. iv.), and this precept of Christ, "Be ye perfect, as your Father in heaven is perfect"! (See the conscientious work of M. EM. HAVET, *Le christianisme et ses origines.*)

[2] These books, which he denounced as the works of the devil, are here rehabilitated. (See Introduction, p. 23.)

suffer without any trouble if they had not already the beginning of bitterness in their mind. In fine, it is almost always true that, if men do not love us, it is because we cannot make ourselves loved.

We contribute, then, ourselves to this disquiet and opposition, and to these troubles that others cause us; and as it is partly this that renders us unhappy, nothing is more important for us, even from a worldly point of view, than to set ourselves to avoid them. And the science that teaches us to do this is a thousand times more useful than all those that men learn with so much pains and time. There is reason, therefore, to deplore the bad choice that men make in the study of arts, exercises, and sciences. They take great pains to acquire a knowledge of matter, and to find the means of making it useful for their needs. They learn the art of taming animals and employing them in the labours of daily life, and do not give a thought to that of making men useful to them, and preventing them troubling them and rendering their lives unhappy, although men contribute infinitely more to their happiness or unhappiness than all the other creatures. . . .

Charity not only includes all men, but includes them at all times. Thus we should have peace with all men and at all times, for there is no time in which we ought not to love them and desire to serve them; and, consequently, there is none in which we should not, for our part, remove all the obstacles that we may meet with, of which the greatest is the aversion and coolness that they may feel towards us. So that, even when we cannot preserve with them an interior peace, which consists in unity of sentiments, we should endeavour to preserve an exterior peace, which consists in the duties of human civility, in order not to make ourselves incapable of serving them some day, and to bear witness before God of our sincere desire to do so.

Besides, if we do not actually serve them, we are obliged, at least, not to hurt them. Now leading them to become cool towards us by offending them is hurting them. It is doing them a real harm to dispose them by the coolness they conceive towards us to take our actions and words in bad part, to speak of them in an unjust manner which would hurt their conscience and, in fine, to despise even the truth from our mouth, and not to love justice when it is we who defend it.

It is, then, not only the interest of men, but also that of truth itself, which obliges us not to embitter them needlessly against us. If we love it, we should avoid making it odious by our imprudence, and closing its entrance into the heart and mind of men by closing it to ourselves; and thus, to lead us to avoid this defect the Scripture warns us, *that wise men adorn knowledge*, that is to say, render it venerable to men, and that the esteem that they attract by their moderation makes the truth which they announce appear more august; whereas by making ourselves despised or hated by men we dishonour it, because contempt and hatred usually pass from the person to the teaching. . . .

The trouble does not lie in convincing ourselves of the necessity of preserving union with our neighbour, it is really to preserve it by avoiding all that can disturb it, and it is certain that a large charity alone can produce the grand effect. But, among the human means that it is useful to employ, it seems there is none more fitting than to endeavour to learn the usual causes of the divisions that take place among men, in order to be able to prevent them. Now, considering them in general, we may say that we only fall out with men because in offending them we lead them to hold themselves aloof from us; or because being offended by their actions or words we ourselves keep away from them, and give up their friendship. Both may happen either by open rupture, or by gradually increasing coolness; but however it may happen, it is always these reciprocal discontents which cause divisions; and the sole means of avoiding them is never to do anything that may offend another, and never to be offended by anything ourselves.

Nothing is easier than to prescribe this generally. But there are few things more difficult to practise in particular; and we may say that here is one of those rules which, being short in words, are very general in sense, and include in their generality a great number of very important duties. For this reason it will be profitable to develop it by examining more particularly by what means we may avoid offending men, and may put our own minds in a condition not to be offended by what they may do or say against us.

The means of succeeding in the practice of the first of these duties is to learn what it is that offends them, and causes aversion and coolness. Now it seems that all these causes may be reduced to two, namely, contradicting their opinions and opposing their passions. . . .

Men are naturally attached to their opinions, because they always have some desire to rule over others in every possible manner. Now we rule in a certain way by our reputation; for it is a kind of authority to make others receive our opinions. And thus the opposition we meet with wounds us in proportion as we are fond of this sort of domination. *Man puts his joy,* says the Scripture, *in the thoughts that he sets forth.* For in setting them forth he makes them his own, he makes them his goods, he clings to them by interest; to destroy them is to destroy something belonging to him. It cannot be done without showing him that he is mistaken, and a man has no pleasure in being mistaken. He who contradicts another on any point claims to have more knowledge of it than he has. And thus two disagreeable ideas are presented to him at once—one, that he fails in knowledge; the other, that he who corrects him surpasses him in intelligence. The first humiliates him, the second arouses his jealousy. These impressions are more deep and clear as the desire to rule is more lively and active; but there are few persons who do not feel them in some degree, or who submit to contradiction without some displeasure.

Besides this general cause, there are several others which make men cling to their ideas, or make them more sensitive to contradiction. Although it may appear that piety, by diminishing the esteem we may have for ourselves, and the desire to dominate over the minds of others, ought to diminish our attachment to our own opinions, it often has the contrary effect. For as spiritual persons[1] look at all things from a spiritual point of view, and yet are sometimes deceived, sometimes also they spiritualize certain falsehoods, and support some unsettled or ill-founded opinions with conscientious reasons, which cause them to cling to them with obstinacy. So that, applying their general love of truth, virtue, and the interests of God to those opinions

---

[1] That is, those who live a spiritual rather than a bodily life.

which they have not sufficiently examined, their zeal is aroused and inflamed against those who oppose them, or who show that they are not persuaded by them; and what remains of the desire to rule, mingling and blending with these impulses of zeal, spreads so much the more freely as they make less resistance, and do not discriminate this double movement which acts in their heart, because their mind is only perceptibly occupied with these spiritual reasons, which appear to them the sole source of their zeal. . . .

The impatience which leads us to contradict others with warmth comes from the fact that we find a difficulty in allowing others to hold different opinions from our own. These opinions offend us, not because they are contrary to truth, but because they are contrary to our feelings. If our aim were to be of use to those whom we contradict, we should employ other means and measures. We only wish to subject them to our opinions, and exalt ourselves above them; or, rather, we wish, by contradicting them, to take a small vengeance for the annoyance they have given us by offending our feelings. So that there are altogether in this proceeding pride, which causes this annoyance, want of charity, which leads us to revenge ourselves by an injudicious contradiction, and hypocrisy, which makes us cloak our corrupt feelings under the pretext of love of truth, and the charitable desire of disabusing others, whereas, in fact, we are only seeking to gratify ourselves. And thus what the sage says may be applied to us, that the warnings that a man who wishes to insult gives are false and deceitful: *Est correptio mendax in ore contumeliosi.* Not that he always says false things, but that, in wishing to appear to have the desire to serve us by correcting us for some fault, he only has the desire to displease and insult us.

We ought, then, to regard this impatience that leads us to oppose without discernment what appears to us false as a very considerable fault, which is even greater than the pretended error from which we wish to free others. Thus, as we owe the first charity to ourselves, our first care should be work upon ourselves, and endeavour to put our mind into such a state as to bear without emotion the opinions of others which appear false to us, in order never to oppose them, but with the desire to be useful to them. . . .

We must not, however, carry the principles which we have laid down so far as to scruple generally in conversation, to show that we do not approve some of the opinions of those with whom we live. This would be destroying social intercourse instead of preserving it, because this restraint would be too great, and everyone would prefer to stay at home. This reserve, then, should be confined to the most essential things, and to those in which we see men take most interest; and there are methods of contradicting them by which it would be impossible for them to be offended. And this should be especially studied, since public intercourse could not exist if we had not the liberty of showing that we do not hold the opinions of others.

Thus it is very useful to carefully study how we may express our opinions in a manner so gentle, reserved, and agreeable, that no one can be offended by them.

Men of the world do this admirably with respect to the great, because cupidity makes them find the means. And we should find them as easily as they do if charity were as active in us as cupidity is in them . . . and made us as apprehensive of offending our brethren . . . as they are of offending those whom they have an interest in making use of to further their fortune.

This practice is so important and so necessary during the whole course of life, that special care should be taken in using it. For very often it is not so much our opinions that offend others as the haughty, presumptuous, passionate, disdainful, and insulting manner in which we express them. We should, then, learn to contradict politely and gently, and to consider the faults we make in this as very considerable.

It is difficult to comprise in special rules and precepts the various ways of contradicting the opinions of others without offending them. Circumstances give rise to them, and the charitable fear of offending our brethren makes us find them. But there are certain common faults that we should be careful to avoid, and which are the ordinary sources of this bad conduct. The first is an air of superiority, that is to say, an imperious manner of expressing our opinions, that very few people can put up with, as much because it indicates a proud and haughty spirit, which is naturally disliked, as because it seems that we wish to dominate and make ourselves masters over the minds of others. . . .

For example, it is a kind of superiority to show displeasure that we are not believed, and to complain of it; for it is like accusing those to whom we speak either of a stupidity that prevents them understanding our reasons, or of an obstinacy which prevents their yielding to them. We ought to be persuaded, on the contrary, that those who are not convinced by our reasons will not be shaken by our reproaches, since these reproaches give them no more information, and only show that we prefer our own opinion to theirs, and that we are careless of offending them.

Another great fault is to speak with an authoritative air, as if what we say cannot reasonably be contested; for we offend those to whom we speak in this manner by making them feel that they are opposing an indubitable fact, or by making it appear that we wish to deprive them of the liberty of examining and judging by their own intelligence, which appears to them an unjust assumption.

It was to lead religious men to avoid this offensive manner that a saint advised them to season their discourse with the salt of doubt, as opposed to that dogmatic and authoritative air: *Omnis sermo vester dubitationis sale sit conditus*, because he thought that humility did not allow us to claim such a perfect knowledge of the truth as not to leave room for doubt.[1]

For those who have this peremptory manner bear witness that not only they have no doubt of what they advance, but also that they will not have others doubt of it. Now this is demanding too much of others, and claiming too much for ourselves. Every man wishes to be the judge of his own opinions, and only to accept them because he approves them. All that these persons gain, then, by this is that men attach themselves more than they otherwise would to reasons for doubting what they say, because

---

[1] We must not, however, on this pretext, adopt the ridiculous position of Marphurius: "Seigneur Sganarelle, change this mode of speaking, if you please. Our philosophy commands us not to enounce a decisive proposition, but to speak of everything with doubt, and always to suspend our judgment; and for this reason you should not say 'I am come,' but, 'It seems to me that I am come.'" (MOLIÈRE, *le Mariage forcé*, act i. sc. 8.)

this manner of speaking arouses a secret desire of contradicting them, and of showing that what they propose with so much assurance is not certain, or not so certain as they imagine. . . .

Employing insulting and depreciatory terms in an argument is so visible a fault that it is not necessary to refer to it. But it is proper to remark that there is a roughness and incivility that proceed from contempt, although they may come from another principle. It is sufficient to convince those whom we oppose that they are wrong and mistaken, without making them feel, by using harsh and humiliating expressions, that we think they have not the least spark of intelligence. And the change of opinion to which we wish to drive them is sufficiently hard for human nature without adding new difficulties to it. These terms can only be useful in written refutations, in which the design is to convince those who read them of the small intelligence of him who is refuted rather than to convince the man himself.

In fine, abruptness, which does not so much consist in harshness of terms as want of certain palliatives, offends also, usually because it includes a species of indifference and disdain. For it leaves the wound made by the contradiction without any remedy to diminish the pain. Now it is not showing sufficient regard for men to give them pain without feeling it ourselves, and without endeavouring to relieve it; and abruptness does not do this, because, properly speaking, its essence consists in not doing it, and in saying harsh things harshly. We treat tenderly those whom we love and esteem, and thus we openly testify to those whom we do not treat so, that we have no friendship nor esteem for them.

It is not enough to avoid offending men in order to preserve peace with them; we must also bear with them when they commit faults against us. For it is impossible to preserve internal peace if we are so sensitive to what they may do and say contrary to our inclinations and feelings; and it is difficult for the internal displeasure that we have conceived not to break out and dispose us to act towards those who have offended us in a manner capable of offending them in their turn, and this gradually increases the differences, and often carries them to extremities.

We must endeavour, then, to stop divisions and quarrels in their very beginning. Self-esteem never fails to suggest to us on this subject that the means of succeeding in it would be to correct those who incommode us and to bring them to reason, showing them that they are wrong in acting towards us as they do. This leads us to complain of the proceedings of others and to notice their faults, either to correct what displeases us in them, or to punish them by the vexation our complaints may cause them and the disapprobation they may draw upon them.

But if we ourselves were really reasonable, we should easily see that this design of establishing peace by the reformation of others is ridiculous, because its success is impossible. The more we complain of the proceedings of others, the more we exasperate them against ourselves without correcting them. We cause ourselves to be considered fastidious, proud, and haughty, and the worst is that this opinion will not be altogether unjust, since, in fact, these complaints only proceed from fastidiousness and pride. Those even who show that they accept our reasoning, and who think that some injustice has been done us, will not fail to be ill-satisfied with our sensitiveness. And as men are naturally inclined to justify themselves, if those of whom we complain have a little tact, they will turn things in such a manner as to put us in the wrong; for the same defect of narrowness of mind and want of equity which attributes to people the faults of which we complain, prevents them also very often from acknowledging them, and makes them take as true and just all that may serve to justify them.

For if those of whom we complain are higher than ourselves in rank, influence, or authority, the complaints that we might make would be still more useless and dangerous. They can only give us the malignant and transitory satisfaction of getting them condemned by those to whom we complain, and produce in the sequel durable and permanent bad effects, by exasperating those persons against us and destroying all harmony that we might have with them.

Prudence, then, obliges us to take the opposite road, to entirely abandon the chimerical design of correcting everything that displeases us in others, and to endeavour to found our peace and repose upon our own proper reformation and on the moderation of our passions. Neither the mind nor the language of men is at our command, and we are accountable for their actions only in so far as we have given occasion to them, but we are accountable for our own actions, words, and thoughts. We are charged to watch over ourselves and correct our faults; and if we do so properly, nothing that comes from without will be able to trouble us. . . .

It is not sufficient, in order to preserve peace with ourselves and others, not to offend anyone, and not to demand either friendship, esteem, confidence, gratitude, or civility from anyone; we must have a patience proof against all sorts of humours and caprices. For as it is impossible to make all those with whom we live just, moderate, and faultless, we must despair of being able to preserve tranquillity of mind if we confine it to this means.

We must expect, then, that, living with men, we shall find disagreeable tempers, people who get angry without a motive, who take things amiss, who argue, who show a haughty superiority or a base and displeasing complacency; some will be too passionate, others too cold; some will contradict without any reason, others will not bear the least contradiction in anything; some will be envious and malicious, others insolent, full of themselves and without regard for others; some will be found who think that everything is due to them, and who, never thinking of how they act towards others, will not fail to exact from them excessive deference.

What hope should we have of living quietly if all these defects disturb, trouble, and upset us, and unsettle our minds?

We must, then, bear them patiently and firmly, if we wish to possess our souls, as the Scripture says, and prevent impatience making us break out every moment, and throw us into all the difficulties that we have spoken of; but this patience is not a very common virtue. So that it is very strange that, it being on the one hand so difficult and so useful on the other, we take so little pains to exercise ourselves in it, at the same time that we study so many other useless and unprofitable things.

One of the principal means of acquiring it is to minimise the deep impression that the defects of others make on us. And for this purpose it is useful to consider:—

1. That, defects being as common as they are, it is foolish to be surprised at them and not to expect them. Men are made up of good and bad qualities; they must be taken on this footing, and whoever wishes to reap advantages from their intercourse ought to resolve to submit patiently to the inconveniences that are attached to it.

2. That nothing is more ridiculous than to be unreasonable because another is so, to injure ourselves because another injures himself, and to become a participator in all the follies of another, as if we had not enough with our own defects and the misfortunes of all the rest. Now this is what we do in losing patience at the faults of others.

3. That, however great the defects that we find in others may be, they only injure those who have them, and do us no harm unless we voluntarily receive the impression of it. They are objects of commiseration, not of anger, and we have as little reason to be irritated against the maladies of others' minds as against those that attack their bodies. There is even this difference, that we may contract bodily maladies against our will, whereas only our own will can give entrance to mental maladies.

4. We should not only regard the defects of others as maladies, but also as maladies that are common to us, for we are subject to them as they are. There are no defects to which we are not liable, and if there are some that we have not, we have, perhaps, others greater. Thus, having no reason to prefer ourselves to them, we shall find that we have none to take offence at what they do, and that if we suffer from them we make them suffer in our turn.

5. The faults of others, if we could regard them with a tranquil and charitable eye, should be lessons for us so much the more useful as we saw the deformity in them much better than in our own, a part of which self-esteem always hides from us. They might give us an opportunity of remarking that the passions usually have a different effect from what is asserted. We get angry in order to make ourselves believed, and the more angry we become

the less we are believed. We are offended because we are not so much esteemed as we think we deserve, and we are less esteemed the more we seek to be so. We are angry at not being liked, wishing to be so by force, and we draw upon us still more men's aversion.

We might also see with astonishment how far these same passions blind those who are possessed by them. For these effects, which are so perceptible to others, are usually unknown to themselves. And it often happens that, making themselves odious and disagreeable, they are the only persons who do not perceive it.

And all that may help us to remember either faults into which we formerly fell through like passions, or those into which we still fall through other passions, which are not, perhaps, less dangerous, and to which we are not less blind; and in this way, all our attention being drawn to our own faults, we shall become more disposed to bear with those of others.

In fine, we should consider that it is as ridiculous to get angry for the faults and whims of others as to be offended because the weather is bad, or is too cold or too hot, because our anger is as little capable of correcting men as of changing the seasons.[1] It is even more unreasonable in this point, that by getting angry with the seasons we do not make them either more or less incommodious; whereas the exasperation that we feel towards men irritates them against us, and makes their passions more lively and active.

---

[1] Nicole compromises his thesis by insisting too much on this excellent precept of indulgence, especially by means of these comparisons more striking than exact. Cold and heat are necessary consequences of physical phenomena. Do men's vices and faults obey the same law? If so, what becomes of morality? And if we can no more correct men than change the seasons, what is the aim of education or preaching? We must not try to prove too much.

EULOGY ON DESCARTES' PHILOSOPHY.

... A man must ill understand the philosophy of M. Descartes to believe of it what this author[1] says: *That it consists in some truths, or seeming truths, mixed with some errors or uncertain conjectures; that it draws bad conclusions from good premisses; that it defends and explains truths by false reasoning; that if it sometimes finds the truth it is more by a happy accident than by a sure method; that it supports it rather by imagination than by science; and that it is more fertile in discussion than in doctrine.* We have only to take the opposite of all this to form a true idea of the philosophy of M. Descartes; for never has a philosopher reasoned more clearly and exactly, avoided long discourses, and said more things in fewer words, been less satisfied with seeming truths and uncertain conjectures, and taken more pains to build on the rock and not on the sand, that is to say, to lay down nothing but on clear and certain principles. It is only necessary to read the first book of his *Principles* or his *Meditations* to be convinced of that. Nothing is more ill-founded in this respect than the parallels that this writer draws between heresy and philosophy. . . .

The author of the treatise then objected to philosophy that it passed off as common opinions and the prejudices of habit, the notions most universally received by all men, as heresies make the things most universally received pass for popular opinions. Arnauld accepts the parallel, but with the conclusion that if "the heretics are wrong the philosophers are right."

Many judgments that men form on natural things may be false, although they may be common to all men, because they have a cause of error common to all men, namely, the prejudices of their childhood. For as long as we are children, judging things only by the senses, we are inclined to think that what we do not perceive by any sense does not exist. Thus we all think, in our

---

[1] Le Moine, dean of the chapter at Vitré, in Britanny, had composed a treatise on the essence of the body and of the union of the soul with the body, against the philosophy of Descartes. Arnauld, then at Delft, in Holland (1680), replied to it in a letter to his niece, the mother Angélique de Saint-Jean, which was found and published in 1780.

childhood, that there is nothing at all in a bottle when there is no more wine in it, because we do not see the air that has taken the place of the wine. We think, in the same way, that all heavy things fall of themselves; but there is this difference between these two false judgments, that many correct the first, because by degrees we learn about the air; for, being sometimes hot and sometimes cold, and being able to be moved with force by the wind or a fan against our faces, the sense of touch teaches us that we were deceived when we thought that it was nothing. But because we could not discover by any sense the subtle matter that draws down heavy bodies, it has been an opinion almost universally received by men before M. Descartes that they have themselves a certain quality, called heaviness, which is the cause of their fall. Now I maintain that he was right in not resting on this opinion, although it is universally received, because it is false, and destroys one of the clearest proofs of the divinity, which is that matter can never move of itself; so that, since there is movement in nature, matter must necessarily have received it from a higher cause, which can only be God. There are many other things in which M. Descartes has done well to reject as vulgar errors what is believed without reason, because it was believed in childhood, however universally received these opinions may be. . . .

In creating the philosophers of the present day, God does not give them a larger, more enlightened, and less defective intellect than He did to those who lived two thousand years ago. The general corruption of human nature does not diminish with the progress of the ages; rather it increases, and with it the blindness of the natural intellect. Nothing is less sound than this assertion. It is not a question of intellect in itself, whether it be greater and less defective in the men of the present day than in those of former times. It is, perhaps, equal in all men, and possibly it is only the manner of using it that makes some men more able than others. It is only a question, then, of ability itself, and not even of general ability, but only of that which regards the natural sciences. Now it is a ridiculous paradox to suppose that the most ancient have always been the most learned men, for the reason that the number of centuries increases the general corruption of human nature, and with it the blindness of the natural intellect. If that were so it follows that there were before the deluge more able physicians, more learned geometricians, and greater astronomers than Hippocrates, Archimedes, and Ptolemy. Is it not clear, on the contrary, that human sciences are perfected by time? I do not condescend to discuss it. It is plain that nothing is more ill-founded than what this writer advances on the *increase of blindness of the natural intellect*, in order to conclude from it, as he does, that M. Descartes is not comparable to the philosophers of antiquity. *We must not flatter the men of this age*, he says. *If they are compared, having only the light that they bring with them into the world and without that which they receive through instruction in the Christian verities, they are not comparable for energy of mind, soundness of judgment, and accuracy of reasoning with the great men of pagan antiquity.*

But it is rather those great men of pagan antiquity who are by no means to be compared in respect to the natural sciences, of which alone we are speaking, with the great men of these latter times. For all that Ptolemy and the most able astronomers of past ages knew of the heavens and of the courses of the stars does not approach what is known at present, since Copernicus and Tycho Brahé have carried this science very much farther than it was before their time; that Galileo has still more improved it by the use of telescopes; and that such men of our time as M. Huyghens and M. Cassini are still making new discoveries.[1] Galen understood anatomy best of all the ancients, and better described the uses of the parts of the human body; nevertheless, this is almost nothing if we compare it to what Harvey, Sténon,

---

[1] Ptolemy, a Greek astronomer, second century B.C.—Copernicus, a Pole (1473-1543), demonstrated the falsity of Ptolemy's theories, and founded the planetary system, which places the sun in the centre of the universe.—Tycho Brahé, a Swede (1546-1601); a better theory of the moon and numerous observations of the stars are due to him.—Cassini, Jean-Dominique (1625-1712), an Italian naturalized in France, the head of an illustrious family of scholars, author of some remarkable works on Jupiter, Mars, Venus, the satellites of Saturn and the Zodiacal light; organizer of the Observatory of Paris.—Huyghens, a Dutchman (1629-1695), a celebrated mathematician and astronomer. To him are especially due the discovery of Saturn's ring, the adaptation of the pendulum to clocks, &c. The disastrous revocation of the Edict of Nantes obliged him to leave France.

Willis,[1] and so many others have discovered in our time. How many things has chemistry (of which the ancients had no knowledge) made known in minerals, plants, and the parts of animals, of which the ancients had not the least suspicion, the least idea? The invention of the microscope has given us, as it were, new eyes to see an infinite number of God's works, of which the ancients had no knowledge. Is it otherwise than by reasoning more accurately than the ancients that it has been discovered that a vast number of effects, which they attributed to a fantastic horror of a vacuum, ought to be attributed to the gravity of the air? And, in fine, although Archimedes, Apollonius, and many other great men of antiquity have left us some very fine things in geometry and other parts of mathematics, a man must be a very bad judge of these things not to admit that M. Descartes has gone incomparably farther than all of them in his *Geometry* and *Dioptrics*.[2] I might say as much of music and mechanics; the two small tracts that he gave upon them, which are almost nothing, and which he wrote for pastime, are worth more than all the ancients wrote on both these sciences. . . .

OF THE UNION OF THE SOUL AND BODY.

I cannot avoid showing here some indignation against this opponent of M. Descartes' philosophy; for who can bear with patience that he should single out, in order to decry it, what all enlightened philosophers, if they are at all equitable, must admit to be his greatest glory, and what all pious persons must regard as a singular effect of God's Providence, which has willed to prevent the frightful leaning that many persons in these latter times seem to have towards irreligion and freethinking, by a means suitable to their disposition? They are people who will

---

[1] Galen, a Greek physician, second century A.D., much attached to the ideas of Aristotle, dominated medicine throughout the Middle Ages as his master did philosophy.—Harvey, an English physician (1578-1658); his most celebrated discovery was that of the circulation of the blood (1628). —Sténon, a Swedish anatomist (1638-1687).—Willis, an English physician (1622-1675).

[2] Dioptrics is that part of optics that especially treats of refraction and catoptrics of reflection.

accept nothing but what can be known by the light of reason, who have a thorough disinclination to begin by believing, who suspect all who profess piety to be weak-minded, and who close every avenue to religion by the opinion which they hold, and which is, in the greater number, a result of their moral corruption, that all that is said of another life is nothing but fables, and that everything dies with the body. There are minds of this sort in all religions, and still more now among heretics than among Catholics. And it is sufficiently clear that as long as they hold these false principles, it is not to be hoped either that the former will become sincere Catholics or the latter embrace piety and become good Christians. It seems, then, that it was most important, in order to remove the greatest obstacle to the salvation of all these people, and prevent this contagion from spreading more and more, to disturb them in their false repose, which only rests on their persuasion that it is a weakness of mind to believe that the soul survives the body. Now could God, who uses His creatures as it pleases Him, and in this way hides the operation of His providence, cause them this trouble, so well fitted to make them return to themselves, better than by raising up a man[1] who possessed all the qualities that this sort of people could desire, in order to abase their presumption, and force them at least to a proper mistrust of their pretended lights? a grandeur of mind quite extraordinary in the most abstract sciences; an application to philosophy alone, which is not suspicious to them; an open avowal to throw off all ordinary prejudices, which is much to their taste, and which, by that very fact, has found a way to convince the most incredulous, provided they will only open their eyes to the light that is presented to them, that nothing is more contrary to reason than to wish that the dissolution of the body, which is nothing but the disarrangement of certain parts of the matter that composes it, should be the extinction of the soul? And how did he discover that?

---

[1] Arnauld, alone at Port-Royal, exhibits this lively admiration for the genius of Descartes. I have shown in the Introduction, p. 28, Nicole's inconsistency on this point, and, p. 11, the prejudice of de Saci, who smiles at seeing Aristotle despoiled by a robber, who will be despoiled in his turn.

Precisely by doing what this author thinks it so bad that he has done, so depraved is his taste.

By establishing on clear principles solely founded on natural notions, with which every man of good sense should agree, that the soul and the body, that it is say, that which thinks and that which has extension, are two substances totally distinct; so that it is impossible that the extended substance should be a modification of that which thinks or that thought should be a modification of extended substance. For that alone being well established, as it is in the *Meditations* of M. Descartes, no free-thinker who has an equitable mind can remain convinced that our souls die with our bodies. For there are none who more readily agree that nothing that exists returns into nothingness, and that thus what is called the death of the body is the destruction of some parts of matter, which always remains in nature. They cannot, then, imagine that the thinking substance can be reduced to nothing, since the bodies themselves are not so reduced. And they must, besides, admit that what may be called destruction in the body cannot be suitable to that, because there can be neither change nor disarrangement of parts in a substance which has none, such as a thinking substance.

But this author, far from being grateful to M. Descartes for having so clearly established the distinction between soul and body, which is the only solid foundation of its immortality, makes it a reason for insulting him, as if he had spoilt everything by that. *If M. Descartes*, he says, *has found some new secret in nature, it is that of having separated soul and body rather than uniting them.* . . . He could not more highly praise those whom he undertakes to decry. Yes, we admit it, if anything renders M. Descartes commendable, it is to have so clearly separated soul and body, and to have so well established that they are two totally distinct substances, of which one only is material, that we need no longer trouble ourselves, after that, how two substances so different can be united to form one man. He need not carry his views very far before recognizing that it is infinitely more important to convince men that the thinking part in them is entirely different from that part of matter which forms their bodies, than to prove to them that this part of matter is joined to their soul.

They are sufficiently convinced of this union, and there is more reason to fear that they will carry it too far by conceiving of their soul only as a more subtle part of their body, like the Epicureans and the Stoics, than there is to fear that they may believe that their soul is to their body what a pilot is to a ship that he navigates. We know that this last was the idea of the Platonists; hence the definition that they gave of man was that he is a soul that governs a body. And St. Augustine deemed so little that this was a pernicious error, that he reproduces the opinion of these philosophers without condemning it in the book, *Morals of the Catholic Church*, ch. iv., admitting that it is a rather difficult question to solve. . . . M. de Pibrac,[1] also, has not been censured for saying the same thing in one of his quatrains, which have had great vogue, and have been translated into many languages :—

> That which you see of man is not man ;
> It is the prison in which he is shut up ;
> The tottering bed on which he sleeps a short sleep.

It is, therefore, very strange that this author was ignorant of such a common thing, which makes him exclaim, after having falsely attributed this operation to M. Descartes, *This thought is irrelevant, ridiculous, false, and heretical in philosophy itself, in the judgment of all men, in all times, and in every part of the world, except among the Cartists.*[2]

That is doubly false ; for it is not true that this was the operation of the Cartists ; and it is true that it was that of the great philosophers of antiquity. However it may be, although it might be said that the distinction that M. Descartes has so well estab-

---

[1] Gui du ▓▓▓, seigneur de Pibrac, born at Toulouse in 1529, died 1584, *président d▓▓▓rtier* and chancellor of Queen Marguerite at Nérac. Et. Pasquier calls him "one of the lights of the age." De Thou, in his *Mémoires*, says of him, "A man of incorruptible probity . . . a noble heart and generous mind." Montaigne also celebrates "the worthy Monsieur Pibrac, a mind so gentle, opinions so sound, manners so agreeable." (*Essays*, iii. 9.) His *Quatrains moraux, contenant préceptes et enseignements utiles pour la vie de l'homme public* were printed for the first time in 1574. "Translated into all the languages of Europe, and even into Arabic, Turkish, and Persian, they did more than secularize the teaching of virtue, they popularized it ; this very small book has truly been the catechism of several generations." (E. COUGNY, *Pibrac, sa vie et ses écrits*, 1869.)

[2] We say *Cartesians*, from the Latin name of Descartes, *Cartesius*. His philosophy is called *Cartesianism*.

lished between the soul and body might give reason to think of man as the Platonists did, this would be the prick of a pin in comparison with the great plague that he cured in destroying by this distinction the impious opinion of the mortality of the soul, which is principally founded on the idea that it is of the same nature as the body, and which is the most damnable of all errors, those who hold it being led to abandon themselves to all their passions, because, being persuaded that there is nothing to expect after this life, they have no curb to restrain them. Where, then, is the judgment of those who, being obliged to acknowledge, if they are at all fair, that the philosophy of M. Descartes has, without comparison, broken up more than any other the foundation of freethinking, hold it in small esteem, and do not show any gratitude towards him but are disturbed by the fear that it will lead men to think that they are not composed of body and soul? It is like a man who should quarrel with the doctor who had cured a mortal ulcer by a small incision, which it might be feared he would not be able to close. The comparison is exact, for here in the same way the fear is imaginary, the union of soul and body being at least as well explained in this philosophy as in any other.

(Arnauld, *Œuvres*, t. xxxviii. p. 90.)

EXCELLENT MAXIMS, INCLUDING SOME OF THE RULES THAT A PRECEPTOR SHOULD LAY DOWN FOR HIMSELF IN THIS EMPLOYMENT.

No art is without its rules, and no science without its principles and particular maxims.

It must not, then, be doubted that the Christian education of children has its own, which are as much more excellent as the end proposed is infinitely above the temporal conveniences and advantages that are the object of the other arts and sciences.

There would be a greater number of these maxims if we wished to repeat them all; I shall here set down only the principal, on which each man may, if he shall think fit, make others for his own special use.

To be very Assiduous with Children.

Nothing is so useful as assiduity for learning the temper, mind, and genius of children ;[1] they may be hid for some hours, but it is impossible for them to use a constant dissimulation. Thus we are in a better position to counteract their bad inclinations by seeing from what sources they spring. . . .

In order to judge how useful this assiduity is, we have only to consider that what Plautus says of the general of an army may be said of a preceptor, that disorders always happen when he is absent, which his presence, no doubt, would have prevented. . . .

To be very Watchful of Himself and Them.

It is not sufficient for a preceptor to be assiduous with the children confided to his care; besides that, he must be very watchful over himself and them.

Over himself, because children are lynx-eyed for the smallest actions, words, and movements of their masters, to make them the subject of their conversations and often of their raillery if they are not well disciplined; for this reason he should always be on his guard, as if he were in an enemy's country.[2]

He should also carefully watch over his children, for three reasons.

The first is that it is much easier to prevent faults than to correct them when they are once fixed in their hearts. Therefore it is necessary to reprove them constantly. That which has been once cut, as St. Bernard says, will quickly shoot out again in them; what has been driven away returns; what has been extinguished is relighted; and what has only been lulled to sleep soon awakens.

---

[1] These pedagogic reasons have quite another value than the motive so often given by the masters of Port-Royal, namely, the necessity of watchfulness to prevent the devil devouring his prey. (See Saint-Cyran, p. 76.)

[2] "Remember," says Mme. de Maintenon to the Ladies of Saint-Cyr, "that you must appear irreproachable to children. You cannot imagine how clear-sighted they are, and what small account they make of persons whom they do not esteem. . . . You must not think that you will impose upon children, they can discover the bad faith of persons who seek for pretexts to hide their defects or their passions. Truth, as you know, pierces through walls, and sooner or later appears, whatever care may be taken to hide it." (*Entretien*, Dec., 1706.)

The second reason is that the faults of children are usually imputed to the teachers, and attributed to their want of care or negligence.

In fine, the third and most important is the indispensable obligation they are under to answer for them to God. . . .

This watchfulness of the preceptor refers not only to those who are firm, whom he should, if possible, prevent from falling, but also to those who have fallen, to whom he should give a hand to raise them from their fall.

It should go so far as to take note of the tempers and dominant inclinations of the children, in order to quickly apply the remedies that prudence will show them to be the most useful, for it may be said that the strength of desire, which only ceases in us with death, is so much the more violent in them as the reason is weaker, and that they have as yet no experience of the world. It is necessary, then, to weaken and diminish it by retrenching all that is capable of fortifying and encouraging it.

In order to do this, it is necessary to note their inclinations and the direction of their natural disposition; that is to say, whether they are gentle, affable, and obliging, or, on the contrary, whether they are proud, irritable, and disdainful; whether they are sober and temperate, or whether they like drinking and good cheer; whether they have the fear of God, or are hasty and disobedient, &c.

But how are we to know this? you will say. I answer that their disposition soon shows itself in their conversation and actions.

But it is not sufficient to know what the disposition of children is, it must also be remedied. And this is the difficulty; for wherever there is opposition there is a struggle, which is unpleasing to human nature, which does not like to be reproved.

It is in this, then, that the vigilance, wit, and tact of a preceptor should appear; he should rouse a naturally slow child, and, on the contrary, soften and restrain a too impetuous and excitable nature.

On this subject, it has been remarked that those who had charge of the education of Sebastian, King of Portugal,[1] made a

---

[1] Sebastian, the successor of John III., in 1557. Philip II. perfidiously encouraged him to go to war in Morocco, where he met his death in the bloody battle of Alcazar-Kebir (1578). Portuguese nationality was lost until the awakening in 1640.

very great mistake, for he was of an ardent and fiery nature. As he burnt with the excessive desire of acquiring glory, there was material to form an Alexander if he had had the good fortune to find an Aristotle; but that failed him. Instead of moderating the excessive ardour that he showed in everything, he was allowed to follow his course. The most violent exercises were his ordinary diversions. He affected, in hunting, the chase of the wild boar, and went on the sea when it was most stormy, and he was praised for this. But at last this courage, which had not early been trained to submit to reason and allow itself to be conducted by its light, became fatal to him. He was carried away by his zeal to turn his arms against the Moors; and this zeal, which was good but not sufficiently under control, caused the loss of the battle of Alcacer, which brought on his subjects numberless miseries, and caused them to fall under the yoke of their greatest enemies.

It must, however, be admitted that more difficulty is found in the practice than in the theory of this maxim.

To have Special Regard to their Good Morals.

I have already said that there is much difference between the education that the pagans gave to their children and that which Christians should give theirs. As the former had only the world in view, they paid especial attention to making their children recommendable by the sciences and polite literature. But it is not so with Christians; they have heaven in view, for which the sciences are much less necessary than good morals.

We must imitate sometimes the sculptors, who are constantly removing their imperfections, and sometimes the painters, who finish their works by daily adding some new touch of the brush or some new lines of beauty.[1]

St. Chrysostom compares the soul of children to a golden city, in the midst of which the King of Heaven wishes to place His residence; and he compares the preceptor to the governor, who should watch over its preservation.

He says that its citizens are thoughts which go in and out by three principal gates, the eyes, the ears, and the mouth.

---

[1] These graceful expressions are borrowed from St. Chrysostom.

He wishes the council to take every precaution and to do its duty by setting trusty guards at these three gates, through which death may enter into the soul.

As to the eyes, which are, he says, very difficult to guard, he wishes children not to be taken to balls or the theatre.[1] For the mouth, he wishes care to be taken that the children hold proper discourse, that they do not sing secular songs, that they do not pass their time in answering, slandering, or laughing at persons. And as there is a great tie between the ears and the tongue, in order to provide for the safety of the ears, he forbids too great freedom of speech to be used before children, because they resemble echoes that only repeat what they have heard.

To Separate them from those whose Company might be Injurious to them.

As vices, whether bodily or mental, are easily communicated, and as they work their way by an imperceptible contagion even into the hearts of children, through their inclination to evil, one of the principal objects of the vigilance of a preceptor is to prevent the children under his care from having any intercourse with those of their own age who might corrupt them, especially if they are swearers, not decent in conversation, or given to wine and dishonesty, for children are usually very much disposed to imitate others in evil as well as good . . .

To have the Heart full of Charity towards them.

As in this employment the preceptor holds the place of the parents, he should endeavour to enter into their spirit, and fill his heart with the tenderness and love that nature has given them for their children; or, better, with the charity that . . . has all the tenderness of natural affection without its defects and weaknesses.

---

[1] All the masters of Port-Royal are unanimous in condemning the theatre. Lancelot gave up his preceptorship with the princesse de Conti, rather than take her children to the theatre. Nicole calls dramatic authors public poisoners, and does not even spare the *Cid*. Racine, who on this occasion quarrelled with Port-Royal, succeeded, however, in getting *Phèdre* approved by Arnauld.

This charity will teach him not to treat them in a base and flattering manner, overlooking the imperfections that he should correct; nor in a domineering manner, which would become hateful and insupportable to them, but in a manner always gentle and condescending, so that the children fear him as their master, respect him as their father, and love him as their best friend.

This will make him take every precaution to make them avoid what will be injurious to them.

This will lead him always to speak to them, not in a rough and repellent tone, but with a moderation and gentleness which will give them the confidence that they should always have in him. . . .

And, in fact, as heavy rains run over the surface of the ground without penetrating and fertilizing it, so rough words make no impression on the mind, into which they do not sink.

As studies give most trouble to young children, it will cause him to seek every means of relieving them; for example, by telling them the words that they cannot find, explaining the difficulties that stop them, and thus making their understanding of their authors more easy; in fine, by encouraging those of moderate capacity, and aiding them to learn their lessons, &c.

This charity also will make him bear with much patience a hundred small defects that age will cure; by showing very often greater signs of affection to those who have greater natural imperfections, and imitating in this way the conduct of mothers who caress more, says St. Bernard, the weakest of their children.

No doubt nothing is so useful both to the preceptor and to the children as this kindly and charitable conduct, because it is an infallible means for the preceptor to make himself loved, and to incline his children, in consequence, to study and virtue; for as the heart is the source of all actions, being once master of that, he gets done all that he wishes.

Love with all your heart, says St. Augustine, and afterwards do what you like to your neighbour. If you reprove him and become angry with him, he will not take offence, because he knows that you act in this way only because you love him; and even if you go so far as to chastise him, he accepts it, because he is convinced that you only wish for his good. . . .

To bear their Inattention to Study and all their other Defects with much Patience.

We must not be astonished to find defects in children. . . . Whether these defects proceed from the corruption of nature or the weakness of their age, it is necessary to bear them with much patience and compassion, and assist the children to correct them little by little. . . .

But, you will say, how is it possible to bear so many small trifles, whose repetition makes them tiresome, as also their inattention to study and their small liking for the finest things that are told them?

I admit that it is troublesome and annoying, and the more intelligence and energy a person has the more trouble he has to descend to these minutiæ.

But it is necessary, however, thus to descend, in order to elevate them little by little, and to imitate nurses, who are satisfied with giving milk to their little ones, waiting for them to grow and arrive at a state in which more solid food may be given them.

And, in fact, demanding reason from children and exacting from them firmness and attachment to what is good is like seeking fruit on a tree newly planted. We must put up with their weakness for some time. . . . We must remember the fine saying of St. Chrysologus, that a physician who will not suffer with the patient, and who does not become infirm with the infirm, is not in a position to restore him to health. . . .

To treat them, as far as possible, with great Gentleness.

It is not sufficient to bear the faults of children with great patience, but this toleration must be accompanied with great gentleness.

Experience sufficiently shows that children who are treated too severely, under the pretext of making them accomplished men, imperceptibly accustom themselves to dissimulate, and that under an appearance of virtue they conceal a fund of corruption and horrible licentiousness.

It is the same as regards studies, for too great severity in the master very often induces aversion for them. We must, then, as far as possible, and following Plato's advice, rather lead children to virtue and study by the gentleness of persuasion than by excessive rigour. . . .

Away, then, with those looks in which the marks of an odious severity are continually depicted ! We cannot expect by frightening children to make them respect us and to lead them to their duties, love being incomparably more powerful than fear in obtaining from them what we desire. . . .

"Labour rather," says St. Bernard, "to make yourselves loved by children than feared. And if sometimes it is needful to use severity, let it be the severity of a father, and not that of a tyrant. Show that you are the mothers of the children by treating them with much tenderness, and their fathers by reproving them for their faults. Cease to be haughty and cruel, and become gentle. Lay aside punishments and rods. . . ."

But when I say that a preceptor should treat his children with much gentleness, I do not mean that it should degenerate into an indulgence that encourages vice and tends to multiply faults which he is bound to punish, since this gentleness would be equally prejudicial to himself and the children.

And as the corruption of human nature seems at present to have reached its height, although it is to be wished that all children could always be treated with great mildness, there are some, nevertheless, with respect to whom we must be contented to keep it in our hearts, it being more advantageous to their wellbeing that we should always appear rather severe; and this it seems is what the Holy Spirit meant to confirm by opposing, as He does, that indulgence which is natural to parents, in many passages where He seems always to put the rod into their hands.

"He that loveth his son causeth him oft to feel the rod, that he may have joy of him in the end." (Eccles. xxx. 1.)

"He that spareth his rod hateth his son." (Prov. xiii. 24.)

"The rod and reproof give wisdom, but a child left to himself bringeth his mother to shame." (Prov. xxix. 15.)[1]

---

[1] The worthy Rollin will equally tax his ingenuity to soften the most precise texts by an interpretation inspired by his love of children: "The

To employ Exhortations rather than Threats in order to lead them to Piety and Virtue.

What a man does against his will and by a sort of constraint not only is not praiseworthy, but cannot even be lasting; for what is forced soon returns to its previous state, as a tree that has been forcibly bent soon returns to its former direction, whereas what is done from free choice is usually stable and permanent.

We must, then, always endeavour to render virtue lovable in itself, sometimes by praising before the children [1] those who are really virtuous, and sometimes by making them understand the shame and confusion by which bad actions are usually followed.

They must also always be exhorted to look to God rather than man in all their actions, and to fear much more in their thoughts the judgment of Him who penetrates the depths of the heart than men's reproof by words.

When they do well they must be encouraged to do better, because not to advance constantly on the road of virtue is to recede; and they must remember this proverb, that however good a horse may be, he always needs the spur. . . .

To add Good Examples to Good Teaching.

It is not enough to give children good instruction, we must also endeavour to give them good examples. . . .

Nothing has more influence on the mind, and especially the mind of children, who notice much more what they see their

---

Holy Scripture, by these and other similar words, means perhaps punishment in general, and condemns the false tenderness and blind indulgence of parents. . . . Supposing it necessary to take the word *rod* literally, there is great appearance that this chastisement is advised for those hard, gross, unteachable, and intractable characters which are insensible to reprimands or honour. But can we think that Scripture, so full of charity and mildness, and of compassion for weaknesses, even at a more advanced age, means that children should be treated harshly whose faults often spring rather from thoughtlessness than perversity?" (*Traité des études*, liv. viii.)

[1] This was not the opinion of M. de Saci. (See p. 93.) He advises Fontaine *to thank God in secret* for the good that he recognizes in children. Pascal, who laments that "admiration spoils everything in children," states, on the other hand, that "the children of Port-Royal, to whom this stimulus to envy and glory is not given, fall into heedlessness." (*Pensées*, éd. Havet, p. 449.)

teachers do than what they may say to them, and can have only contempt for the good that they propose when their actions are not conformable to their words.

And, in fact, can we listen to a man who does not listen to himself? And have we reason to think that he is convinced of the truths that he endeavours to make others believe, when he will not take the trouble to practise them?[1] . . .

A preceptor should be to his children like clear glass and like a beautiful mirror, in which they may see their spots and imperfections, or, again, like a rule, which corrects by its straightness whatever was uneven and defective. He must speak to them, I say, more by his actions than by his words, and must show them the way in which they should go more by acting than talking.

If he does himself what he intends to enjoin on those under his charge, not only will he correct their faults, but also he will shield himself from the just reproach that the Apostle addresses to those who do not act thus: "Why do you not teach yourselves, you who pretend to teach others!"

Now, nothing serves a teacher to set a good example so much as uniformity of conduct.

Lay down for yourselves, then, a good mode of life, and set yourselves a rule to follow, said Seneca; regulate all your actions by it, for irregularity of conduct is the mark of an inconstant mind which has no firm foundation. . . .

---

[1] Mme. de Maintenon sets this excellent lesson in a clearer light in a letter to a lady of Saint-Cyr: "You will make them reasonable only by imparting reason to them by your discourses and by your example, which will be still more efficacious than your words. They will be very nearly what you are; if you are sincere, they will be sincere; if you act uprightly, they will act uprightly; if you are remiss, they will be remiss; if you are superficial, they will be superficial; if you act otherwise when you are seen than you do when you are not seen, they will do the same; if you are in earnest, they will be in earnest in the things you give them to do; if you hide yourselves from your superiors, they will hide themselves from you." (A Mme. de la Mairie, 1714.)

OF CIVILITY AND POLITENESS IN CHILDREN.

It is not sufficient to do good, but we must always endeavour to do it in the best manner possible. . . . And, in fact, as meats good in themselves but badly seasoned are not very agreeable, so a good action awkwardly done cannot be pleasing.

What I here call politeness and civility is an easy, open, and becoming manner; and I maintain that, in order to acquire it, not only is it necessary to learn its maxims early, but to put them in practice, according to this axiom of the philosophers, that things that are learnt for use are best learnt by use. Now the politeness of children should especially appear in their deportment and their behaviour at table, as well as in their conversation.[1]

Of the Manner in which they should Sit and Behave at Table.

They should always sit upright, without moving their arms and legs about, and, if possible, without inconveniencing those who are near them.

It is very impolite to be constantly looking at the dishes, and devouring with our eyes all the viands that are served up.

You must not put your hand in the dish first, nor show signs of impatience before you are served, or too much haste and eagerness in eating what has been given you.

Put gently on your plate what is offered you, bowing your head slightly, to thank him who serves you, without taking off your hat,[2] unless to persons who are of higher rank than yourself, and for whom you are bound to have a marked respect.

---

[1] Coustel justifies himself for entering into details that may appear trivial by this judicious saying of Quintilian: "What must be done deserves to be learnt." The annexed extract on behaviour at table is a very curious study of manners.

[2] *La Bienséance de la conversation entre les hommes*, published at Pont-à-Mousson in 1618, mentions this custom of wearing the hat at meals: "When you are at table, it is sufficient to make a slight bow, *for it is not seemly to uncover at table*."

Father de la Salle recommends the guests to remain standing and uncovered until grace has been said, and not to put on their hats until they are seated, and the most distinguished persons have put on theirs." (*Les Règles de la bienséance et de la civilité chrétienne.*)

Never refuse what is offered, for this would be a tacit reproach either that it has not been well chosen or to show that it is not to your taste.

It is advantageous to habituate yourself early to cut the meat neatly, to present it gracefully, and even to learn which is the best part of a capon, a partridge, or waterfowl.[1]

If you may take the liberty of putting your hand in the dish, take what is before you, without seeking right and left what may seem to you better.

If there is a nice piece, never take it for yourself, but present it to those whom you have invited, or who are the most distinguished in the company.

Keep your eyes on your plate, without constantly looking over others to see what they are eating.

Take what is served you with your fork, and not with your fingers.

Do not put very large pieces into your mouth nor inflate your cheeks in eating, as if you were blowing the fire.

Do not break your bread with your hand, but always use your knife to cut it.

Masticate the meat you have in your mouth slowly; this contributes very much to health, for the second digestion does not correct the imperfection of the first.

Never dip in the dish a morsel you have already put in your mouth.

Avoid as much as possible a diversity of meats, for nothing ruins the stomach so much, or is so prejudicial to health.

Never begin a meal by drinking; that has too much the appearance of the drunkard, who drinks more by habit than necessity. Never be the first to drink. Wipe your mouth, and swallow what you have in it before drinking.

Always put water in your wine. Pure wine is to the body what oil is to fire; for it inflames it more, instead of moderating and diminishing the heat that is consuming it.

---

[1] Father de la Salle enters into kitchen details on the different meats, boiled or roast, and fish, "in order that you may not take the best parts for yourself (which might happen by mistake, for want of knowing), and may offer them seasonably to those to whom it is fitting." (*Civilité chrétienne*, p. 107.) Coustel, a few lines further on, gives the same reason.

If anyone does you the honour of drinking your health, modestly thank him who does so.

Do not make a boast of drinking to excess; a barrel has a much greater capacity than the largest stomach.

The custom of forcing others to drink the healths which have been proposed, to the prejudice of their own, is neither honest nor praiseworthy; a man must be a glutton and unmannerly to do so.

Equals do not offer things to one another, presuming to do so is attempting to take the upper hand and act the host.

It is showing too great daintiness to complain that the viands are ill-cooked, or that they are not to our taste.

If the company remain too long at table you may retire quietly, after saluting them in a civil and obliging manner.

OF CONVERSATION.

Conversation must not be judged by the oddities and bad temper of certain melancholy persons, but by the general feeling that the Author of Nature has imprinted on the mind of all men. God did not give them the use of speech to make them pass their lives in the deserts, but to converse with one another, that they may learn what they did not know, and may perfect themselves in the knowledge of what they already know. As, then, conversation sharpens the wit, forms the judgment, makes us know ourselves, and not have a blind attachment to our own opinions, in fine, as it teaches us to live with everybody in an honest and seemly manner, we are right in calling it the school of wisdom and the teacher of civility. We may say that it is certainly very useful, and may even go farther and maintain that it is necessary. And, in fact, there are very many things that Jesus Christ commands in the gospel that can only be done by conversing with men, as, for example, consoling the afflicted, instructing the ignorant, correcting those who commit faults, and setting on the right road those who have strayed.

Admitting, then, the necessity for conversation, it may be asked here, What ought to be its qualities? with what persons should we converse? how should young persons conduct themselves in it? what are the principal faults to be avoided? . . . Oaths, blasphemy, indecent and equivocal words should be banished from it, and, in a word, nothing should ever be said that may pain the listener or shame the speaker.

It should be very circumspect. Thus it is ill to play the cheerful man before persons who are afflicted or the sad with those who only think of amusing themselves. . . .

It should be respectful and full of deference, especially towards women and the aged, to whom good breeding should lead us to give the best places. . . .

In the fourth place it should be sincere; for, as soon as we accustom ourselves to disguises and deceit, we lose all influence, and get involved in many awkward affairs.

In fine, it should be charitable towards ourselves and towards others; towards ourselves, by profiting by what is said; for if a learned man is speaking all that he says instructs, and if a thoughtless person he should make those who listen to him more reticent, in order not to commit the same faults.

It is also necessary in conversation to be charitable towards others by falling in with their humour, by interpreting favourably all that they say, by overlooking their defects, and, in fine, by preventing improper talk and slander, if we have sufficient authority for that, or, at least, in showing by our coolness and silence that we will take no part in it.

It may be asked here if women's conversation is advantageous to young men; to which it is not difficult to respond, if we follow the light of Christianity rather than the corrupt maxims of the age. . . . There is danger, no doubt, in the conversation of women, who are called, on this subject, the snares of the devil, and the net in which those who are not on their guard are caught.[1] . . .

To show here that young men seldom think of forming their minds by conversing with women, and of learning, as they say, politeness and civility, they do not usually like the conversation of those who are somewhat old, although their seriousness and

---

[1] Nicole says, not very gallantly: "Having a woman for adviser is having a double concupiscence." (*Essais de Morale*, t. vi. p. 266.) This was not Franklin's opinion.

great experience might be more useful to them; but they like bodily much more than mental beauty; and the brightness of a young face has more charms for them than the marks of extraordinary virtue and merit in an old person. . . .

It is necessary to become acquainted with the ceremonies that are practised in the country where we are. I mean by ceremonies the outward marks of honour and respect that are paid to certain persons. . . .

Ceremonies must be used with much prudence and propriety, not too sparingly nor too prodigally.

To use none is boorish; to use them through interest is disguise and flattery; to use them with persons who are very busy is indiscreet; and to use them with those whom we do not intend to oblige is an insult.

Useless ceremonies should not be affected, refusing, for instance, the first place when it is undoubtedly our due, and offering battle, as they say, in order not to enter a door first.

You must not walk about when the others are sitting down, nor bite your nails nor pick your teeth before company, thus showing that their society is not agreeable, and that you seek amusement by these little pastimes.

When you are seated you must not lean upon others nor turn your back to them, nor stretch out your arms nor make unbecoming gesticulations; such liberties are only allowable in persons of much higher rank than the others.

It is a fundamental maxim of our religion always to treat others as we wish to be treated ourselves. Always excuse, then, the faults of others, and put a good construction on their actions and words. Thus, if on entering someone does not salute you, do not say that he despises or disdains you; but rather suppose that he did not see you, or that his mind was elsewhere and occupied with something else.

Endeavour to keep an even temper, and fall in with the temper of others when it is not in sympathy with your own.

Complaisance is the soul of society and the seasoning of conversation. It should, then, be very great with respect to everybody, yet without ever making us approve of what is manifestly unjust and bad. . . .

Always be more pleased to listen to what others say than to talk yourself, and on this subject remember what Plutarch says, "that Numa taught the Romans to reverence more than any other a goddess to whom he gave the name of *Tacita* (the Silent). . . ."

The advantage gained by silence is that it makes those who know how to observe it pass before the world as very wise, however ignorant and stupid they may be.[1]

There are times when nothing should be said, there are others when it is necessary to say something; but there are none when it is necessary to say all that we know.

Be very reserved when you are in company where there are persons of rank, very learned men, and old men to whom age has given much experience.

When you take upon yourself to speak, be careful of these three things: of what you speak, before whom you have to speak, how you ought to speak.

Do not open your mouth before you have well arranged and digested in your mind what you have to say,[2] lest your thoughts be like those abortions which have not had sufficient time to be perfectly formed; for the trouble we have in expressing ourselves usually comes from the fact that we have not thoroughly arranged what we have to say; for we always express ourselves well when we have arranged in our minds what we wish to say. . . .

Do not undertake to speak of things which are above your capacity, and only speak of those that you think you know best with great moderation and reserve.

If you wish to pass for an able man strive to be really so; for

---

[1] Grimarest, in the *Life of Molière*, relates a very amusing scene. Molière and Chapelle, returning by water from Auteuil to Paris, were discussing about Gassendi and Descartes before a friar minim who was on the boat, and the two speakers took him for judge. The friar minim only replied by "*hum! hum!*" or by motions of his head. Our philosophers were a little confused on perceiving a little later by his wallet that he was a serving brother, and quite a stranger to these questions. Molière then said to the young baron who accompanied them, "See, my lad, what silence does when it is carefully observed."

[2] "There are people," says La Bruyère shrewdly, "who speak a moment before they have thought." (*Caractères*, ch. iv.)

time, which discovers all, will show you such as you are; and there may be someone in the company who will perhaps expose your ignorance to your mortification.

If an opportunity offers of telling some story, come to the point at once, without stopping to make a long and tiresome preface, and always use in telling it proper, natural, and pleasing expressions. . . .

Always endeavour to excuse him of whom evil is spoken; and if you cannot excuse the action that is blamed, excuse at least its motive by saying that he was surprised, and that he did not sufficiently reflect. If you cannot excuse the motive, attribute his act to human infirmity and the strength of the temptation which would very likely have carried away others if they had been in the same position as he.

If anyone says something indecent, either pretend not to have heard it, or show by your coolness or silence that you are unwilling to take any part in it.

It is not necessary in company to remain always silent nor to be continually talking; the first would be a mark of stupidity or contempt, and the other would show a too great assumption of capacity. It is right for everyone to pay his share as much for food for the mind as for food for the body.

Conversation should always be adapted to the places and the persons with whom we are. Thus it is ungraceful to play the Cato[1] before women, or the preacher before people who are thinking only of amusing themselves.

Points of theology or questions difficult to resolve should not be brought forward at table, but only those things on which each may express his ideas without too much concentration of mind. . . .

If a man has advanced an extravagant or pernicious opinion it is useful and even praiseworthy for him to change it; whereas it would be a shameful thing to change an opinion that is just and true. It is only persons of understanding and judgment, says St. Augustine, who recall things ill said; and a man is

---

[1] Cato the Censor (233-183 B.C.), celebrated for his severity against luxury, especially that of women.

usually more admired when he becomes, against himself, the censor of an opinion advanced out of season than if he had never held it, or if he had corrected another. . . .

Jokers, boasters, and great talkers are not usually liked.

Here, however, innocent joking must be distinguished from that which is altogether odious.

For there is joking that is not only permissible but which even enlivens conversation, and, therefore, those who succeed in it are always well received. Now I call a joke a sensible thing said to the point, and which amuses. For this it should be:—

1. Subtle and refined, for both the joke and the joker are laughed at when it is not so.

2. The things that are joked upon should not be serious or criminal, for there is no subject for joking when there is no subject for laughing.

3. Great defects of body or mind should not be taken as subjects for it. Man did not make himself; God made him as he is; it is upon Him then that the jokes fall.

4. Joking must be used with discretion; thus we should never joke about the powerful.

5. We should never joke about the wretched, because they are worthy of compassion.

In fine, joking should be used in moderation, for excess is always blamable, and there is no pleasure in driving people to extremes.

I do not speak here of those whose jokes are stinging, and who do not care if they give pain and trouble to others, provided that they show themselves off and acquire the reputation for wit. Nothing lowers and makes a young man disliked more than that.

Boasters, again, are very disagreeable persons in conversation, for they have always in their mouths the names of their ancestors and their estates, and talk only of their own clever schemes.

Be afraid of pleasing yourself, lest you please yourself alone. It is the same with the good qualities of our minds as with the nudity of our bodies. We should always hide them from our servants, and modesty does not permit us to dwell on them.

There are also odd people who love only themselves, whom

everything that others say displeases, and who think nothing well done which they do not do themselves.

Obstinate and opinionated persons are also very disagreeable.

When things are of small consequence we should not wish to carry them with a high hand; victory is always dangerous in this sort of encounters, since we often lose a good friend for a thing of no value. Besides, we show our bad humour in good company.

(Coustel, *Règles de l'éducation des enfants*.)

ON THE PERSECUTIONS OF PORT-ROYAL.[1]

... There must be a strange confusion in the affairs of this world, since we see those who may certainly be said to have done some service to the Church persecuted, ill-treated, calumniated, and oppressed under the fictitious name of an imaginary sect, and scarcely daring to defend themselves against the most unjust and outrageous accusations; and those, on the contrary, who dishonour the Church by their ignorance and passion, as M. Mallet has done, held in honour and credit, and not only free from fear of punishment for their excesses, but making themselves feared, through the power that is given them, by all those whom they consider their enemies, because they are the enemies of their errors, their extravagances, and their falsehoods.

Nevertheless, after all, we have no reason to be astonished at this conduct. God permits it, God ordains it, for the good of His elect. And, considering it in this light, we should not only submit to it, but adore and kiss the hand which strikes us. I adore the infinite variety of Thy commands, O my God, ever just, ever holy in the government of Thy creatures, both old and new, that is to say, the world and the Church.

---

[1] "We can scarcely read now those great volumes of heavy discussion. Their conclusion alone need be noticed for its eloquence and sentiment. It is said that the Chancellor Le Tellier could never tire of reading these pages nor of making his friends read them; his enthusiasm, however, did not lead him so far as to repeat anything of them to the king. Racine, it is said, re-read them with a lively admiration which I wish we could share for the moral beauty of it!" (SAINTE-BEUVE, *Port-Royal*, t. v. p. 297.)

It would be showing little faith in Thy promises to be moved by what is passing in these days of clouds and darkness, *in diebus nubis et caliginis*, as Thou in Thy Scriptures callest these times of trouble and tempest, in which it seemeth that Thou abandonest innocence to the rage of the wicked, and takest pleasure in permitting vice, injustice, and violence to triumph. What, after all, can they do to those who put their confidence only in Thee, and only love eternal things?[1]

They deceive princes, and cause them to take their most faithful servants for enemies. But the heart of kings is in Thy hands, and Thou canst change it in a moment by discovering what is hidden from them, and removing the false impressions that have been given them. If it do not please Thee to dissipate these clouds, should it not suffice Thy servants that the depths of their hearts are known to Thee, waiting till Thou give grace to princes, who are incited against them, to penetrate the artifices by which they are prejudiced, and to use their power only for the punishment of the wicked and the protection of the good, for it is for this only that Thou hast given it to them, as Thy apostles declare.

In the meanwhile they are proscribed, banished, and deprived of liberty. Can a Christian, to whom all the earth is a place of exile and a prison, be much troubled by a change of dungeon? Thou art found everywhere, O my God. Even loaded with fetters, those who possess Thee are more free than kings. No prison is to be dreaded but that of a soul whose vices and passions hold it confined and prevent it enjoying the liberty of the children of God, and this it was that made one of Thy saints[2] say that the conscience of a wicked man is full of darkness, more fatal and more horrible, not only than all prisons, but even than hell itself.

But we may die from the fatigues and labours of a wandering life. Should we avoid it if we were more at ease? A little sooner, a little later, what is that when compared with eternity?

---

[1] This sentiment of confidence also greatly animated the Mother Angélique Arnauld when she supported the courage of her nuns: "What! are we weeping here? Come, my children, what is this? Have you no faith? At what are you surprised? What! men are bestirring themselves; well! they are flies that make a little noise when they fly. Do you trust in God and yet fear? Believe me, fear Him alone, and all will be well."
[2] Saint Augustine.

Thou hast numbered our days; we came into the world when Thou wouldest, and go from it when it pleaseth Thee. The evils of this world affright us when they are seen from afar; we grow accustomed to them when they are present, and Thy grace renders all things endurable; and besides, they are always less than we deserve for our sins. Thou hast taught us by Thine apostle that all who serve Thee should be willing to say like him: *I know both how to be abased, and I know how to abound: everywhere and in all things I am instructed, both to be full and to be hungry, both to abound and to suffer need. I can do all things through Him who strengtheneth me.*

But how far are we still removed from the state of those of whom the same apostle says: *they were destitute, afflicted, tormented, of whom the world was not worthy, wandering in the deserts and on the mountains, and hiding in dens and caves of the earth!*

We have but to acknowledge Thy bounty, O Lord, who hast condescended to treat as weak those whom Thou knowest to have yet not much strength. Thou fulfillest the promises of Thy Gospel, and givest them, in place of what they have left for love of Thee, fathers, mothers, brethren, and sisters, in whom Thou breathest a charity so tender towards those whom they regard as suffering for the truth, and so great diligence in supplying all their needs, that by singular goodness Thou changest the cross that Thou layest upon them into sweetness and consolation. But they trust in Thy mercy that if Thou preparest for them harder trials Thou wilt also give them more grace and a greater abundance of Thy Spirit to support them as true Christians. This is the sole foundation of their confidence; for they know well that we can do nothing without Thee, and that however persuaded we may be of the truths that Thou teachest us, they are only practised when Thou makest them pass from the mind to the heart, and that Thou fulfillest that which one of Thy saints has said, that Thou alone settest the will to the good work, and removest the difficulties to make it easy for the will. . . . I am ready then, O my God, to follow Thee wherever it shall please Thee to lead me; and though I walk through the shadow of death, I will fear nothing while Thou leadest me by the hand. On this hope I rest, and shall await with patience until, being softened by the prayers of so many good men, Thou restore to Thy Church the tranquillity that she cannot enjoy unless Thou quellest, by the authority of Thy ministers, the stormy winds of human opinions that strive to raise themselves above the truths of Thy Gospel, and until Thou appease by Thy Word the storms that carnal men raise when they are troubled in the right they think they have to live as heathens and none the less to expect the rewards of the other life, which Thou hast only promised to true Christians.[1]

(Arnauld, *Œuvres*, t. vii. p. 902.)

THE CONSTITUTIONS OF THE MONASTERY OF PORT-ROYAL DU SAINT-SACREMENT.[2]

Of the Instruction of the Girls.[3]

Girls may be received in the monastery for instruction in the fear of God during several years, but not for one year only, because that is not sufficient to form them in good morals according to the rules of Christianity.

Those only will be received whose parents desire them to be instructed in this way, and who offer them to God without an expressed desire for them to be nuns or lay persons, but as it may please God to ordain.

The girls shall be in a department separate from the nuns, with a mistress to instruct them in virtue, to whom assistants will be given to instruct them in reading, writing, needlework, and other useful things, and not those which only minister to vanity.

---

[1] Many men have spoken of their misfortunes, their unmerited troubles, and their noble poverty, and have even turned them to account to make an ostentatious display. What renders the words which we have just read really noteworthy is that there is not a syllable that is not sincere, that Arnauld says nothing more than he feels and is ready to do on the instant; the character of the writer confirms and completes the eloquence. I have been obliged to quote the whole passage, which was formerly celebrated. It is classic in the history of the exiled Arnauld. (SAINTE-BEUVE, *Port-Royal*, t. v. p. 300.)

[2] "The Constitutions of the monastery of Port-Royal du Saint-Sacrement, which are the result of the instructions of M. de Saint-Cyran, were written by the Mother Agnès (at the time of the foundation of the Institut du Saint-Sacrement in 1647), after having been long practised. They were printed for the first time in 1666." (*Mémoires* de Lancelot, t. i. p. 423.)

[3] See Introduction, p. 46.

They will wear the novices' dress; nevertheless, they shall not be compelled to do so at first, if they show any dislike to it, until familiarity and the sight of their companions make them desire it. If anyone persists in not wishing it, she shall wear secular dress, but not silk, and without lace, in order that the others may not envy her.

They shall sing in the choir at certain hours when they shall be of age to do so, and demand it; as also in the refectory, where they shall sit at a separate table with their mistress.

No more than twelve girls, under ten years of age, will be received, lest the charity that the sisters show in that be prejudicial to them, by giving them too much occupation, and withdrawing them from their other duties; and also that they may fulfil their duties more perfectly, without failing in any attentions necessary to their good education.

They may be kept until the age of sixteen years, although they do not wish to be nuns, provided that they are docile and modest, that they take no liberties, and profit by the instruction given them, confirming themselves more and more in Christian virtue. If, on the contrary, they have a vain and worldly temper, they shall be promptly dismissed, at any age, lest they corrupt the rest.

If one had lost her mother, and it were beneficial for her to remain after the age of sixteen, permission may be asked of the superior to keep her, and action will be taken as he shall think fit.

The number of junior girls shall be at the most twelve, as we have said; nevertheless, when they have passed the age of ten years they shall not be considered juniors, and younger girls may be taken in their place, although they still live in the monastery, because there is much less care and work with them than with the younger.

The nuns shall not ask to receive girls, nor use any influence with the parents to make them give them, not even with those who are related to them; this should proceed from their own proper impulse, and a sincere desire for the good education of their children.

Girls of three or four years of age, who have no mother, will be more easily and willingly received, and all necessary assistance will be affectionately given them in their helplessness, considering in this that the charity is so much greater as these young orphans are sometimes badly brought up, having no mother to watch over them.

And let not the sisters think this an occupation ill-fitted for their position, namely, to undertake the bringing-up of children who are not yet capable of receiving any instruction for their salvation, since in that they imitate God Himself, who first formed the body of the first man, into which He then inspired the breath of life.

Let them take, then, for their share the nourishment of their small bodies with all necessary care, until their age is fitted for the infusion of grace, by this means becoming like the mothers of these children, which will make their virginity fruitful before God, whose spouses they are, as He is the Father of souls and spirits according to St. Paul.

The sisters who shall be employed in this duty having undertaken, as has been said, a work of charity, should consider that it is at the same time an exercise of patience, there being much to suffer from these little creatures, and a great restraint with them.

Let them not complain of either, but make themselves, for the love of Christ, who became a child for us, the servants of these children in whom He Himself dwells, humbling Himself in their weaknesses. Let them also bear with their little tempers, which are sometimes very tiresome. Let them never reprove them by a movement of anger, but let them suspend punishment until their emotion has passed, and that the children themselves may think that they do not love them less when they punish than when they caress them.

The mistresses will take great care not to be partial towards the children, not loving more those who are more agreeable and pretty, in order not to make the others jealous. Let them not amuse themselves by playing with them more than is necessary for their diversion, while they are still incapable of joining the other girls, nor permit the children to caress them too much, nor attach themselves too much to them, which would make them ill-humoured with others who might be given to them.

They must only gain their affections in so far as they are their mistresses, and not as private persons. And although children are not able to make this distinction, the mistresses should do so, and oblige the children to give as much to one of the mistresses as to another. For example, if a child would not obey one of the mistresses because she liked her less, the other mistress, instead of being gratified that this child liked her more, should show severity, and make her give her companion the obedience which is due to her.[1] And as a proof that the sisters do not wish to be loved by the children, except for the good of the children themselves, when they are removed from this office they will no longer caress them when they meet them any more than the other sisters do, who should never so amuse themselves, even if they should be their relations, except in so far as the mother should think convenient, in order to accustom the children on their first entrance, or under some special circumstances. With these exceptions, they will not show any tenderness they may feel for them, and they will make a sacrifice of it to God, to obtain from His goodness that these children may benefit by the good education that will be given them.

When the mistresses take the children to the parlour they will not exhibit a too marked affection for them before the parents; but only show that they love them so far as they are obliged, and that they take the greatest possible care of them. They will not praise the children too much, if some were very pretty, but will simply say that they are very docile, or something of the sort. They will not blame them for their faults nor accuse them of anything, unless the mother has expressly told them to do so; if they are questioned to know if they are bad or tiresome, they will say that much still remains to be done, without showing that they are wearied or disgusted with it, in order not to give pain to the

---

[1] Mme. de Maintenon gives the same recommendation to the Ladies of Saint-Cyr, but with less measure and accuracy: "If the girls carry flattery so far as to give you to understand that they like you more than they like the others, show *such a profound contempt for this baseness*, and so great a desire that your sisters may be not less esteemed and loved than yourself, that they may understand that you are far from taking pleasure in their discourse. It would be very wrong to let them perceive that you had this weakness." (*Entretiens*, 1703.)

parents. They will ask nothing for the children without the permission of the mother, not even toys, nor books, nor anything else, as much not to importune the parents as not to give occasion for jealousy to the others, to whom nothing will be given. And for this reason it would be desirable that they were all equal;[1] therefore we shall continue, as heretofore, to undertake their maintenance in order to avoid the inequality that is found among their parents, some of whom would give liberally and others would withhold what would be necessary for them, which would make the former proud and give pain to the others; this is avoided by treating them almost all equally, so far as discretion permits.

The junior girls shall not be left in the parlour alone when they are very young, nor when they are older, unless with their father and mother, if they desire it, and only for a very short time.

The very young children should never be lost sight of, lest they fall and hurt themselves; they will not even be allowed to play together in a remote part of their room, but will be constantly watched, to correct them in the small irregularities they may commit.

The senior girls shall not be exempt from this supervision; on the contrary, the inconveniences may be greater; therefore equal or greater care will be taken that they shall not be left without a person to take charge of them.

They are not to be allowed to whisper together, however little. One of the mistresses is to sleep in their room, and in going through the monastery to the choir and the refectory, they are always to be conducted, care being taken that they do not go together. In fine, constant attention must be given to remove from them, as far as possible, all occasions of doing harm to one another, which is usually what most corrupts the young. . . .

The sisters who shall be employed in the care of the children

---

[1] It was unavoidable to make some exception in an age when ranks were so distinct. We see in Leclerc that Mlle. d'Elbœuf, who entered Port-Royal at the age of nine years, was the object of special care in the boarders' room; the Mother Angélique had a small space divided off where she slept. "As to food, she was served first, and her ordinary fare was also different. . . . At thirteen she had a room to herself and a sister to wait on her. . . ." (*Vies intéressantes*, t. iii. p. 183.)

shall act, as has been said, with great affection and fidelity, and at the same time great indifference, dreading this charge on account of the many opportunities it gives of committing errors, of diverting themselves too much, and of losing the spirit of meditation, which it is not easy to preserve in such an important occupation; if, nevertheless, obedience retains them in it, let them trust that God will support them, and that the charity which necessarily accompanies this duty will cover their faults. Let them know also, for their consolation, that in taking care to bring up these children well, they are recalling before God the years of their own childhood and youth, which they perhaps employed ill for want of a similar education.

REGULATIONS FOR THE CHILDREN OF PORT-ROYAL.
Advertisement.

Although this regulation for children is not a mere fancy, but has been drawn up on what has been practised at Port-Royal des Champs during many years, it must, nevertheless, be admitted that, for what is external, it would not always be easy nor even useful to put it in practice with all its severity. For it may be that all the children are not capable of such strict silence and so strained a life without being depressed and wearied, which must be avoided above all things, and that all mistresses cannot keep them under such exact discipline, gaining at the same time their affection and love, which is absolutely necessary in order to succeed in their education. It is the part of prudence, then, to moderate all these things, and, according to the saying of a pope, to join the strength which retains the children without repelling them to a gentleness that wins them without enervating them: *Sit rigor, sed non exaspe*... *; sit amor, sed non emolliens.*

Regulation for the Children.
To Monsieur Singlin, April 15, 1657.

I humbly beg your pardon for having so long delayed to give you an account of the manner in which I act with children.[1]

---

[1] Jacqueline Pascal, younger sister of Pascal, born in 1625, retired from the world in which she had early shone by her wit and a certain poetic

What prevented me doing so from the first word you said to me about it was, that I thought you asked me to set down in writing how they ought to be treated, which I did not think myself able to undertake without great temerity, having so little knowledge for so difficult an employment. For I can assure you that obedience alone can make me do the least thing in it, and if I do not spoil all, it is to be attributed to the efficacity of the words of our mother, who told me, when giving me the charge, not to be anxious about anything, and God would do all. This so appeased the trouble in which my impotence had put me, that I remained full of confidence and with as much tranquillity as if God Himself had given me this promise, and I acknowledge to my confusion that, when I look at myself and fall into despondency, as you know I do very often, these words alone, *God will do all*, repeated with confidence, restore peace to my mind. But what removed my trouble was that you told me afterwards that you did not ask me to write how they should be treated, but only how I treated them, in order to notice the faults that I commit, which not only destroy what God does in it through me, but even place great obstacles to the grace that He puts in these souls. . . .

I. *In what spirit we should render service to the children. Union of the mistresses. Some general advice for their conduct, chiefly towards the younger children.*

1. I think, then, that to be useful to the children, we should never speak to them, nor act for their good, without looking to God and asking His grace, desiring to take in Him all that is needful to instruct them in His fear.

2. We should have great charity and tenderness for them, neglecting them in nothing whatever, either spiritual or bodily, showing them upon every occasion that we set ourselves no limits

---

talent, and entered Port-Royal in 1652, where she took the name of sister Sainte-Euphémie. From 1657 to 1659 she had charge of the education of the children, and, in virtue of this, drew up the annexed regulation. She was afterwards sent to Port-Royal des Champs, as sub-prioress, to direct the novices. She died in 1661 from sorrow and remorse at having signed the formulary against her conscience in deference to the authority of Arnauld. M. Cousin has devoted a volume full of interest to this distinguished woman.

for their service, and that we do it with affection and with all our heart, because they are children of God, and that we feel ourselves obliged to spare nothing to render them worthy of this sacred title.

3. It is very necessary to devote ourselves to them without reserve and not to leave their quarters without unavoidable necessity, in order to be always present in the room where they are working, if we are not talking to them or visiting them when they are ill or employed in other things which concern them.

4. No difficulty should be made in missing all the service for this, unless the elder children are present at it. The constant care of the children is of such importance, that we should prefer this duty to all others,[1] when obedience lays it on us, and much more than our own private gratification, even when it concerns spiritual things. The charity with which all the services which are useful to them will be given, will cover not only many of our faults, but will take the place of many things that we think would be useful for our own perfection.

5. There will be a sister on whom we can rely, without in any way relieving us of our duty. This sister who will be given us should be attached, as far as possible, to the schoolroom. Therefore it would be desirable to have two, animated with the same zeal and the same spirit for the children, and who most often should be together in the schoolroom, even in the presence of the head mistress, in order that, seeing the respect with which the children behave before her, they may both have the right to demand for themselves the same respect in her absence as in her presence.

6. We should act in such a manner that the children may notice a great harmony and perfect union and confidence with the sister who is given to us for a companion. She should not, therefore, be reproved for what she has done or ordered, if what she has ordered is not well, in order that the children should

---

[1] For greater security, Mme. de Maintenon will make the Ladies of Saint-Cyr, in addition to the usual vows of poverty, chastity, and obedience, take a fourth and special vow, namely, to devote themselves to the education of the girls of Saint-Cyr.

never notice any contrariety, but should be warned privately. For it is important, and almost necessary, in order to govern the children well, that the sister who is given as assistant should be inclined to think everything good that is said to her. If it were not so, it would be necessary to report it to the mother superior. If what she might do contrary to us only touched our temper, and did no harm to the children, we should demand God's grace to rejoice that we had an occasion to be vexed.

7. We should pray to God to give the children a great respect for the sisters who are with us. We should also give them great authority, but especially to her who is next to us. It is well, then, to show the children, and even tell them at times, that she has a great charity for them, that she loves them, and that we order her to tell all that takes place in the schoolroom, and to tell her before the children that she is obliged by duty and charity to tell us not only all their greater faults, but even their slight failings, in order to aid them in correcting them.

8. We put a sort of confidence in the sisters who aid us, by telling them the inclinations of the children, especially of the younger ones, and also those of the elder which might cause some disorder, that they may the better watch over them. We should not, however, so readily tell them things that the children tell us privately if we do not see in this a necessity for their good, lest they should inadvertently let them know something of it. I think it of great importance that the children should see that we can keep a secret, although what they tell us may not be of great importance for the time, because it might happen that they would have something important to tell us another time, especially when they advance in age, which they would have some difficulty in telling us if they had found out that we had not been faithful in small things.

9. As it is very important that we should be in perfect harmony and complete accord with the sisters who are appointed to assist us, it is still more so that these sisters act only according to the order that they find and see established, and that they should so conform to the ideas of the head mistress as to speak only through her mouth and see only through her eyes, in order that the children

may notice nothing that is not in perfect agreement between them;[1] and if the sisters find anything to object to in the conduct of the head mistress they should tell her, if they have sufficient confidence in her, and have permission from their superiors. If God does not give them this confidence they should inform the mother of it, lest unintentionally they let something of it appear before the children.

10. When two nuns are in the schoolroom when the bell rings for service, they may say it one after the other, that there may be one to overlook the children; but she will say nothing of the faults she may see them commit if they are unimportant until her companion has finished her prayers, in order to inspire them with great respect when they see anyone engaged in prayer. But as soon as the service is over, which is very short when it is said in a low voice, they must be punished according to the gravity of the fault, and more severely than when prayers are not being said.

11. When there is only one, she need make no difficulty in casting a look at them, but must say nothing until she has finished her prayer. We have seen by experience the good this does them, and when we are strict in not speaking to nor reproving them during the prayer,[2] this makes them more re-

---

[1] Mme. de Maintenon equally insists on this recommendation: "In order to succeed in your government it would be necessary for all to have the same ideas and the same maxims, or at least, if you have different ones, to be sufficiently humble to renounce your own opinions and follow those of your superiors, maintaining what is established by them against your own judgment. . . . Lay aside the private projects that self-love makes in order to compensate the necessity of falling in with the opinion of an official. You have still the pleasure of inwardly disapproving of her conduct and of saying, If I ever have that place I shall act in a different manner, I shall do this or that, I shall be more gentle or more firm. Never, I repeat, will your authority be established by such diversity of conduct. It would be better not to do quite so well but to do always the same, than to show this unevenness in the manner of educating your young ladies and fulfilling your duties." (*Entretiens*, 1703.)

[2] No detail, perhaps, shows better the depth and sincerity of the religious feeling that animated the monastery of Port-Royal. The Constable Anne de Montmorency had fewer scruples. "He never missed his devotions nor prayers," says Brantôme; "for he did not fail to repeat his Paternosters every morning, whether he remained at home or mounted his horse and went through the fields to the armies, where they used to say that they must beware of the Constable's Paternosters; for while saying and mumbling

spectful when they pray, and more afraid of interrupting us. We cannot too much inspire the young with respect for God as much by our example as by our words. For this reason we shall be very precise in repeating our prayers at the hours when they are said in the choir, in leaving off what we are doing at the second bell, and never letting ourselves be carried away by the desire to finish something. Not that, if the necessity of rendering some service to the children occurred, we should not attend to it before our prayers; but it is right that the children and our own conscience should be convinced that we are only working for God, our example being the best instruction we can give them, for the devil gives them memory to make them remember our least faults, and takes it away to prevent them remembering the trifling good that we do them.

12. Therefore we cannot pray to God too much, nor humble ourselves and watch over ourselves too much, in order to discharge our duty to the children, since obedience binds us to it; and I think that it is one of the most important duties of the house, and we cannot be too apprehensive[1] in fulfilling it, although we must not be pusillanimous, but put our trust in God, and force Him, by our groans, to grant us what we do not deserve of ourselves, but what we ask of Him through the blood of His Son, shed for these innocent souls that He has put into our hands. For we should always look upon these tender souls as sacred deposits that He has entrusted to us, and of which He will make us give account; therefore we should speak less to them than to God for them.

13. And as we are obliged to be with them always, we must behave so that they cannot see in us any inequality of temper,[2]

them, when the circumstances occurred, because many outbreaks and disorders now happen there, he used to say, 'Hang me such a one, bind that man to this tree, send that man through the pikes immediately. . . . burn me that village,' and thus he pronounced such or suchlike sentences of justice and military police according to emergencies, without leaving his Paternosters, until he had finished them."

[1] The saying of Saint-Cyran, "a tempest of the mind," will be remembered.
[2] "The sole desire of children is to find out the weak side of their teachers, as of those to whom they are subject; as soon as they can encroach upon them they gain the upper hand, and assume an influence over them that they never lose. That which makes us once lose this superiority over them also prevents us recovering it." (LA BRUYÈRE.)

by treating them sometimes with too much mildness and at other times with severity. These two faults usually follow each other; for when we allow ourselves to caress and flatter them, giving them liberty to go as far as their temper and inclination lead them, reproof infallibly follows, and this causes that unevenness of temper which is much more painful to the children than always keeping them to their duty.

14. We must never be too familiar with them, nor show them too much confidence, even when they are grown up; but we must show them real kindness and great gentleness in all that they need, and even anticipate them.

15. We must treat them with courtesy and speak to them with deference, and give way to them as far as possible. This wins them over, and it is well to condescend to them sometimes in things which in themselves are indifferent, in order to gain their hearts.

16. When it is necessary to reprove their levity and awkwardness, they should never be mimicked nor excited by harshness, although they may be in a bad temper; on the contrary, they must be spoken to with great mildness and given good reasons in order to persuade them; which will prevent them becoming soured, and make them accept what is said to them.

17. We must pray to God to make the children straightforward, and labour ourselves to turn them from all tricks and artifices, but this must be done so simply as not to make them artful while exhorting them to be artless.[1] Therefore, I think that we should not let it appear that they have so much artifice. For sometimes by constantly telling them that they must not be

---

[1] This wise advice recalls this lively passage of a letter of Mme. de Maintenon to Mme. de Fontaine, 20 September, 1691, at the time of the reformation of Saint-Cyr: "Pray to God, and make the others pray that He will change their hearts (the girls'), and that he will give us all humility; but, Madam, it is not necessary to talk much of it to them. Everything at Saint-Cyr is turned into discoursing; they often talk of simplicity, seek to define it correctly, to understand it, to distinguish what is simple from what is not so; then in practice they amuse themselves by saying, 'Through simplicity I take the best place, through simplicity I am going to praise myself, through simplicity I desire what is farthest from me on the table.' Really, this is playing with everything, and making a joke of what is most serious."

artful we make them so, and that they make use of everything which was told them, when they were not so, at another time, when they need to use artifice to hide some faults which they do not wish to be known.

18. Therefore the children must be constantly watched, never leaving them alone in any place whatever, in health or in sickness, but without letting them see that this is done so strictly, in order not to foster in them a distrustful spirit constantly on the watch. For that accustoms them to play tricks on the sly, especially the young ones. Thus, I think, that our constant watching should be effected with mildness and a certain confidence which may make them think they are loved, and that it is only for the sake of accompanying them that we are with them. This makes them like this supervision rather than fear it.

19. As to the youngest children, they must be, more than the rest, familiarized and brought up, if possible, like young doves. When they have committed a considerable fault which deserves punishment, few words should be used; but when you are perfectly certain, they must be punished without saying a word why they are punished until it is over. And even then it is good to ask them, before telling them anything, if they know why they have been punished; for usually they have not failed to recognize it. This punishment, promptly administered without a word, prevents them telling untruths in order to make excuses for their faults, to which young children are very prone; and I think that they correct their faults better themselves, because they fear being surprised.

20. I think also that in slight faults small warning should be given them, for insensibly they get accustomed to be always talked to. Therefore you should pretend only to see one out of three or four faults; but after having looked at them some time, they must be caught and made to give satisfaction at once. That corrects them much better than many words.

21. When young children are very obstinate and rebellious, they should be made to undergo the same punishment three or four times, which subdues them completely when they see that you are not wearied. But when you do this one day and forgive them the next or neglect them, it makes no impression on their minds, and

it is found to be necessary to adopt more stringent measures than those which would have been necessary with any sort of regularity.

22. Lying is very common with young children. Everything therefore should be done to accustom them not to fall into this vicious habit; and for that it seems to me that they should be cautioned with great gentleness, to make them confess their faults, saying that we know very well what they have done, and when they confess of themselves they should be forgiven, or their punishment should be mitigated.

23. While the children are still very young, as four or five years old, they should not be left all day with nothing to do, but their time should be divided, making them read for a quarter of an hour, then play for another quarter, and then work again for a short time. These changes amuse them, and prevent them falling into the bad habit, to which children are very liable, of holding their book and playing with it, or with their work, of sitting sideways and often turning their heads. But when they are told to employ a quarter or half an hour well, and are promised that if they attend to their lesson or their work they shall be allowed to play, they work quickly and well for this short time in order to be rewarded afterwards. And when you have made this promise before work, although they play during the time, you must say nothing; but at the end, when the time is up, and they think they are going to play, they must again give the time to the work, pointing out to them that you do not always wish to speak, but that, since they have done nothing but trifle, they must begin again. That surprises them, and puts them on their guard another time.[1]

II. *To what we lead them in general conversations and in conjunctures in which they give us cause to speak to and warn them.*

They are made to understand that perfection does not consist in doing many special things, but in doing well what they do in common, that is to say, cheerfully and for the love of God, with

---

[1] This is an application of natural sanction, so dear to Rousseau and Spencer. That is better than all arbitrary punishments and reprimands. The child feels the justice of it, and corrects himself.

a great desire to please Him, and always to do His holy will with joy.

They are taught to value the small opportunities that God gives them of suffering something for His sake, as some slight contempt shown by their sisters, some accusations wrongly made against themselves, some privations of their desires and inclinations, some occasion for renouncing their own will which may be given by their teachers, or by some other occurrence. They are asked to receive all this as a gift of God, and a witness of His great love, and of the care that He takes to give them opportunities of perfecting themselves every day.[1]

They should often be spoken to of the pleasure and satisfaction of giving themselves entirely to God and of serving Him in truth and simplicity, without wishing to keep anything back from Him; . . . that some will gain heaven and others deserve only chastisement for the same action, according to the impulse of their heart and the purity or impurity of their motives. It is well to make them understand this by some slight comparisons, as, for example, that a good action done for God's sake, and from a desire to please Him and to do His holy will leads us to heaven; and that, on the contrary, the same action done in a spirit of hypocrisy or vanity, and only with the desire to be well thought of by our fellow-creatures, deserves only punishment;[2] for having done nothing for God, we ought not to expect a reward, but only punishment in recompense of our hypocrisy.

Children should be strongly exhorted to know themselves, their

---

[1] This morality is very ill adapted to the intelligence and character of children. It is simpler and more practical to tell them that in order to render social life possible, we ought mutually to bear our imperfections, to avoid offending our neighbours, and to arm ourselves with patience. These are the reasons that Nicole develops in his celebrated treatise on the *Means of living in peace with men.*

[2] Mme. de Maintenon will be less severe. "You cannot too much inspire your young ladies with the love of reputation. They must be very scrupulous on the subject. Consider those who are the vainest as the best of your pupils . . . they must die to this scrupulousness when they are more advanced in piety; but before dying to it they must have lived in it. Nothing is so bad as certain natures without honour and without vanity; we do not know how to take them in order to make them surmount the obstacles they find in their path; thus it would be very dangerous to stifle these sentiments in young persons who usually are incapable of an exalted piety." (*Entretiens,* 1703.)

inclinations, vices, and passions, and to go to the root of their defects. It is well, also, that they know to what their nature inclines them, in order to remove what may be displeasing to God, and to change their natural inclinations into spiritual. To tell them, for example, that if they are of a sympathetic disposition they should change the love they have for themselves and their fellow-creatures into loving God with all their hearts, and thus with their other inclinations.

They may be shown sometimes that one of the greatest faults of the young is indocility, and that it is, as it were, natural to them; that if they do not take care this vice will ruin them, making them incapable of accepting advice, and that this is always the mark of a proud spirit. Therefore, they will often be told that they should wish to be treated with firmness, and that they should show, by the meekness with which they receive advice that is given them, that they are willing that everything that may be displeasing to God should be destroyed in them.

We exhort them not to be ashamed of doing good. For sometimes those who have been unruly are ashamed to do what is right before those who have seen their unruliness. They must be told to pray to God to strengthen them that they may do good freely, and that, although at first they often fall back, they must raise themselves again often and more courageously. These instructions should be given generally, and even at times when none are disorderly, that they may serve for another time, and that those who should be more orderly may apply them to themselves if needful.

We tell them that their difficulties in acquiring virtue proceed from this, that as soon as some vice to be overcome or some virtue to be acquired appears, they fall back upon themselves in order to consult their own temper, inclination, self-love, and weaknesses, and the trouble that they have to conquer themselves; but instead of weakening themselves by these human views, they must turn to God, in whom they will find all strength, even in their weakness;
. . . that if they were told to throw off their troubles and weaknesses by themselves they would have good reason to be discouraged; but since they are told that God will Himself remove their difficulties, they have only to pray and hope. . . .

We ought not to anticipate them touching religion, especially in general, nor let them see how few persons we think are saved in the world; it is sufficient to let them see that there are many difficulties in being saved in it. . . . What they ought to avoid if they return to society should be pointed out to them. . . .

If they enter on the subject of religion of their own accord, in order to express their opinions on it, the opportunity may very well be taken to tell them something of the happiness of a good nun.[1] . . .

It is well to let them know sometimes that they are loved for God's sake, and that this affection makes us so sensitive to their faults and renders it so difficult to support them, and that the ardour of this love makes the words we use in reproving them sometimes so severe. At the same time, we shall assure them that, in whatever manner we act, we are led only by the affection we bear them and the desire to make them such as God would have them to be; that our heart is always tender towards them, that our severity is only for their faults, and that we do great violence to ourselves, having much more inclination to treat them gently than severely.

III. *How children should be spoken to in private.*

The habit of speaking to children in private makes their government easier. In these conversations their troubles are relieved, we enter into their spirit to make them strive against their faults, we lay bare their vices and passions to the roots, and I may say that when God gives them a thorough confidence in their teacher, there is much to be hoped for; and I have not seen one who enjoyed this perfect confidence who has not succeeded.

The conversations with them should be very serious, and great kindness should be shown them, but no familiarity; and if there were one who was seen to seek talking for amusement, she should be treated more coolly than the rest. Therefore we have need of great discretion, not only in the conversation itself, but also in the time chosen for it. I think about every fortnight is sufficient, unless for some special need, for which no rule can be given.

---

[1] The recommendation was not needed. Everything in this education tended to conventual life.

We must take great care, and not allow ourselves to be deceived; and it is a great advantage when they are forewarned that we know all the artifices of children, which makes them give up the design, and unconsciously return to simplicity and sincerity, without which it is impossible to serve them usefully.

It is, then, very necessary not to allow ourselves to be surprised, and we cannot avoid this without God's continual help. Therefore we shall never speak to them without having prayed to God, and considered, even in His presence, what we think they should tell us, and what we think He wishes that we should reply to them [1] . . . and if, while speaking to them, they tell us something of the truth of which we are not quite certain, we shall tell them that we will take time to pray to God before replying to them, in order that He may prepare them to receive with a heart entirely free from all human interest, all that we shall tell them from Him for their good. We shall also use this retardation as soon as we see that their mind is soured by what we have said to them, or that they do not take in good part some advice that we have given them. We may tell them that we see that they are not very well disposed to listen to us, or that perhaps we are not well informed, and that by both praying to God, if we do it with humility, He will no doubt have pity on us. This slight condescension and all these things should not be told to all, but is of great use to the elder girls and to those who are intelligent. Great discretion is needed to speak to them at a proper time and place. Therefore I repeat here what I cannot say too often, and what I do not do enough, namely, to pray more than talk, and I think we must always have our heart and mind raised to heaven to receive from God all the words that we should say to them.[2]

Constant vigilance is necessary in order to form an opinion of them and to discover their tempers and inclinations, that we may learn, by regarding them attentively, what they have not the courage to disclose to us. It is well to encourage them when we see that they are ashamed to tell of their faults in order to give them more freedom to disclose them; it is well to hide from

---

[1] This is, indeed, the teaching of Saint-Cyran. (See p. 77.)
[2] See the saying of Saint-Cyran. (p. 70.)

them many truths that we think would be too hard for their imperfect state. . . .

If they ask to be set to do many private things, few or none will be given them, pointing out to them that they will not please God in that way if it does not come from a heart really touched by love of Him and a sincere desire to please Him and do penance; that we do not judge them by these actions, but by their obedience to the smallest rules of the schoolroom, by the support they give their sisters, by the kindness with which they help them at need, and by their care in mortifying their faults; these things will make us think they wish to serve God, and not a number of private actions. . . .

We shall tell them these things, although sometimes we shall not fail to allow them to do in other circumstances what they ask us, without appearing to take notice or taking any account of it; on the contrary, during the time that they are asking for something extraordinary to do, we shall pretend not to be occupied with them, not failing to notice their actions much more than at other times, in order to point them out afterwards when opportunity offers. By behaving thus to them we shall soon discover if they only ask these things through hypocrisy. For then, if they have only done it to be noticed, when they see that we do not notice them they will let them go and ask nothing more. . . .

IV. *Of General and Private Penances that may be imposed on them.*

They must be obliged to beg pardon of those sisters or of their companions of whom they have spoken ill with mockery, or given some other offence or shown a bad example.

This pardon may be asked in several ways, according to the gravity of the fault, either in public or in private, in the refectory or during lessons. They may also be commanded to kiss the feet of the companion whom they have offended. Above all, care must be taken that if the fault was only witnessed by two or three persons, they must make amends only in private, at least, if the fault was of little consequence, it being very dangerous to inform needlessly those who have not seen the faults of others.

I say the same of the faults of some of the leading girls; when a considerable number have fallen into them it will be necessary to wait and reprove each privately or all the guilty together, in order not to inform the weak needlessly.

They may be obliged to wear a grey cloak, to go to the refectory without a veil or a scapulary, and even to stand at the church door in this state.

They should also be deprived of going to church for one or more days, according to the gravity of their fault, or made to stand at the church door or in some other place separate from the rest; above all, care must be taken that the deprivation of going to church is not indifferent to them.

The children of the lower and middle classes may be made to wear a paper written in large characters expressing their faults; it is sufficient if there is a word or two, as idle, negligent, untruthful, &c.[1]

To make them ask the sisters of the refectory to pray for them, telling them the fault into which they have fallen or the virtue which they lack.[2]

The elder girls should be made to fear for God's sake, and through fear of His judgments, and in certain circumstances some of the penances that are imposed on the younger may be imposed on them, as making them go without a veil, or ask the prayers of the sisters in the refectory. But it must be considered if that would be useful and not harmful to them by only exasperating them. This obliges us to pray to God that He will enlighten us and guide us in everything for His glory and the salvation of these souls that He has committed to our care. . . .

V. *Of Confession.*

. . . The youngest girls will not go so soon or so often to confession; before making the younger go, you will wait until they are reasonable and show a wish to correct their small failings, nothing being so much to be dreaded as making the-

---

[1] This public humiliation has the grave disadvantage of weakening the sentiment of honour in children; it depraves instead of correcting.

[2] It was demanding great perfection from the children to impose a burden which, moreover, ran the risk of being insincere.

children go so young without seeing any change in them, and you should at least wait until they have persevered for some time in trying to do better. . . .

We take care that the children are benefited by the confession before permitting them to return to it; and when they have committed some considerable faults, we exhort them to make amends for them first; and if they have the confidence to tell them to us, which is the most useful, we advise them to make amends according to the gravity of their faults, but especially in things which mortify them and are opposed to their faults.[1] As, for example, if they have failed in the charity that they owe to their sisters, they will be made to serve them and fulfil towards them all the duties of charity with more unction and gentleness; and if the fault has been seen, they will ask pardon both of her who has been offended and of those who have seen it; they will also repeat some prayers for those whom they have offended. We shall act in such a way that they do not return to confession until their heart is really humbled, and they are sorry that they have offended God. We shall act thus with respect to the greater faults that the children commit in order that they may not make their confession by routine, which is much to be feared for everybody, but especially for children. . . .

VI. *Of Reading.*

The books used for the instruction of the children are the *Imitation of Christ*, Fr. *Luis de Granada*, *The Philothée, St. John Climacus, The Tradition of the Church*, the *Letters* of M. de Saint-Cyran, the *Familiar Theology*, the Christian maxims in the *Book of Hours*, the *Letters of a Carthusian Father*, lately translated, and other books whose object is to form the true Christian life.

For the reading by one of them after vespers other books may be used, as some letters of St. Jerome, the *Christian Almsgiving,*

---

[1] This is one of the important points of the moral reform of Saint-Cyran. He thought it shameful that Christians should think it sufficient to go and tell their faults to a priest, and consider themselves absolved by God and their conscience for having afterwards recited a few prayers by way of penance, without altering their conduct in the least. (See Introduction, pp. 61 and 62, the violent outburst of Arnauld against this abuse.)

some passages of St. Teresa's *Way of Perfection*, and also of *The Foundations* in what concerns the narrative, the Lives of the Fathers of the Desert, and other lives of saints which are in special books.

We ourselves do all the reading in public except that after vespers, but we are always present to explain what is read to them and address them upon it. The object should be to habituate them not to listen to the reading for the sake of amusement or curiosity, but with a desire to apply it to themselves; and for that it is necessary that the manner of explaining it should aim rather at making them good Christians and leading them to correct their own faults than making them learned. . . .

In the readings that we do not do ourselves we mark what they have to read, and they are not permitted to change either the passage or the book, for there are very few books in which there is not something to pass over.

At the reading after vespers they are allowed and even enjoined to ask questions constantly upon everything that they do not understand, provided that it be done with respect and humility; and in replying we teach them how to apply this reading to the correction of their manners. If, in reading, we see that they ask no questions on something that we think most of them do not understand, they are asked if they understand it, and, if we see that they cannot answer, they will be reproved for remaining in ignorance, since they have been told to ask for instruction in what they do not know.

As soon as the reading is finished the book is taken away, for we leave them no other book in private than their *Hours*, the *Familiar Theology*, the *Words of our Lord*, an *Imitation of Christ*, and a Latin and French *Psalter*. Their mistress keeps all their other books, which they think very proper, having recognized that it is more advantageous to them, and that the most pious reading is of no use to them when it is done through curiosity. . . .

They are never allowed to open a book that does not belong to them, nor to borrow from each other without permission from their mistress, which is seldom given, in order to avoid the confusion that these loans occasion.

VII. *Of the Sick and their Bodily Needs.*

Very great care must be taken of those who fall sick, attending upon them properly and exactly at the stated hours; calling in the physician if the malady requires him, and carrying out punctually all that he orders for the relief of their sickness. . . .

We accustom them not to make difficulties in taking the most disagreeable remedies. We are always present, in order to speak to them of God, to encourage them, and make them offer their sickness to God. . . .

They are exhorted never to find fault with the doctor's prescriptions, because he holds the place of God with respect to them in their sickness. Therefore they ought to obey him as they would God Himself, abandoning their life, their health, or their sickness to the order of Divine Providence, who uses the good or ill success of the remedies for our welfare. Therefore, in everything untoward that may happen, the blame must never be laid on the physician nor on the remedies, but, in silence and humility, the order that the Divine Goodness lays upon us must be adored; and to give occasion to the sick to be in this frame of mind, I presuppose that we always have, if possible, physicians who are good Christians as well as good physicians.[1]

There will always be a room set apart for the sick, which the other children will not be allowed to enter, unless in case of great necessity, and with the permission of their mistress. During the time of recreation one of the more steady may be sent to amuse them. The sister in attendance must not leave them, unless there be some older children, as those who are ready to enter upon their

---

[1] Port-Royal, in fact, counted some distinguished physicians among her solitaries; first *Pallu*, from 1643 to 1650, of whom Fontaine has left us this delightful portrait: "Everything belonging to him was small, except his mind; a small body, a small house, a small horse, but everything well fitting, well proportioned, and very agreeable. Who would not have loved this worthy recluse? It was almost agreeable to fall ill in order to have the pleasure of enjoying his conversation." Then *Hamon*, from 1650 to 1687, graver, more authoritative, and an ardent mystic, which made this simple layman, during the years of persecution, the consoler and director of the sisters. The Mother Angélique wrote to him: "After the great gift of a perfect confessor, nothing is more important than that of a truly Christian physician, who expresses, in all his words and actions, the pious maxims of Christianity." His pupil, Racine, desired to be interred at the foot of his grave. And lastly, *Hecquet*, from 1688 to 1693.

novitiate, and who may be entirely trusted, who may watch and even attend upon them if the illness is not very serious.

. When there are many patients a sister is placed there, besides her who takes care of them in health, and the sisters must be discreet and gentle; discreet, to keep them to their duty, lest during the sickness they lose what they have acquired with so much labour in health, and also not to humour them in their inclinations or the repugnance they have in taking the remedies that are ordered them, and the abstinence they should practise from certain food which would be hurtful to them; but they must also be gentle, in order to soften, by the kind way in which they act and by gentle words, all that must be refused them for their health.[1]

We pay great attention to the sick, leaving rather even the healthy, as much to treat them properly, as to keep them in order and teach them to be sick like Christians. . . .

As soon as the children are cured they go back to the others, lest they should become unruly, which is to be feared in the young, who most often only ask for liberty.[2] But, although they have returned to the schoolroom, great care will be taken to feed them, and give them repose when they need it for the perfect recovery of their health.

For slight ailments which may come upon them every attention will be paid them, but they will not be petted too much; for children sometimes pretend to be ill. I have seen some of this sort, although, through God's grace, it has not happened among ours for a long time. But, when it does occur, you must not show that you think that they wish to deceive you, but, on the contrary, pity them a good deal and tell them that they are really

---

[1] Pascal said during his sufferings: "Do not pity me, sickness is the natural state of Christians." According to the fine expression of Saint-Cyran, "the sick should regard their bed as an altar, on which they offer to God continually the sacrifice of their life, to restore it to Him when He shall please!" Pliny the younger wrote upon this thought one of his finest letters: "We are all good people when we are ill; for what sick man does avarice or ambition tempt? . . . I can give here, between us two and in few words, a lesson on which the philosophers make whole volumes. Let us persevere in being such in health as we should wish to become when we are sick."

[2] What a criticism on this monastic system of education!

ill, and immediately put them to bed in a separate room, with a sister to nurse them, but who is not to speak to them at all, telling them that talking will do them harm, and that they require rest.[1]

They are put for a day or two on a diet of broth and eggs. If the illness is real this diet is very good for them, and if not there is no doubt they will say next day that they are not ill; and thus they will be cured of their deceit, without giving them an opportunity of complaining, a thing that happens when they are told that they have not the illness that they complain of, and even risks making them tell untruths and pretend still more.

SISTER ANNE-EUGÉNIE DE L'INCARNATION, MISTRESS OF THE BOARDERS.

The Mother Angélique recalled sister Eugénie, after a residence of three and a half years at Maubuisson, in 1631.

Her return to Port-Royal was a subject of great joy for the house. She was entrusted with the care of the younger boarders, and performed this duty with very great success. This will easily be understood when it is known on what principles and on what method she acted in this office. First, she had a special zeal in making the children value the grace of baptismal innocence. She often spoke to them of it, and did so with incredible energy, and, consequently, she took them to the parlour, to the visitors who came to see them, with very great reluctance; and when she was there, took very great care to avoid conversation which might inspire them with love of the world. She taught the children that the society of worldly people was contagious for the soul, as the plague is for the body.[2] She knew how to impress upon them a great respect for the mysteries of religion, for the grandeur of God, and for the truths of the gospel. She never told any of these truths to the children, except after having prepared them,

---

[1] This little comedy, so legitimately acted, shows another application of natural sanction. (See note, p. 234.)
[2] This was a strange preparation for social life. Mme. de Maintenon, notwithstanding her desire to educate better than the convent, paints the world in frightful colours, without recalling to mind the wise definition of Fénelon: "The world is not a phantom, it is the assemblage of all the families."

and often after having made them do something to deserve it.
She announced several days in advance that she had a great
truth to tell them, and thus made it expected and desired. She
only taught these truths one by one, dreading lest the habit of
hearing them should accustom the children to them, and that they
should be no longer touched by them, having known them before
they had sufficient grace and understanding to comprehend and
feel them. She gave a constant attention to everything that
concerned the spiritual welfare of the children, she was quite
taken up with it, she prayed without ceasing for them, she even
made a practice of regularly attending all the prayers of the
children that were said in common, and of saying them with
them, considering herself charged to pay to God the worship
that these children were not yet able to pay Him, and to supply
by her will that which the children lacked.

The children's faults affected her as much as her own; she did
penance for them, and incited them to do it for themselves according to their slender capacity. If she found one who was not
willing to acknowledge her fault she said nothing more to her,
prayed for her in private, and left her with a kindness and toleration that sooner or later bore fruit. She had this maxim from
M. de Saint-Cyran, as well as all the preceding, that with the young
it was necessary to speak little, tolerate much, and pray still more.
She contrived little artifices of charity to make them love what is
good, she composed devout little notes on the virtues, and made
them draw lots for them, which piously amused the children.
She represented some virtue by an emblem, she made an enigmatical portrait of it, and left them to guess what virtue it was.
Recreation usually began with that, and then she left them to
amuse themselves with their little games; for she never failed
to be present at the commencement of their recreation every day,
which astonished the sisters, who knew how devout she was, and
not being ignorant of how much natural dislike she had for
teaching children, wondered how she constrained herself to
become a child with the children and willingly remain among
these little people. Moreover the great punishment she employed
with regard to them when she had any reason for displeasure,
was not to be present at their recreation. All the party then,

burst into tears, and the other sisters had to go and beg Sister Eugénie to return and dry their tears. She was fifteen or sixteen years in this employment.

Her humble simplicity was towards the end put to a proof which turned to her glory, but not to the welfare of the children. The mothers, who had received and admitted to the house a sister from Gif, named Sister Flavie Passart, were thoroughly deceived in her. They saw that she was capable of many things by the mental qualities that she possessed, and they thought that she had also those of the heart. They made her assistant mistress of the boarders under Sister Eugénie. This young woman, who was full of ambition, set to work to draw all authority to herself.[1] She substituted a high-handed and despotic manner for that of Sister Eugénie, who was full of gentleness. She even succeeded in making Sister Eugénie believe that hitherto she had acted wrongly, that her gentleness was the cause that the children did not correct themselves, and that they would succeed better by severity. Sister Eugénie was simple and humble enough to adopt the views of this young woman. She allowed her to act, believing that she was doing better than herself, she bewailed without ceasing the pretended faults that she had committed in her place; at last she earnestly begged to be relieved of her employment, especially as she was getting very infirm.

(Besogne, *Hist. de l'abbaye de Port-Royal*, t. i. p. 348.)

A RECREATION AT PORT-ROYAL.

"In the monastery of Port-Royal des Champs," Desmarets[2] relates, "the mistress of the boarders had instructed her scholars in matters contested between the disciples of Jansenius and the jesuit fathers, and having inspired them with a terrible aversion for these fathers, had given them the idea of making a doll and

[1] Sister Flavie, Nicole tells us, was mistress of the boarders for fifteen years. (*Les Visionnaires*, p. 347.)
[2] Desmarets de Saint-Sorlin (1595-1676), a member of the French Academy, the author of the comedy of the *Visionnaires*, and of the poem *Clovis*; he was distinguished among the most violent enemies of jansenism. His reason went astray in the folly of a mystical illuminism. Nicole defended Port-Royal against him, as Boileau undertook to avenge antiquity for his attacks.

dressing it like a jesuit. Then they made another doll and dressed it like a capuchin. They took them to the sisters for their amusement, and after several questions between one and another, one, who was the president, summed up and condemned the jesuit. Then all the boarders and the sisters clapped their hands in token of victory, rose up tumultuously, and carried the jesuit doll in triumph into the garden, where there was a pond, plunged it in several times, and at last drowned it. This was done with transports of joy, bursts of laughter, flying veils and wimples in disorder, and laughing frenzy, and the poor counterfeit jesuit was like a wretched Orpheus in the hands of furious Menads. Nevertheless, that was called a becoming recreation for pious nuns and devout school girls, and passed off with the great satisfaction and approbation of the mothers, who are very pious, if you will believe their apologist."

EXPLANATIONS.

"Here," replies Nicole, "is one of the strangest examples to be found of the artifices that malice can inspire to raise the blackest calumnies on the slightest and most simple grounds. This is all that can have given rise to this scandalous story. When nothing but Escobar was spoken of in Paris and throughout France, some engravers made a ridiculous picture of him. A young child of good family, who was then about eight or nine years old, gave one to his sisters, who were about his own age, and were brought up in the monastery of Port-Royal des Champs. These little girls having seen it, and being struck with the name and the expression of the personage of whom their brother had sometimes spoken to them laughing, brought him to trial and condemned him to be drowned. To carry out this sentence they made a paper boat, and their intention was to put Escobar[1] in it, and send him to be drowned into the middle of the canal that ran through their garden. But this design was discovered before it was executed . . . so that it was very near costing these poor little girls more than Escobar. . . . This is all that is true in this tale, which only shows the wisdom of the nuns of Port-Royal." (*Les Visionnaires*, p. 350.)

---

[1] Escobar y Mendoza (1589-1669), a Spanish casuist of the Society of Jesus, whose lax morality Pascal has branded with immortal ridicule.

APPENDIX.

A STUDY OF THE WRITERS OF PORT-ROYAL BY FATHER BOUHOURS.[1]

... WHAT do you think, said Ariste, of those solitaries who have written so much during the last twenty years?—I do them justice, replied Eugène, and I candidly admit that they have contributed much to the perfection of our language.

Have you seen, said Ariste, the translation that they have made of the *Imitation of Christ*? I have heard say that it is one of their best works, and that they propose it themselves as a model of the purity of the language.

I have been reading it for some days, replied Eugène, and I esteem it at least as much as the *Confessions of St. Augustine* and the *Life of Dom Barthélemy des Martyrs*, in which the long sentences rather fatigue the reader.

It is true, replied Ariste, that these very famous writers cannot be accused of brevity; they like long discourses naturally, long parentheses please them very much, long periods, and especially those which, by their excessive length, make one out of breath to read them, are quite to their taste. The fine *Life of the Archbishop of Prague*

---

[1] Father Bouhours, a jesuit (1628-1702) and a meritorious critic, author of the *Entretiens d'Ariste et d'Eugène*, of *Remarques sur la langue française*, and of the *Manière de bien penser dans les ouvrages d'esprit*. "He overflows with wit," Mme. de Sévigné wrote of him. Racine, addressing to him, about 1676, the first four acts of *Phèdre*, begs him "to mark the faults that he may have committed against the language, of which you are one of our most excellent masters." But his character and morals do not deserve the same praise: "He is a wretch of whom nothing good is to be expected," writes Arnauld to M. du Vaucel (18 August, 1690). If this testimony seems suspicious, why did the archbishop of Paris not permit Bouhours to put his name, "as being too undignified," to his translation of the New Testament?

begins with an inordinately long sentence ; a man must have good lungs to deliver it all in one breath, and pay great attention to understand it the first time of reading.

That may be called getting tired at the beginning of the journey, said Eugène ; but the fact is, he added, these gentlemen have been going on in this style for a long time ; they are used to it, and apparently they will have some difficulty in giving it up. After all, we must not quarrel with them for a fault that only proceeds from copiousness ; if making long sentences is a vice, it is the vice of great orators ; and this makes me think that these gentlemen will not get rid of it.

Why should they not get rid of their long periods ? replied Ariste ; with time they have got rid of their exaggerations. Nothing was more common in their earlier books than extravagant expressions, as : *la plus grande et la plus punissable de toutes les hardiesses, la plus sanglante de toutes les invectives, la plus étrange témérité et la plus grossière ignorance qui fut jamais.* There was seen, even in titles and narratives that ought to be plain and simple, *une audace qui n'eut jamais de pareille, une ignorance insupportable, une insolence punissable, la plus insigne de toutes les fourberies, la plus lâche prévarication qui fut jamais.* One of the most judicious critics of our time formerly reproached them with this.

They have not entirely given up this kind of expressions, said Eugène. They still put *le plus* in many places where it is not wanted ; or, if they do not use this term to exaggerate what they say, they use big words and grand epithets, which have nearly the same effect. For instance, *une impertinence signalée, un égarement prodigieux, un attentat insupportable, un emportement diabolique, un effroyable excès de malice et de folie.* As to the length of the sentences, far from shortening them, they add tails, which make the discourse extremely long. For example, after long sentences, which are tiring in themselves, they usually put some participle, as : *étant certain que . . . , rien n'étant plus avantageux que . . . ,* which does not give much repose to the mind, nor allow readers to take breath.

I do not, indeed, find hyperbolical expressions nor inordinately long sentences in the *Imitation of Christ;* notwithstanding, to hide nothing from you, there is a something, I do not know what, that I do not like. These are scruples, perhaps ; you shall judge, if you like, and I begin with the epistle dedicatory.

Tant s'en faut que ce glorieux rabaissement soit indigne du courage de votre naissance. I confess that this *glorieux rabaissement* does not please me very much.—It does not please me at all, said Ariste, and I doubt whether *rabaissement* is French. I have heard talk of the *rabais* of money; and perhaps we might say the *rabaissement* of a person who has been deprived of his dignity and rank; but I do not think we say *rabaissement* for *humilité*, and this *glorieux* does not suit very well, according to my idea.

There is a word which surprised me in the *Avertissement au lecteur*, continued Eugène. *Il égale la hautesse et la magnificence des ouvrages des saints Pères.* What do you say of *hautesse*? Until now, said Ariste, I thought that the title *hautesse* was given to a nobleman, and I did not think the title *hautesse* ought ever to be given to the Fathers. I would as soon call them *altesse*, and I should think the *altesse* of their works as good as *hautesse*. Joking apart, *hautesse* offends me still more than *rabaissement*. But let us see the rest (Eugène then read the following passages): *L'œil est insatiable de voir; ils travaillent plus à s'acquérir de l'éclat qu'à se fonder dans l'humilité. Ceux qui sont encore nouveaux et inexpérimentés dans la voie de Dieu.*

I think your previous doubts are very well founded, said Ariste. *Insatiable* is one of those words that have nothing after them, that govern nothing. We say insatiable avarice (*une avarice insatiable*), an insatiable heart (*un cœur insatiable*), but we cannot say *insatiable de manger*, nor *insatiable de voir*. We may, indeed, say *un désir insatiable d'apprendre;* but then *d'apprendre* is governed by *désir*, and not by *insatiable*.

Se fonder dans l'humilité does not seem to me very good; but *acquérir de l'éclat* does not seem to me to be French. We say indeed *aimer l'éclat, faire de l'éclat;* but we do not say, that I know, *acquérir de l'éclat* in any sense whatever.

Inexpérimenté is a word in the style of these gentlemen, as well as *inallié, inalliable, incorrompu, inconvertible, intolérance, clairvoyance, inobservation, inattention, désoccupation, désoccuper, désaveugler, coronateur, insidiateur;* to which may be added *élèvement, abrègement, brisement, déchirement, resserrement, attiédissement;* and these adverbs *déclarement, inexplicablement,* and *incontestablement.* For they have no difficulty in making new words, and even claim to have the right to do so; as if private persons and solitaries had a power that kings themselves do not possess.

It is apparently in virtue of this assumed authority, said Eugène, that the translator of the *Imitation* has coined a word, of which we have never heard speak, namely, *indisposer*, with an active signification —*Celui qui, après m'avoir reçu, se répand aussitôt en des satisfactions extérieures, s'indispose beaucoup pour me recevoir.* . . .

This *indisposer* is pleasant, replied Ariste, and I shall be very much deceived if that word makes its way; for it is with words something like it is with men: some have a lucky star, so to say, and are received as soon as they present themselves; but there are some unlucky ones that cannot be tolerated, and to which we can never get accustomed. *Indisposer* is one of these unfortunate ones, as well as *élèvement*, which these gentlemen put everywhere, and nobody but themselves uses.

Well, what would you have? said Eugène; they are fond of new words, and like making them. But let us go on. Do you like *se trouver dans l'obscurcissement, dans l'enivrement et dans le resserrement?* . . . Do you like *l'enivrement* of the amusements of the world? *Complaire* à Dieu instead of *plaire?* . . .

To be plain with you, said Ariste, I do not like all that.

I do not know, said Eugène, if you will like better what remains to read. . . . *Vous serez sujet malgré vous à la mutabilité et au changement. Celui qui est encore assujetti au trouble de ses passions.* These two phrases do not please me. A man is subject to change, but is not subject to mutability; *mutabilité* means a disposition to change; to be changeable is to be subject to change, so that to be subject to *mutabilité* means the same as to be subject to a disposition to change and to the power of changing, which does not seem to me very reasonable. I say the same of *assujetti au trouble de ses passions*, a man is subject to his passions, he is the slave of his passions, but is not *assujetti au trouble*, nor *esclave du trouble de ses passions;* that is neither according to reason nor usage.

Qu'il est triste, au contraire, et pénible de voir des personnes sans ordre et sans règle! Il est triste de voir, il est pénible de voir displease me.

Celui-là est vraiment sage qui ne prête point l'oreille aux amorces et aux enchantements de ces sirènes qui tuent en caressant. I would pardon this *prêter l'oreille aux amorces* in insignificant writers, who are not expected to be so correct; but I cannot pardon it in great writers, who should excuse nothing in themselves. *Amorces* (bait) is one of those metaphorical words in which something of their primary meaning still remains. We say indeed the *amorces* of vice; we might say, To allow ourselves to be caught by the *amorces* of the sirens; but I doubt if we can say, *Prêter l'oreille aux amorces* (to listen to the bait). It seems to me that these two words, *oreille* and *amorces*, do not go well together.

Que cette vie est malheureuse, puisqu'elle est toujours assiégée de pièges et de filets, et pleine d'une infinité d'ennemis qui l'environnent de toutes parts! This word *assiégée* does not very well agree with *pièges* and *filets;* it would agree better with *ennemis*, and this passage would be better thus: *Que cette vie est malheureuse, puisqu'elle est toujours assiégée*

d'ennemis, et pleine d'une infinité de pièges et de filets qui l'environnent de toutes parts!
Afin que vous soyez le dominateur de vos actions.
Good heavens! what a way to talk! I would as soon say *le seigneur et le roi de vos actions.* Not that *dominateur* is not French; but *dominateur* and *actions* do not harmonize.

Il faut que vous conserviez votre âme dans une privation de toutes les douceurs. Abaissez mon cou et ma tête superbes, afin de faire plier ma volonté déréglée et inflexible sous la rectitude et la sainteté de la vôtre.—
Here are what may be called phrases. To preserve his soul in the privation of all delights; to make his will bend under the rectitude of the will of God: either I am no judge, or else this is rather like Nervèze.[1]

Je suis dans une défaillance générale de toutes choses. This is not well expressed, meaning I am in want of all things; *défaillance* does not mean *manquement* and *défaut*, in that sense. We say *défaillance de cœur, défaillance d'esprit, défaillance des astres;* but not *défaillance* in speaking of money, of clothes, or of things necessary to life.

L'impuissance où je me trouve d'être consolé par aucun homme. Être dans l'impuissance agrees very well with an active verb, but not with a passive verb. We say, *Je suis dans l'impuissance de vous assister, de vous servir;* but I do not think we can say, *Je suis dans l'impuissance d'être assisté de mes amis, d'être consolé par aucun homme.*

Si impuissant à vous taire; si facile pour la dissipation et le ris; si fécond à former de bonnes résolutions, et si stérile à en produire les effets. These phrases are not French. What style! *Je suis impuissant à parler, je suis impuissant à me taire,* meaning I cannot speak, I cannot be silent. Foreigners who are beginning to learn French speak in that manner; they should say, *Si peu maître de votre langue,* instead of *Si impuissant à vous taire. Facile* does not go well with *pour,* nor with a *noun;* either it requires nothing after it or *à* and a verb. *C'est un esprit facile, c'est une chose facile à faire. Fécond* and *stérile* are not joined with verbs. The earth is *féconde,* a field is *stérile;* but the earth is not *féconde à former* metals in its bowels; a field is not *stérile à produire du blé;* at most the earth is *féconde en métaux,* a field is *stérile en blé.* The translator should have said, *Si fécond en bonnes résolutions, et si stérile en bons effets.*

---

[1] De Nervèze, the author of *Essais poétiques,* dedicated to Henri de Bourbon (1603).—Furetière, in his *factums,* speaks of the strained metaphors which make his songs, sonnets, heroic epistles, ballets, &c., ridiculous. Father Bouhours says a little above: the nervèze, the gibberish, and the bombast.

De peur que m'abstenant plus longtemps de votre sacré corps, je ne me refroidisse peu à peu de mes saints désirs.—*Se refroidir de ses saints désirs* is a new phrase that I have not yet heard. I have always heard say: *Se refroidir dans ses exercices de piété, dans une entreprise où l'on s'est engagé avec chaleur.*

O état sacré de la vie religieuse, qui rend l'homme chéri de Dieu! Si vous aviez soin de rendre votre âme vide de l'affection de toutes les créatures.—I am sure that persons at all fastidious in language will not like this style of speaking: *Rendre chéri, rendre vide. Rendre* does not agree with participles, nor with all kinds of adjectives. We do not say *Il se rend aimé*, although we may say *Il se rend aimable*. Nor do we say *rendre vide* any more than *rendre plein*, meaning *vider* and *remplir*. These expressions are like *rendre connu*, which Balzac has absolutely condemned in the sonnet on *Job*.

Comme ils n'ont pas en moi une pleine confiance, ils s'entremettent encore du soin d'eux-mêmes. That is not French. We say indeed, *S'entremettre d'une affaire;* but we do not say, *S'entremettre du soin d'une affaire*, nor *du soin d'une personne.*

Tous mes désirs soupirent vers vous. It is the heart, the person that sighs (*soupire*); but desires do not sigh, they cause to sigh. *Soupirent vers vous* is not good; it should be *Soupirent après vous*, or *pour vous*.

Je ne trouve du repos en aucune créature, mais en vous seul, ô mon Dieu. This construction is not regular. *Je ne trouve du repos* does not agree well with *mais en vous seul*. The phrase should be turned differently, or at least it should be *mais j'en trouve en vous seul*. The verb should not be understood in these constructions; it should always be expressed, and we should not be afraid to repeat the same word; repetition is not disagreeable when it contributes to regularity of construction and clearness of style.

Vous vous aimez trop par un amour déréglé. Considérer tout par un œil si pur et si éclairé. As soon as a person loves himself too much, he loves himself extravagantly; thus *par un amour déréglé* is useless after *trop*. Besides, *s'aimer par un amour déréglé* is not well expressed, no more than *considérer par un œil si pur et si éclairé;* we must say, *S'aimer d'un amour déréglé, considérer tout d'un œil si pur et si éclairé.*

Il y en a peu qui sortent entièrement de leurs inclinations et de leur humeur. This is not good French for saying, *Qui renoncent entièrement à leurs inclinations et à leur humeur.* We say of a man carried away by passion, *il est hors de soi, il est rentré en soi-même;* but we do not say, *Il est sorti de soi-même;* thus we say, *Sortir de son péché, sortir de son caractère;* but we do not say, *Sortir de ses inclinations et de son humeur.* . . .

Appendix.

We should never end, said Eugène, if I were to read you all the passages that I have marked. There is not a chapter on which I have not some doubts. Nevertheless, the *Imitation of Christ* is the smallest book of these gentlemen, and has had the greatest popularity of all their books; it has gone to thirteen editions.

I conclude from all this, said Ariste, that the greatest masters are liable to be mistaken sometimes.

(*Deuxième entretien d'Ariste et d'Eugène*, p. 187.)

The *Bureau typographique* or Typographic Table was a method of teaching the alphabet invented by Louis Dumas (1676-1744), a French *littérateur* of Montpellier. It was a table with compartments like a printer's case, containing the letters of the alphabet and the orthographical signs written on cards; over the compartments the names of the letters were written as they are given in the note (p. 111). The child picked out the letters to form the words that were given him to spell, and afterwards distributed the letters into their proper divisions, thus learning, in play, orthography and the elements of grammar. This was a favourite system in the 18th century.

(*Note by the Translator.*)

INDEX.

Abgarus : 38.
Agnes, The Mother, (Jeanne-Cathérine Agnès Arnauld, sister of Dr. Arnauld): 6, 46, 49, 51, 53, note; 65, note; 75, note; 95, note; 221, note.
Aguesseau, D': 40.
Aldrovandus : 174 and note.
Alembert, D': 64.
Alet (Bp. of): 63, note.
Alvares : 14, note.
Ambrose, St.: 13.
Andilly, D', see Villeneuve, son of.
— Arnauld d' (elder brother of Dr. Arnauld): 25, 45, 46, note; 78, note; 81, 82.
Angélique, The Mother (Marie Angélique Arnauld, sister of Dr. Arnauld): 45 and note; 46 and note; 48, 50, 54, note; 55 and note; 60, note; 110, note; 219, note; 225, note; 243, note; 245.
— de Saint-Jean (Arnauld), The Mother (niece of Dr. Arnauld): 46, 193, note.
Annat, Father, jesuit : 19, 44.
Anne of Austria, 63.
— Eugénie de l'Incarnation, Sister (sister of Dr. Arnauld): 50, 54, 245 seq.
Archimedes : 195.
Aristotle : 11, 28, 29; definition of the verb, 113 and note; 125, 132 seq.
Arnauld (advocate): 43, note.
— Antoine, Dr. (son of preceding): 1, 9 and note; Author of Port-Royal books, 12, 17, 19, 21, note; 22, 25; *Logic*, 26; a Cartesian, 27, 28 and note; *Logic*, 31, 43 seq. and note; composition of the *Logic*, 44, 52, 55, 56, 59, note; 61, 62 and note; 65, note; 82, 89, note; 96 and note; 110, note; 114, note; letter on grammar, 117 seq.; on classical studies, 123 seq., 193, note; 197, note; 204, note; 221, note; 227, note; 241, note; his opinion of Bouhours, 249, note.
Arsenius, St.: 71 and note.
Aubry, Mlle.: 21, 39.
Augustine, St.: 13, 36, 83, note; 96, 103, 104, 107, 199, 205, 216, 219, note.
Avaux, M. d': 21, note.

Bacon : 31 and notes his opinion of the jesuits as educators, 59, note; 128, note.
Bailly : judicial astrology, 129, note.
Bain : indirect moral instruction, 169, note.
Balzac, M. de : 16, 84, note; 254.
Barbier, notice on Guyot : 42.
Barcos, M. de : 21, 82.
Basil, St.: 180.
Bauny, Father : 36.
Bayle : 66.
Beaubrun, M. de, on Nicole's jansenism : 22.
Beauzée : 113, note; 117, note.
Bembo : 146 and note.
Benedict, St. : 71, 76.
Bernard, St. : 85, note; 201, 205, 207.
Bernières, M. de : 86, note.
Bérulle, De : 60.
Besogne : Nicole's classical knowledge, 22, 41, 44, 47 and note; 50, 55, note; 62.
Bignon, M. Jérôme : 3, note; 8, 13, 31, note; 70 and note.
— Jérôme and Thierri : 3, note; 45, 70, note.

Index.

Bignon, Marie: 3, note; 47, 70, note.
Boileau: 20; *Arrêt burlesque*, 30, 66, 147, note.
Boisguilbert, 45, 46, note.
Boissier, M. G.: 178, note.
Bona, Card.: 65, note.
Bossuet: 19, note; 24, 27, note; 29, note; 34, 37, note; 44, 96, note.
Bouhours, Father: 16 and note; 19, note; 249 and note; 253, note.
Bourbon, Henri de: 63, 253, note.
Bourdoise: 60.
Boutiot, M. Th.: 47, note.
Boxhorn: 113, note.
Bréal, Michel: 17.
Brisacier, Father: 19, note; 44.
Bruno, Giordano: 29.
Burnouf: 17.
Bussy: 14.
Buxtorf: 114 and note.

Calvin: 19, note; 62.
Camper: 79, note.
Canaye, Father: 59.
Cassini, astronomer: 195.
Cato the Censor: 216 and note.
Chambre, M. de la: 117 and note.
Champagne, Philippe de: 97 and note.
Channing: 2, note; 80, note.
Chapelain: 17, 20, 25, 26.
Chapelle: 215, note.
Charron: 109, note.
Chazé, Mme. de: 50.
Chevreuse, Duc de: 20, 44.
Chiflet, Father: pronunciation of *oi*, 157, note.
Choisy, Mme. de: 66.
Chrysologus, St.: 206.
Chrysostom, St.: 13, 203 and note.
Cicero: 125, his letters, 178 and note.
Clémencet: 47, note.
Clénard: 14.
Comenius: 15.
Condillac: 17.
Contarini: 60, note.
Conti, La princesse de: 63, 204, note.
Conti, Le prince de: 20, 63 and note.
Copernicus: 195.
Corbinelli: 14.
Cordier, Mathurin, teacher: 153 and note.
Corneille: 18, 24, 46, note.

Cousin, M.: 46, 63, 110, note; 227, note.
Coustel or Coutel: 12, 41, 210, note; 211, note.

Descartes: 10, 11, 17, 18, 27, 28, 29 and note; 30, 65, 96, note; 193 *seq.*, 196 *seq.*, 215, note.
Desmarets de Saint-Sorlin: 247 and note.
Despautère: 14, 157, note.
Diez: 17.
Dübner: 15.
Duclos: 17, 111, notes.
Dufossé: 7, 48, 49, note.
Du Fargis, Mlle: 54, note.
Duguet: 59, note.
Du Marsais: 17.
Duvergier de Hauranne, see Saint-Cyran: 1.

Egger, M.: 14, 15, 113, note.
Elbœuf, Mlle. d': 225, note.
Elzevier, Daniel: 18.
Embrun (Abp. of): 44.
Epictetus: 10, 95, note; Pascal's opinion of, 97 *seq.*
Epicurus: 27.
Escobar: 36, 54, 56, 248 and note.
Espinoy, M. d': 81 and note; see also Saint-Ange (the young).

Fayette, Mme. de la: 24, 34, 39.
Fénelon: 14, 18, note; on eloquence, 144, note; *id.* 147, note; definition of the world, 245, note.
Fermat: 96, note.
Fleury, Card.: 67.
Fludd, Robert: 135 and note.
Foix, Mme. de: 53, note; 65, note.
Fontaine (Nicolas): 2, 8; description of de Saci, 10, 20, 93, note; 208, note; 243, note.
Fontaine, Mme. de: 232, note.
Fontpertuis, Mme. de: 21, note.
Fouruel, M. V.: 39.
François de Sales: 60.
Franklin: 125, 213.
Fromageau, Abbé: 47.
Furetière: 253, note.
Furstemberg, Card.: 41.

Galen: 195, 196, note.
Galileo: 29.

Garasse, Father: 23, note.
Gassendi: 27, 135, note; 215, note.
Gerberon: 66, note.
Gregory Nazianzen, St.: 6.
Grignan, Mme. de: 64, 109, note.
Grimarest: 215, note.
Grimm: 17.
Guedreville, De: 47.
Guénégaut, Mme. de: 63.
Guise, Duc de: 79.
— Duchesse de: 4, 79.
Gui Patin: 60, note; 135, notes.
Guy Joly: 63, note.
Guyot: 4, 6, 12; his translations, 41, 42 and note; 159, note; 160, note.

Hamon, M., physician: 97, 243, note.
Harcourt, D': 63.
Harlai (Abp. of Paris): 44.
Harvey, physician: 141, note; 195, 196, note.
Hecquet, physician: 243, note.
Hément, M. Félix: 173, note.
Hippocrates, 195.
Hocquincourt, Marquis d': 59.
Huet: 27.
Hufeland: 5.
Humboldt: 17.
Huyghens: 96, note; 195 and note.

Innocent X: 60, note.

James II.: 21, note.
Jansenius (Cornelius, Bp. of Ypres): 11, 43, note; 57, 60, 66, note; 83, note.
Joubert: 11, 36, note; his estimate of Balzac, 85, note.
Jurieu: 27, 44.

Kepler: 135, note.

La Boétie: 40.
La Bruyère: 23, 40, 43, note; 151, note; 215, note.
La Fontaine: 20; the Horoscope, 130, note.
La Marans: 32, note.
Lamoignon, Sister Louise — Saint-Praxède de: 46, note.

Lancelot, Claude: 1, 2, 3, and note; 4, 6; pedagogic directions, 7, 8, 12; enters Port-Royal, 13; publishes Latin Grammar, *id.*, Greek Grammar, 14; his opinion on *Janua linguarum*, 15; Grammaire générale, 17 and note; Italian and Spanish Grammars under the name of M. de Trigny, *id.*; declines to write a French Grammar, 18, 19; publishes four treatises on poetry, 20; end of his pedagogic career, 21; his exile and death, *id.* and note, 41, 62, 70, note; 73, note; 81, note; 82, note; 83 note; 117, note; 204, note.
La Rochefoucauld: 35, 40.
Launoi, M. de: 136, note.
Lavaur (Bp. of): 44.
Leclerc: 50, 54, note; 225, note.
Legouvé, M., his defence of Cicero, 178, note.
Leibnitz, his objections to Descartes' philosophy, 27 and note; his opinion of the jesuits as educators, 59, note.
Le Maistre, J.: 34.
Lemaître (Antoine): 5, note; 7, 41, 51, 70, note; 85, note; 95, note.
Lemoine: 27, 44, 193, note.
Le Nain de Tillemont: 45.
Leo X.: 146, note.
Le Tellier: 12, 218, note.
Lipsius, 173.
Littré, 17.
Locke, 5, 93, note.
Longueville, Mme. de: 62, 63 and note; 86, note.
Louis XIII.: 129, note.
Louis XIV.: 62, 63, 90, note; 117, note.
Lucian: 80, note.
Luines, Duc de: 44, 63.
Luther: 62.

Maimbourg, Jesuit: 44.
Maintenon, Mme. de: 4, note; her opinion on the books of Port-Royal, 19, 51, 55 and note; relates two anecdotes 56, 62; sets writing copies, 159, note; 170, note; advice to teachers, 201, note, and 209, note; 224, note; 228, note; 230, note; 232, note; 235, note; 245, note.

Malebranche: 44, 147, note.
Mallet, M.: 218.
Marcus Aurelius: 97, note.
Maria Teresa, Donna: 17.
Marie, Mme. de la: 4, note; 209, note.
Martha, M.: 97, note.
Martin, Henri, method of Saint-Cyran, 65.
Maurepas: 67.
Mégret, Louis: 18, note.
Melanchthon: 80, note.
Ménage, M.: 16 and note.
Mersenne, Father: 27, 29, 96, note; 135, note.
Michelet: 46.
Minucius Felix: 180, note.
Mirabeau: 46, note.
Mirandola, Francis Picus: 146.
Molière: 51, note; 129, note; 215, note.
Montaigne: 5, 10, 32, note; 40, 93, note; Pascal's opinion of, 97 *seq.*, 132, 199, note.
Montmorency, Constable Anne de: 230, note.
Morel: 44.

Nervèze, De: 253 and note.
Nicole: 12, 21, 22; his prejudice against ancient literature, 23; criticism on French literature, 24; his literary taste, 25; *Logic*, 26, 28, 31; *Essais de morale*, 32 *seq.*; education of a prince, 40, 41, 43, 44, 46, 59, note; 62, 89, note; 130, note; 132, note; 167, note; 172, note; 176, note; on study of rhetoric, 177, 192, note; 197, note; 204, note; 213, note; 235, note; 247, note; reply to Desmarets, 248.
Nouet: 44.

Olivet, Abbé d': 25.
Olympia, Signora: 60, note,
Origen: 83 and note.

Pallu, physician: 243, note.
Palsgrave, French Grammar: 18, note.
Paracelsus, physician: 135 and note.
Pascal: 10, 19; *Pensées*, 24; their style corrected, 25, 32 and note; 36, note; 39, 40, 44, 45, 59, note; 85, note; at Port-Royal, 95 *seq.*; his method of reading, 110, note; 138, note; 139, note; 145, note; Nicole's opinion on the *Pensées*, 179, 208, note; 244, note.
Pascal, Jacqueline (Sister Sainte-Euphémie): 50, 53; Port-Royal method of reading, 110, note; 226, note.
Pasquier, Étienne: 71, note.
Pasquin: 60, note.
Passart, Sister Flavie: 247 and note.
Perdreau, Sister Marie-Dorothée: 49, 75, note.
Péréfixe (Archbishop of Paris): 44, 56.
Perrier, M.: 25.
Pestalozzi: 93, note.
Pétau, Father: 19, 44.
Philip II.: 202, note.
Pibrac, M. de, his quatrains: 199 and note.
Plato: 207.
Plautus: 201.
Pliny the Younger, his letters: 178, 244, note.
Plutarch: 32 note.
Pomponne, M. Arnauld de: 46, note.
Ptolemy: 195 and note.

Quesnel, Father: 22.
Quintilian: 13, 14, 125, 179, 210, note.

Rabelais: 5, 93, note.
Racine (Jean): 8, 15, 20, 24, 45, 47, 48, 59, 63, 204, note; 243, note; 249, note.
— (Bonaventure), Abbé: 45, note.
Ramus: 14; French Grammar, 18, note; 134, note.
Rancé, De: 60.
Rapin, Father: 2, 14, note; 19, 22, 52, 55, 62 and note; 64, 67, 92, note.
Raymond of Sabunde: 101 and note.
Renan, M.: 63.
Retz, Card. de: 62, 63 and note.
Richelieu: 3, 69, note; 78, note; 82, 97, note.
Rivet, D.: 49.
Roberval: 96, note.
Rollin: 17, 40, 125, note; 207, note.

Rousseau: 5, 6; negative education, 71, note; 93, note; 234, note.
Sablé, Mme. de: 28, note.
Saci, Louis-Isaac Lemaître de (brother of Antoine Lemaître): 3, note; 6; his poetical talent, 8 *seq.*; his translation of the Bible, 11, 21, 59, note; 62 and note; 70, note; 73, note; 82; Patience and silence, 92, 93, note; 96 *seq.*, 197, note; 208, note.
— M. Sylvestre de: 40.
Sainte-Agnès de Féron, Sister Elizabeth de: 50.
Sainte-Aldegonde des Pommares, Sister Marie de; 49.
Saint-Ange, M. de: 81, note.
— (the young): 7. See also Espinoy.
Saint-Amour, Dr.: 18.
Sainte-Beuve: 11; Lancelot's inconsistency. 20, 45, 46, note; 95, note; 97, note.
— Jacques de: 89 and note.
Saint-Cyran, Abbé de: his ideas on education, 1 *seq.*, 13, 21, 23, 43 and note; 46, note; 50, 55, 57, 59, note; 60, 62, 65, 69, notes, *et seq.*; on corporal punishment, 75 and note; 221, note; 231, note: 241, note: 244, note; 246.
Sainte-Domitille, Sister Jeanne de: 54, note.
Saint-Evremond: 59.
Saint-Pierre, Abbé de: 24.
Sainte-Suzanne, Sister: 97, note.
Salle, Father de la: 210, note; 211, note.
Sanctius: 14, note.
Scaliger, Julius Cæsar: 113, note; 114 and note.
Scioppius: 14, note.
Sebastian, King of Portugal: 202 and note.
Seneca: 178, 179, 180, note; 209.
Senecey, Marquis de: 63.
Sévigné, Marquis de: 24, 32, note; 63.

Sévigné, Mme. de: 16 and note, 21; her admiration of Nicole, 31, 32, 34; her criticism of Nicole, 35 *seq.*, 39, 40, 63, note; 64, 66, 109, note; 171, note; 249, note.
Simon, Richard: 44.
Singlin, Abbé, 3, 8, 21, 22, 50, 62, 63, note; 74 and note; 82, and Pascal, 96, 226.
Sirmond, jesuit: 44.
Socrates, Nicole's opinion of, 28.
Spencer, 234, note.
Sténon: 195, 196, note.
Sully-Prudhomme, M.: 38.

Têtu, Abbé: 32, note.
Theodosius the Great: 71, note.
Thou, De: 199, note.
Torricelli: 96, note.
Tracy, De: 17.
Trigny, M. de: 17; see Lancelot.
Tycho Brahé: 195 and note.

Vabres (Bp. of): 44.
Valant, M.: 122.
Van-Helmont: 135 and note.
Vanini: 29.
Varin: 76, note.
Vaucel, M. du: 21, note; 249, note.
Vaugelas: 18, note; 84, note; 144.
Vauvenargues: 40.
Vavasseur, Father: 25.
Vergara: 14.
Villeneuve, M. de: 81; see also Andilly, D'.
Villeroi: 63.
Vincent de Paul: 2, 60 and note.
Virgil: 6, 73.
Vitard, M.: 13.
Vives, Luis: 138, note.
Voltaire: 21, 40, 45.
Vossius: 14 and note.

Wallon de Beaupuis, M: 12, 42.
Willis, physician: 196 and note.

Ypres, M. d'; see Jansenius.